MW01235297

I'D DO IT ALL AGAIN

I'D DO IT ALL AGAIN

CLIFTON L. GANUS, JR.

XULON PRESS

Xulon Press
2301 Lucien Way #415
Maitland, FL 32751
407.339.4217
www.xulonpress.com

© 2020 by Clifton L. Ganus, Jr.

Printed in the United States of America

Library of Congress Control Number: 2020924576

Paperback ISBN-13: 978-1-6628-0462-5
Dust Jacket ISBN-13: 978-1-6628-0463-2
Ebook ISBN-13: 978-1-6628-0464-9

This book is dedicated to Louise Ganus, as was its author.

CONTENTS

PREFACE

D r. Clifton Loyd Ganus, Jr., was a preacher, a teacher, a scholar, a lecturer, a traveler, a church leader, a university president, an adventurer, a community resource, a benefactor, a devoted family man, and a friend to many people of various backgrounds and nationalities.

He maintained a full schedule of travel and activity through his ninety-seventh year, often noting that "Growing old is not for sissies," as he dealt with heart problems, diabetes, skin cancers, and deteriorating knees and feet which led to many falls.

We children were often asked, sometimes urgently, if Dad was going to write a book about his life, and in late 2016 we met with him in his office to encourage him in that direction. With characteristic humility and a few unexpected tears, he bowed his head and said, "No one wants to read my story." We affirmed that many did. Throughout his life he had made notes of his activities, some written personally and some compiled by Edwina Pace, his secretary. He began assembling and adding to these. After he had over four hundred pages prepared, we engaged Tiffany Yecke Brooks to organize and edit his work into a form that would be interesting to his friends and acquaintances. He continued to compile, write, travel, and maintain a full schedule until May of 2019, when he developed a severe knee infection which spread and led to a cascade of physical difficulties. He passed away on September 9, 2019.

When asked about various events in his past, even the challenging ones, Dad often concluded his comments by saying, "I'd do it all over again." This book is his account of the life he loved.

Cliff Ganus III
Debbie Ganus Duke
Charles Ganus

CHAPTER 1
FAMILY MATTERS

I don't really know the origin of the name Ganus; it may have come from the name Gurganus, as there were a number of members of the Churches of Christ by that name, and many of them were from Alabama, where my great-great grandfather Stephen Ganus was born in 1818 – in Troy, to be exact. Stephen's son Calvin was born in 1849, and Calvin had a son named William Edward in 1872, during the period of Reconstruction following the Civil War. William became my grandfather, and when he was five years old his father decided to move the family West. Thus, however the name Ganus came to be, it became the family name and followed the family on the long wagon journey across southern Alabama, Mississippi, Louisiana, and deep into Texas.

When William Ganus and Mary Jackson, distant cousins from Pike County, Alabama, married on October 27, 1896, they moved to Hillsboro, Texas. That particular branch of the family produced thirteen children over several decades, though, as was sadly normal for that time, not all of the children reached adulthood. A four-year-old was peering down the barrel of a shotgun when an eight-year-old neighbor pulled the trigger. One infant died from meningitis; a twelve-year-old named Billy died from the same. I remember Billy because he was one of the youngest children and was just about my age. We used to wrestle as children and had a lot of fun playing together as friends. It never really occurred to us that we were uncle and nephew; it felt much more like we were cousins. In fact, my youngest uncle, Melvin, was actually two years younger than I was. But no matter the age, I can't imagine how difficult it must have been on my grandparents to have so many children die young.

1

Granddaddy Ganus moved from Hillsboro to Waco, about thirty-five miles away, when I was still a boy. He lived at 2513 Franklin Avenue, right across the street from a lumber mill and a large commercial bakery. Every time the bread was done and the ovens were opened, the smell of baking bread wafted all the way across the street and filled their house. I would often go over to buy fresh bread and bring it back for Grandmother to fix it up with homemade butter and jelly. That was wonderful eating for a youngster. In fact, a lot of my childhood seems to center around food. My grandparents ran a small restaurant in Waco which served hamburgers and my grandmother's fried pies. It was always a pleasure to visit with them. Occasionally we would have a family reunion in the backyard, and I can still see the long tables filled with food. The air seemed filled with vibrant voices as we enjoyed being together once again. So many memories are flavored with the comfortable smells and tastes of honest, square meals.

My granddad was a jovial person – friendly and somewhat comic. That made his death from Alzheimer's at eighty-six all the more difficult, because he was so far gone from the loving, lively person he had always been. I remember saying to him "Granddaddy, I am Cliff, Jr., the son of your son Cliff." Granddaddy just lay there in bed, a large melanoma visible on the right side of his head, then he replied in a weak voice, "I don't recollect a son named Cliff."

My grandmother was an equally dynamic lady in her prime. She enjoyed going to church and loved to sing. One Sunday, as she was standing up for a hymn, the straps on her slip broke and the slip fell down to her feet. Without missing a word of the song, she stepped out of it, gathered up the silk fabric, and put it in her purse. She lived to be eighty but was blind for the last twenty years of her life. Every time I would visit her, she would put her hand on my face and say, "Oh Cliff, you look so good!"

On my mother's side, my great-grandfather Bearden was a soldier in the Confederate army during the Civil War; his wife stayed home in Red River County, in northeast Texas, and took care of the family while he was gone. He was discharged at the end of the war and was able to come home for good when his son Rodney, my grandfather, was only five months old. Eventually, the Beardens moved down to a farm in the Hillsboro area, where Rodney grew up. My grandmother,

Martha Ann Moore, was born in Pulaski County, Tennessee, but when she was thirteen months old her parents moved to Arkansas and later to the Hillsboro area. Rodney and Martha Ann married and had eleven children: eight girls and three boys. My mother was the ninth child and started working on the family farm when she was six years old. Unlike many of her sisters, she preferred farm work to housework and became able to plow, hoe, pick cotton, shock wheat, cut cane, chop wood, pull corn, gather eggs, collect kindling, and all other kinds of odd jobs. Despite her physical strength, she was extremely sensitive as a girl and tears flowed easily; she was tough, but she was tender.

She started school when she was seven and had to walk three miles to the nearest schoolhouse in Menlow each morning. Because her father was a big believer in education for his daughters as well as his sons, they moved to be near a better school in Hillsboro when my mother was ten, despite all the hard work they had invested in building up their family farm. My grandfather believed that a strong education for his all children was worth starting over. The new family home was a ninety-acre cotton and corn farm on the old Brandon Road. It just happened to be across the road from the dairy where the Ganus family had moved in 1913. One of my grandmother's brothers told her that there was a young blond Ganus boy who would be just right for her. She was excited to meet him because the whole Bearden clan were brunettes and a blond sounded exotic. She caught a glimpse of him at school and later borrowed her sister's camera and was able to get him to pose for a picture. The romance began right away. They began to visit with one another, and whenever they played "Drop the Handkerchief" with other children, they would always choose each other, which inevitably displeased their playmates.

———————

When the United States entered World War I, my dad went with his brother to enlist in the service; he was only fifteen, but he was going to try anyway. His brother told the recruiter he was eighteen, and my dad said the same.

"Oh, you're twins!" the recruiter exclaimed.

"No," my uncle replied. "He's three years younger than I am."

3

So my dad was sent back home. Not long afterwards, he got on his bike and started to pedal the sixty-five miles from Hillsboro to Dallas in order to get a job. Along the way, he stopped to rest under a tree, and a man offered to take him and his bike the rest of the way into the city. Dad got a job as a dishwasher at the Southwestern Restaurant, then worked himself up to head waiter. Every other weekend he would go home to Hillsboro to see my mother, who had started seeing the son of a local judge. My dad told her it was one or the other and, luckily, she picked my dad.

Even though they were very young, my dad kept asking her to marry him, but she kept putting him off. Finally, he told her that he was going to head out to California if she turned him down again. It may have been a bluff, but she didn't want to take any chances, so she agreed, and he gave her a ring.

One Saturday morning he borrowed $10 from his boss, went to Hillsboro, borrowed his brother's car, and knocked at Mother's door, asking her to marry him that same day. She told him gently, "I can't. I don't have any clothes bought yet. Let's wait until Monday." He agreed, and on Monday she went downtown and bought the clothes she would need to start her new life as a wife, and they were married at the preacher's house. On the way back to the car after the ceremony, Dad was grinning and kept laughing, "Now I have caught you! Now I have got you!"

Years later, when Mother would tell that story, she would add, "I wasn't really running that fast."

They settled in Dallas, and Dad got a job as a soda jerk at the Palace Drugstore; it was a job that required a lot of knowledge and more skill than you might imagine. He earned a good salary for his age and worked there for a while, but a man in Abilene who owned a pharmacy kept calling and asking him to take his talents to Abilene to work.

Dad went, and Mother stayed behind in Dallas, but the geographical separation was too hard – especially now that they had a baby on the way. She sold a pig her dad had given her as a wedding gift, borrowed a dollar, and paid for her trip to Abilene. One week later the pharmacy closed, and she and Dad had to borrow a dollar to have enough money for them to return to Dallas, eating nothing but peanut butter and potato chips along the way to save money. They wanted to go all the way back to Hillsboro until the baby came, but they didn't have enough cash, so Dad ended up hocking Mother's ring so they could make the trip.

On April 6, 1922, Dad and Mother went over to her parents' house, though her mother was out assisting with the birth of another relative's baby. That night, I began to let them know I wanted out; finally, at 11:55 a.m. the next morning, I arrived. I was fortunate in that a doctor was able to come out to the farm to deliver me. I came into the world hungry, and I have loved to eat ever since!

I still have my first picture as a baby. I am probably six or seven weeks old, propped up in a chair with a white dress, bald head, and big hands and feet. My right eye is closed just a little bit more than my left, which makes sense, because my parents said I used to sleep with one eye shut and the other open. I guess I just didn't want to miss anything, but I surely was a funny-looking baby.

When I was three months old my dad moved us back to Dallas, where he got another job working in a drugstore; but he was always restless. He decided to become a candy salesman, which would allow him to travel, but that only lasted one day before he was back at his old job. My brother Arvis was born in 1924, when I was eighteen months old, and we went back to Hillsboro for nine months to stay with my dad's family. He planted a field of cotton but really didn't enjoy farm work and sold the crop for $75 to be rid of it. We lived in one room with two babies and an incubator for newborn chicks. My parents also sold milk from a Holstein that had been a wedding present from my mother's father, but the cow fell into a ditch one day and injured itself so badly that they had to kill her. Dad skinned the cow, sold the skin, and bought a nice pair of shoes. He knew our family wasn't going to stay on the farm forever and he knew it was essential that he look professional when he went out looking for work in the city; besides, he was always the last to get anything new since every cent he made went into providing for his family.

When we headed back to Dallas again, my dad got a job with Pig Stands. Pig Stands was the original drive-in sandwich shop, a lot like a Sonic today. The car hop would go out to the lot and take the order in person, and then bring the food back on a tray and place it on the car door. There were about one hundred Pig Stands around the south-east, and my dad managed to work his way up through the ranks with the company. Unfortunately, that meant working a lot of late hours – sometimes until midnight – but Mother made the most of her time alone with us boys. Mother liked to say that I could read and recite twenty-three different nursery rhymes when I was three, and by the age of four I would stand on a little box and preach the plan of salvation. She also said I could recite the alphabet as quickly backwards as I could forwards. Maybe some of that was a little bit of a mother's bragging, but I do know that she taught us reading, writing, and arithmetic, as well as to quote from the Bible.

Within a year or two, the Pig Stands management sent my dad to San Antonio to work in a restaurant. I was four years old when we moved, and I don't remember much about it except that I very much enjoyed playing at Brackenridge Park. Just shy of one year later, we were transferred back to Dallas when my dad was made the regional purchasing manager.

My father was in charge of larger sums of money than he had ever seen in his life, and he was doing a great job at it because he was a trust-worthy individual. But he wasn't the only one taking in the big bucks. Dr. Jackson, the owner of the company, gave me a quarter when I was about six, and I couldn't believe my luck. I thought that was the biggest money I had ever seen!

————

I've always been rather accident prone. One day, my brother Arvis and I were working on an oatmeal box, trying to make an engine for a train. He had a butcher knife and was sawing on the box when the knife slipped and went right across my right wrist. The gash was about an inch and a half long, and the blood started oozing out. My mother came into the kitchen and thought I had a red rubber band around my wrist; I showed her that, no, it was actually blood. Thankfully, she wasn't squeamish and was able to stop the bleeding quickly, but I still have the scar to this day.

Around that same time – I was five or six – I was sitting in the back seat of the car while Mother was driving, and for some reason the door flew open as she was turning a corner and I fell out into the road, right on my head! My mother didn't panic – she didn't even seem that worried. She just said, "Cliff, get up and get your hat and get back in the car." We never went to the hospital and I was just fine.

And then there was the time I went into the Pig Stand where my dad was working and took a drink from what I thought was a glass of water sitting on the counter. Turns out it was gasoline. For some time, everyone in my family was afraid to strike a match near me, for fear I would go up in flames. That swallow of gasoline never did seem to hurt me, though.

———

In Dallas, we lived very close to my aunt Clara Sawyer and her three children, Wyatt, Daphne, and Jeanne. Aunt Clara's husband had passed away a few years before, and I faintly remember going to his funeral and playing with my cousins; but much of that time is a blur. I enjoyed being near my cousins and have always loved having lots of family nearby.

Every year when I was young, my family would go back to the old Bearden family farmstead where I was born in Hillsboro. One year we went in the wintertime, and it had snowed very heavily – and not just by Texas standards. The snow was up to my hips! We couldn't drive the car up the quarter mile from the highway to the house, so we had to get two mules to pull the car to the end of the lane.

I loved those visits because there was always something interesting to do. I loved to gather eggs and annoy the pigs and calves. I loved to turn the old cream separator by hand; there was no electricity or running water, so everything felt exotic and exciting compared to city life. My cousins and I would play hide-and-seek in the cornfield, and I was always climbing on the windmill and the barn. When Mother would look out the window and see me on top of the barn, she would yell, "Clifton Loyd – get down off the barn!" She used my middle name, so I knew I was in trouble.

Mother used to tell us about when she lived in the house as a girl, upstairs in the same room where we all slept. One of her younger sisters had died there, and they used to tell ghost stories to give themselves the shivers.

My grandmother had a frame she used for quilting. When I was young, I used to piece quilts for her; she taught me to stitch together the small pieces in order to form the pattern she wanted to make. I thought it was a lot of fun and I loved getting to spend that time with her. It never even occurred to me that other boys might consider it sissy.

It was nice to be close to my grandfather Bearden, as well as to my granddaddy Ganus, who no longer lived across the street, but was not too far away in Waco. Family is so vital, and I am glad my parents made such an effort to keep us connected to ours – especially since big changes were ahead.

CHAPTER 2

GROWING UP GANUS

M y father left for New Orleans in early 1929 to become the district manager of six Pig Stands, and Mother followed with us boys in May. Our old Chevrolet had a leaky radiator, so she hired a young man to drive with us in case we needed repairs. Just as predicted, the radiator gave us trouble, and we ended up having to stop at a number of farmhouses along the way for water. Finally, one old farmer offered us a bit of advice: "Tell you what you can do to fix that; just put some raw eggs in it. That hot water will cook the eggs, and they will get into the hole and congeal. It will put a stop to those leaks." And he was right! We cracked a couple of eggs and went on our way with no further troubles.

We found our new home of New Orleans to be quite a bit different from Dallas. Most importantly, we were surrounded by water. On the north side was Lake Pontchartrain, which was about twenty miles long and twenty miles wide. The Mississippi River circled around the other three sides of the city, which is why it is called "The Crescent City," but the entire place was really just swampy.

We disliked New Orleans intensely for the first few months – even the first few years, if I'm being honest. The Italian, Spanish, and French influences were still very strong at that time (they've mellowed greatly over the past ninety years), and it just felt too unfamiliar for us to really be at ease. We were hoping Dad would get transferred back to Dallas, and we would chase down any car we saw with Texas license plates to see if it might be somebody we knew. Sure enough, one day a car we chased was from Hillsboro, and it had been sold by my uncle Aubrey Ganus, who owned the Ford motor agency there. It was a nice connection to our roots in the midst of a city that still seemed strange

9

and unwelcoming. But New Orleans grew on us and eventually even became home.

Our initial dislike wasn't entirely New Orleans' fault, however; we arrived just a few months before the stock market crash in October of 1929, and the first few years were rough. They would have been rough no matter where we were living.

One of the most interesting things about New Orleans was the way they would deliver various products. Most homes didn't have refrigerators in those days – just an ice box, where the top part held ice and there was a small amount of room for food below. Every day the iceman would come – usually an African-American man driving a horse with a wagon full of ice. He would take your order from a little cardboard plaque that had an arrow on it. You could turn that arrow to 25, 50, 75, or 100 and stick it in the window. He would then bring that number of pounds of ice to your box. Usually we only ordered twenty-five or fifty pounds at a time, but the ice came in big hundred-pound chunks. He would have to take his ice pick and chip off the amount you requested. Of course, that meant that there would be little slivers of ice that would fall off the back of the wagon when he started moving again, and we kids would follow the wagons and pick up those pieces as a special treat during the hot, sultry New Orleans summers. It might not have been very sanitary, but it certainly was cooling and refreshing, and it helped me resolve that I was going to be an iceman when I grew up! I couldn't imagine a better job in the world, especially during the summertime.

Fruit vendors would also come by with strawberries or bananas or whatever might be in season or have just arrived by ship at the port. These were usually African-Americans, too. They would yell out the fruits they had as they rode up the street with their horses wearing little straw hats to keep their heads cool. It was quite a sight to see them rolling along, almost singing out the names of whatever they had for sale. New Orleans was certainly different from anywhere we had lived before.

I loved to watch the boats come in. If you went down to the wharf at the Mississippi, you literally had to go up to the river, because Canal Street, the main street of the city, is lower than the river. Only the levee kept the city from being submerged. There were all kinds of ships from all over the world at the docks, but I remember specifically watching the banana boats from Central America as they were unloaded. Dock workers would go into the hold of the ship and walk back up the steps with huge stalks of bananas on their shoulder, one after another – a steady stream of porters carrying bananas off the boats like ants toting bits of food from a picnic. Bananas were plentiful in New Orleans, even though they were a rarity in much of the rest of the United States at that time. Once Batsell Baxter, who taught Bible at Harding, was visiting the city and asked one of the vendors if he could buy some bananas.

"How much?" the vendor asked.

"Oh, I guess about ten cents' worth," Baxter replied.

The vendor handed him a full dozen bananas, leaving poor Baxter marveling that the fruit could be so cheap, and wondering what in the world he was going to do with so many bananas.

———————

For many years my family rented, rather than owning a home, and we moved every few years. Each time, it seemed, we went to a slightly nicer house. The first home we rented was in the Gentilly area, which is on the eastern side of the city. I don't remember much about it except that it was near the fairgrounds where they had horse races. One day I walked over to the track and watched one of those races; I had never seen horses run like that! I was used to Texas work horses bred for farm work, not thoroughbreds bred to run!

Our next house was on Banks Street, about three blocks from Canal Street. It was too full of the noise and bustle and smell of a big city; to make matters worse, we all came down with the red measles – they call it rubella, now – and had a terrible experience. As I recall, we stayed in the attic area of a house and our mattresses were stuffed with moss, which was hardly airy or comfortable. We didn't stay in that house long.

The next house we moved to was located at 3117 South Roberts. I was about eight years old, and I really liked the fact that it was just a few blocks from one of the Pig Stands my dad was managing on Claiborne Avenue. We had a fig tree in the backyard and also raised chickens. We sold figs, chickens, and eggs to our neighbors up and down the street. One day I was out in the backyard playing with a slingshot and I tried to aim at a little bird, figuring I had no chance of actually hitting it. I grieved terribly when that bird died, and I resolved to be much more careful with my slingshot from then on. But I found other ways to be reckless. A neighbor boy and I crawled up in a tree near the front of our house and sat, eating some oranges. I don't know why, but I had a little box of twelve aspirins, and, for some reason, I decided to eat all of them. Maybe it was the fact that I ate oranges at the same time, but, incredibly, those aspirins didn't harm me.

From there we moved to 328 South Rendon. It was also a couple of blocks off Canal Street – an old shotgun-type house with one room behind the other, but it was two stories tall. The first level included a very small garage. We had a small backyard where I raised pigeons. They were messy, but they were fun to raise and made for some pretty good eating. Right across the street from us there was a house that had a metal picket fence, and one day I decided to try to walk across the top of it. My foot slipped and I fell off, and a sharp prong hit me in the chest but fortunately did not stick in. It was more of a glancing blow that tore my flesh a little, but not nearly as bad as it could have been.

Another time at that location, when I was eleven years old, I found a Civil War cannonball and was breaking rocks with it. I would pick it up and pound it hard on the rocks to break them, but on one occasion I failed to get my right middle finger out from under the cannon ball. As a result, I mashed the finger. It got infected and I had to go to the doctor; he froze it and lanced it. I still have a flat finger that looks very different from the one on my left hand. But I've never pounded rocks with unexploded Civil War ordnance since, so I guess I learned my lesson! It seems that I had a number of accidents when I was young. I guess it was because I was somewhat adventurous and probably a little crazy and was always trying to do something new.[1]

---

[1] A few years ago, I went back to visit a number of the places of my early youth; I found them still to be interesting. At the house on Rendon, I talked with the occupant and asked him if it was a rough neighborhood; it certainly did give the give that appearance. He replied, "Oh yes, it really is. Right around the corner on Sunday morning a man was shot and killed. It's a pretty rough place." It wasn't that bad when I lived there.

When my brother Arvis was about six years old, he was diagnosed with epilepsy, a condition which greatly checked his activity. It was pretty hard on him, and I tried to include him in whatever I could so he wouldn't feel quite so limited. One day, as he and I were walking along a large drainage pipe that ran across a canal near City Park, he fell off on the far side and broke his toe. I had to get across and carry him back to the near side of the canal, then figure out how to get him home. We ended up finding a piece of wood that we could use as an improvised crutch, since he was as big as I was, even though he was younger. There was just no way that I could carry him all the way back to the house by myself.

I went to Howard Number One grade school, which was just two blocks from my house. Whenever my brothers or I were feeling poorly, my parents would take us to the Katz and Besthoff Pharmacy on the corner of Canal Street by the Sacred Heart High School. There the clerks would fix me a dose of castor oil and orange juice, which was a common way to handle a lot of illnesses, but that turned me against orange juice for many years. The castor-oil-and-orange-juice elixir wasn't enough to ward off whooping cough, though, and I ended up being out of school for six weeks until it finally passed. I failed a semester's worth of work due to my absence and had to make it up over the summer. I think it is the only time I ever failed a course in my life, and it distressed me.

Of course, missing out on summer playtime didn't make me too happy either. I loved being outdoors, running around and playing sports. We were just a few blocks from Jefferson Davis Parkway, where there was a large space of what we called "neutral ground," where we could play football, baseball, softball, or anything else we could think of. This was actually a large median in the middle of the boulevard, but it was where many children in New Orleans played at that time because there weren't playgrounds available like there are now.

Staying true to my special knack for finding creative ways to get hurt, I one day decided to try to get to my trumpet lesson more expeditiously. I put on my roller skates, held on tight to my trumpet case, and grabbed hold of the back end of an automobile as it drove down Canal Street. All went well for a couple of minutes until the driver started to accelerate and my skates started to wobble. I fell flat on my stomach and skidded several feet. When I stood up, I was bruised and bloodied, and my clothes were all torn. But I skated on to my lesson and learned something perhaps even more valuable than notes on a trumpet – namely, don't do that again. I never have.

When I was eleven, in 1933, I started working at Hill's Store, which was a national grocery chain of neighborhood markets. My store was located on a corner on Banks Street. I spent all summer from 6:00 a.m. to 6:00 p.m. delivering groceries and shelving products, with one hour for lunch. I was paid ten cents a day, plus a few nickel tips – and I was thrilled. The Depression was a tough time, and we were happy to get whatever work we could find. I had a bicycle, which freed me up to do more jobs, like selling magazines and used newspapers. I think my best job was when I made my dream come true of being an iceman and started selling snow cones. I would purchase a twenty-five-pound block of ice and then use a hand-held shaver to make flakes that I could scoop into a paper cup and cover with syrup – grape, orange, or strawberry. I sold those snow cones for three cents apiece and managed to make a little money doing it! I saved up to buy myself a nice raincoat for school and set a little aside for the movies on Saturday nights.

The Escorial Theater was just a few blocks down Banks Street from the grocery and, like most picture houses of the time, would show serials at the beginning of movies. It might be Tom Mix or one of the other old-time cowboy series, and it would run just a few minutes and then continue again the following Saturday. The theater also held drawings for foodstuffs and other essentials. When you bought your ticket, you held on to the stub until they drew the numbers. Once I won a pair of nylon hose for my mother, which I was terribly proud to give her. Another time I won a basket of food that I shared with the other children, and during the films we devoured everything in it – candy, fruit, nuts – everything except some raw chicken. It was always a thrill to win food during the Depression days.

I loved the pictures. I think I saw *Mutiny on the Bounty* three times. There was also a movie called *The Mystery of the Wax Museum*, in which the villains dumped bodies into vats of wax. It was one of those films that made you hide your eyes a lot.

When I got a little older, I went into the movie business myself. My family had a little projector, so I would purchase short films that would last a few minutes, and I would invite the neighborhood children to come and watch for just a penny or two. We all enjoyed it.

———————

In 1932, after working for Pig Stands for a number of years, my dad decided to go into business for himself. A friend of his named Atkinson, who was an engineer, wanted to go into the restaurant business, so he and Dad pooled their meager resources and started a very small restaurant at 2627 Canal Street, twenty-six blocks from the river on the main drag of the city. They named it A&G Number 1, which was their way of saying that it was just the beginning of many more. It was a tiny building, maybe twenty feet wide and thirty-five feet deep, and it had a few seats inside, but most of the business would come from the car lot. It followed the same model of Pig Stands, with the window ordering and carhop delivery. I enjoyed the food we produced, because it was really, really good. If my dad ever came in and caught me eating a hamburger, though, he would say, "Cliff! You're eating up all the profits!"

A&G Number 1

I worked inside, filling orders. I wanted to be a car hop because they got tips and I didn't, but one day one of the car hops left ten cents on the tray and said that the guy in the car wanted me to have it. Finally, when I was about thirteen, I got the chance to be a car hop one night at one of our restaurants on Claiborne Avenue, where they were short a hop. There was no one else who could go so I seized the opportunity and went over to that location where I made either sixty-three or sixty-seven cents – I can't remember which. But I was thrilled because that sure seemed like a lot of money.

About six months after they opened, Mr. Atkinson decided that the restaurant business was too tough for him, and he declared that he was going back to engineering. He sold his half to my dad, who stayed alone in the business from that point on.

When my dad first started his business in New Orleans, he sold beer. He would never sell liquor or wine, but in New Orleans beer was just like water – and maybe even cleaner than the water. One day, a member of the church who had lapsed in his attendance declared, "No, I'm not going to attend the Carrollton Avenue church because that man, Ganus, is selling beer in his restaurant and I won't go to church with him."

As soon as Dad heard this, he called the general manager, Lloyd Bearden (a cousin on Mother's side), and said, "Lloyd, pull all the beer out of the restaurants; don't sell it anymore. Take it out right now."

"Okay, if that's what you want," Lloyd said, and he went to all the managers of the restaurants to let them know they were ceasing beer sales immediately and to send all of it back to the brewery.

No one believed you could exist in New Orleans in the restaurant business without selling beer and one manager in particular got very upset about it. "Are you crazy?" the manager demanded.

"No," replied Lloyd, "Mr. Ganus is."

It was a move that shocked everyone, but it didn't kill us. I had served beer as I'd worked with my dad, and I never understood how anyone could drink the stuff – the smell of it was bad enough for me – so I hardly felt any loss when we stopped. People noticed, but our restaurants continued, and we simply became known as the restaurant that wouldn't sell beer.[2]

Even though we may have taken something out of the restaurants, we did end up introducing the city to something entirely new – corndogs. While my dad didn't invent them, he was the first restaurant owner in the entire city to put them on his menu.

Back then, corndogs didn't have a stick in them the way they do now; instead, they were made in molds. The cornbread would be placed in the mold, and a wiener was placed into each slot. The top was closed

---

[2] I found out years later just how strongly we had cemented our identity as the restaurant that didn't sell beer when Foy O'Neal, one of my fellow students at Harding, was serving in the Navy on a ship in the Panama Canal Zone. He was talking to a buddy of his who was from New Orleans and mentioned that one of his college friends was from there, too, and his family had a chain of restaurants called A&G – had he heard of them? "Oh, I know that place," the guy said right away. "That's the one that won't sell beer."

and slid into the oven for baking. We even had a tasty sauce that came with them, and people really seemed to enjoy them…at first. But they were more of a curiosity and didn't really catch on as Dad had hoped. I think it was just a taste thing; cornbread simply wasn't popular in New Orleans. Neither was Mexican food. Tastes are regional and the region wasn't quite ready for corndogs at that time.

Dad was a genius at promotions for his businesses. For example, when the song "Pennies from Heaven" was popular, he glued a few pennies to little paper parachutes and had them dropped from a low-flying airplane over Canal Street. People would run to pick them up and, of course, see them printed with an advertisement for A&G. He just had a knack for getting people's attention.

On Sunday mornings after church, Mother and Dad would drive around to various restaurants to check them out, though it always seemed like they waited for us kids to fall asleep in the backseat before they would order anything! I seem to remember them specifically checking out the other places' malted milk, milkshakes, and hot fudge sundaes. But no one could ever top our hot fudge sundae – lily glasses filled with ice cream and covered with thick, warm wonderful chocolate sauce; then whipped cream, nuts, and a maraschino cherry would top it off – and everything was made from scratch. They were a dream.

At the same time that he started the restaurant, Dad also started a sandwich business. He bought the franchise for Mrs. Drake's Sandwiches from a little lady who made sandwiches at home and then loaded them into a basket on her arm and went around New Orleans selling them.

Behind our main A&G Restaurant was the shop from which we ran Mrs. Drake's, along with the company office and the warehouse from which we distributed supplies. We made chili in huge vats and then put it in five-pound tin containers, froze it, and sent it to the restaurants. It was condensed, so they would cut it by adding water when it was time to serve it. We also made doughnuts and little pecan pies.

Our whole family worked at different times for our restaurant, and there were other families similarly involved. One that stands out is the

Swang family. Mrs. Swang was a manager and was followed in that role by her daughter and son, Betty and John. Axel, John's twin, also worked for us for a while. The family didn't go to church at first, but when I was ten years old we started picking up Axel and John and taking them to church with us, and they became Christians. Eventually, Mrs. Swang and Betty did, too, though we never could get Mr. Swang to go with us. Mrs. Swang was a very good worker with a very strong personality. Her family was from Sweden, and she had an Old World mentality about what she did and how she did it. One day, my dad was a little unhappy with a few things and he went to talk to her, telling her that, as the owner of the business, he believed things should be handled in a certain way and he would appreciate if she would follow suit. She didn't say much, so my dad assumed the talk was over and he went back up to his office. A few minutes later, Mrs. Swang came barging in, threw her apron on his desk, and said, "If you want to run the shop, you go ahead and run it. I quit." Then she turned on her heel and left.

Dad was shocked – he just sat there and stared at the apron from a few minutes, then he decided he couldn't afford to lose such a good worker, so he got up the courage and the nerve he needed and went downstairs to make amends. "Look," he told her. "You are the manager. You run it the way you think it ought to be run." I'm sure it was humbling for him, but at least he was able to keep Mrs. Swang.

Dad named his company Finest Foods, Inc. Later, he started adding cafeterias and wholesale as well as restaurants. Dad built it into a sizeable business, not only in New Orleans but also in Houston, Memphis, and elsewhere. Some years later he sold the sandwich business in Houston to an employee named J.W. Chisholm and the one in Memphis to his sister, Nora McHand.[3] These businesses made thousands of sandwiches overnight and distributed them each morning all over those three cities. During the more than sixty years we were open, the company produced millions of sandwiches in a variety of shapes, sizes, and colors. Finest Foods stayed in business until 1998, when my younger brother James died, and we finally closed the last cafeteria and Mrs. Drake's.

---

[3] My aunt operated the business for many years and, at her death, left it to her two sons, my cousins George Reagan and Guy McHand, Jr. They operated it together until George sold his share to Guy.

———

After he joined the family in 1927, James had provided a lot of laughs because he was always a little mischievous. Once he ate a quarter pound of butter, and another time he scarfed down all the wieners we had set aside for dinner that evening. It seems we ate a lot of wieners, pork and beans, and apple butter. It was the Depression; even though we always had enough to eat, sometimes it was just barely enough – especially if James got into the icebox!

My dad was delivering candy and cookies to the restaurants, and on the first floor of our house we had a storage area for these and other items that he would deliver. One day James got in the back of the truck and ate a whole box of Milky Ways. I can't be too hard on James, though, because I did my share of similar activities. One day Arvis and I filled our shirts with cookies that Dad had stored in a closet. We passed my dad who said, "Cliff, what do you have in your shirt?"

"Nothing, Dad."

It would have been much better for us if I had just said, "Cookies, Dad." I learned my lesson.

But James never did seem to learn his. One day, when he was about five, he got the garden hose, turned on the water, and started spraying people as they walked up and down the street. My mother looked out from the second floor, saw what was happening, and yelled down to James to cut it out. In response, he turned the hose upward and sprayed her. Mother sent me down to get him, so I put on my swimsuit and managed to wrestle the hose away from him. Another time, Dad had just left the house and was driving down Canal Street when someone stopped him and told him he had a little boy hanging onto the back bumper of the car; it was James. James also took the spare change Dad had left on the bed after changing his clothes and ran up the railroad track to buy ice cream with it. He didn't care a bit about the danger – he just loved the adventure of it, I guess!

I did some foolish things myself, like when I jumped off the second-floor porch. It was probably eleven or twelve feet high, and I was curious to see what it would be like to jump. That was an experiment that almost broke my leg! Another time I was walking on the tracks that James ran on to get ice cream, and I got my foot caught where the spur joined the main track. I could hear a train coming and managed to wrench my foot free in time, but I never forgot how frightening that was.

When I was about twelve, we moved to 5307 Weiblen Place, which intersected with Canal. I have great memories of that big old white frame house. It was two stories tall and just off the railroad track near one of my dad's restaurants.

I developed a bad habit of walking in my sleep while we were living on Weiblen. I once wandered downstairs and opened the front door before my mother stopped me; another time I got up to use the bathroom but went to the kitchen and started to use the refrigerator instead; again, my mother caught me just in time. She was always afraid of what I'd do, even when I went away to college and lived on the third floor. Fortunately, I never got hurt, but my sleep-walking gave my mother quite a few scares!

––––––––

There were some interesting times, as well, when the peculiar spirit of New Orleans came out in full force for Mardi Gras. One year when I was a teenager, I was selling Mrs. Drake's sandwiches, cookies, candy, and cold drinks at a little stand on Canal and Claiborne, just a few blocks from the river. Business was brisk, but so was the stealing. There were so many people that it was impossible to have my eyes on everything at the same time. There were some people in costumes and some wearing nothing but paint! You couldn't predict what would happen in the chaos. From my little stand, I saw a driver hit a man and kill him and heard of another group of people who were dressed as Native Americans start swinging hatchets at one another in a fight.

––––––––

Our next home was located at 5420 Canal Boulevard, which was only a couple of blocks from Weiblen Place. The median of Canal Boulevard was at one time a real canal, but it was filled in to make a play area, just as had been done on Jefferson Davis Boulevard. We played cowboys and Indians and built clubhouses. One day, when I was about twelve, I was running with the football when someone came up from behind and tackled me. The tackle broke my collar bone, which is the only bone I have ever broken in my entire accident-prone life.

I was home one day, working in the yard with the front door open when I saw an unfamiliar man enter our house. We didn't know him, and I knew he didn't have any business there, so I could only assume he was up to no good. I went around to the back of the house and got a butcher knife from the kitchen; I was ready to confront him, but by the time I came back to the front door he had already gone, and nothing had happened. I guess maybe he was just curious, but I am awfully happy I didn't have to have an altercation with him. After that, I had some very vivid dreams about fighting robbers with my dad. I guess that experience really made an impression on me.

I attended Beauregard School on Canal Street for sixth and seventh grade. I enjoyed my time at Beauregard very much, though the memory that stands out most to me is an unpleasant one. The only time I was ever taken to the principal's office in my life was when I touched the back of a girl's head through an open window. I had thought we were friends and that she would think it was funny – I had ducked back down right afterwards so she couldn't see who had done it – but she apparently took offense to the joke and reported it to the teacher. The principal called me to her office and, in front of all the other students as we were walking down the hall, told me to keep my hands to myself and not to touch the girls. Needless to say, I did not consider that particular young lady my friend after that incident.

Another time a boy called me a sissy. Now, I had never been in a fight in my life except for wrestling with Arvis. Somehow, he and I were always banging around in the living room and hitting furniture and making so much noise that the neighbors thought it was thundering when it was really just one of us hitting the floor. But this situation was different: it was going to be a real fight with a real winner and a real loser. I told that boy to meet me after school and we'd see who the sissy was. Of course, I had no idea what I would actually do once we met after school, but I knew this was the proper response to his challenge.

When the school day was over, he and I met in the empty lot next to the school and had just started to flail away at each other when a lady came by, fortunately, and threatened to take us both to the principal if we didn't break it up. So we did, and that was the closest to a fight I ever came.

Despite my handful of brushes with the administration, Beauregard was a great school and I enjoyed my time there. At lunchtime I would go to Holdsworth, a very small grocery store just across the street from the school. They had po'boys that were eight or ten inches long, piled high with roast beef, ham, and Swiss cheese – and they cost ten cents. A quart-sized bottle of Jumbo or Gimme soda – in cola, orange, or grape flavor – was a nickel. For fifteen cents you could get the best lunch in New Orleans (outside of A&G, of course), and I thought I was just about the luckiest boy in the world to have that life.

It's hard to explain to someone who isn't from New Orleans how fully the river really does affect every aspect of life in the city. Sometimes the fog was very, very thick on the river. In fact, you could watch it rolling in, getting closer and closer until you couldn't even see your hand in front of your face. More than once I had to walk home from school with one foot on the curb and one foot in the street so I would know where the corners were.

The bogginess of the land also made camping difficult, which meant we had to learn to adapt the usual Boy Scout curriculum to match our unusual circumstances – interacting with nature in a swamp city. But I absolutely loved scouting.

When I was twelve I started as a tenderfoot in Boy Scout Troop 41, which met in the basement at Beauregard. Rip Haas was the Scoutmaster, and his brother helped lead the troop. I enjoyed it so much that I rose through the ranks to become an Eagle Scout with five merit badges beyond – I believe the honor was called Bronze Palm. I also served as a junior assistant scoutmaster, and by the time I was seventeen I was in charge of one of the divisions of the troop. We had a lot of fun in those meetings on Friday nights. We learned to tie knots, make bandages, and do first-aid, and even how to box.

If you didn't come to attention when the scoutmaster gave the signal at the meeting, someone could hit you on the arm with his fist. It was a pretty effective method for getting a person's attention. We were a well-disciplined troop and we had a great deal of fun together. I was playing trumpet in my school band at the time, so I decided to learn to play bugle, too. I became the bugler for Troop 41 and was called upon to play at a number of different occasions. When the janitor at the school died, I was asked to play "Taps" at his funeral. I was also invited to perform a demonstration of bugle calls at the Municipal Auditorium with the New Orleans Symphony Orchestra in 1939.

Our evening meetings would sometimes run as late as 10 p.m., and I would have to walk by a cemetery on my way down Canal Street to Canal Boulevard. I could save about a block of walking by cutting through the cemetery, so I usually opted to do that, but the whole time I would have to remind myself that bravery is part of the Boy Scouts' motto. Due to the high water table in New Orleans – sometimes you can hit water by digging less than a foot – people aren't buried underground there. Instead, they are interred in sarcophagi and mausoleums, many of which were dilapidated and broken down from time and the elements. You could literally look in and see, or even reach in and touch, the bones. Sometimes a neighbor boy who was also a Scout would walk with me, and then I wasn't nearly as scared. But when I was by myself, I would usually start out walking, then I would walk a little faster, then I would whistle to fool myself into thinking I was brave, then I would finally break into an all-out run – all the time telling myself that I was just in a hurry to get home and see my family and certainly not running because I was afraid.

The troop would go on hikes from time to time. Some of them were extremely long; we called them twenty-mile hikes, but they were probably closer to fifteen miles. However long they actually were, they were great fun. We would take our tents and equipment and hike out to the Mississippi River to camp on the river side of the levee, sometimes going all the way out to the Huey P. Long Bridge, approximately seven miles outside the city. Once, as we were camping there, I decided to climb the bridge, which was still under construction. The girders were basically semicircles over the highway portion of the bridge, and I crawled right up on top of them. Looking back on it now, I can't believe I did something that crazy as a twelve- or thirteen-year-old.

I never had a gun – not even a BB gun – until one day when my troop was coming home from one of those twenty-mile hikes on the river and we passed by a store that sold BB guns. I bought one even though I knew that my mother would not approve. When I got home, I walked into the house having concealed it in the leg of my trousers. Of course, my mother knew what was wrong when she saw I couldn't bend my knee, but, amazingly, she let me keep the gun. I was thrilled because now I could play cops and robbers with my cousin George, who lived right on the Mississippi in Memphis. The rule was that we could only aim below the waist, but we really shot at one another and, thankfully, no one was ever hit in the eye.

One of my favorite scouting activities was to go across Lake Pontchartrain to Camp Salmon in the summer. It was a Boy Scout camp with a lot of cabins and even more activities. The ground at Camp Salmon was higher than it was in New Orleans, which meant that it was dry enough to find good camping ground easily. One year I took my brother Arvis with me, and he rolled right out of an upper bunk and hit the wooden floor with an awful noise. Thankfully, he wasn't hurt, but I will never forget the sound.

The most memorable camping trip I had with the Boy Scouts was when I had been placed in charge of seven or eight boys, as was Arvis, even though he technically wasn't a Scout. We went over the river to an area in Mississippi where we could find good camping ground that wasn't as marshy in Louisiana. My parents drove us over – probably about forty miles away from home. You have to go a long way from New Orleans to find decent ground. We stayed there several days and did all of our cooking and various activities. There was a spring nearby, so we had all the water we needed, and the rain held off so that it was warm and dry the whole time. It was a wonderful experience.

Except for one thing.

One of the boys came rushing over to me at the campsite and said Arvis had been bitten by a snake and I'd better come in a hurry. I was barefooted at the time, but I grabbed a knife and a tourniquet and a few other things I might need, and I ran over the briars and brambles until my feet were all torn up – but I didn't care. I just had to get to

Arvis in time. When I finally got where they were waiting, they all started laughing and said, "We fooled you! It was a trick!" I was pretty severe with them and they never did pull something like that again. But I was glad that Arvis was safe and that we all had a great camping experience together.[4]

---

[4] My scouting activities didn't cease when I left for college. When I finished at Harding, I moved to Charleston, Mississippi to preach, and I served as the local scoutmaster while I was there. Later, when I returned to teach at Harding, I was asked to serve on the Board of Directors of the Quapaw Area Council, which was headquartered in Little Rock.

CHAPTER 3

HIGH SCHOOL AND THE WORLD BEYOND

B esides scouting, most of my time outside of school was spent
either playing sports, working for Dad, or being at church. When
we first moved to New Orleans, we found only one Church of Christ,
which was located at Seventh and Camp Street in the Garden District.
The preacher, Robert Turner, worked with the railroad but preached on
Sundays when he was at home. A sweet lady called Sister Baptist was
my Sunday School teacher, though I'm sure there were others whose
names I have forgotten. I was eleven years old when I was baptized,
and shortly afterwards I was asked to lead the closing prayer. I worried
about that the whole service, and when it finally came time for me to
speak a big old frog jumped into my throat and clogged it up. Thank
goodness I was able to get rid of it and go on the lead that prayer, but
I didn't speak again in church for many years after that.

When I was thirteen, my parents and some other members decided
to start another congregation. Seventh and Camp was premillennial,
which was a concept that was new to my parents when we joined and
became an issue of some dissent among the Churches of Christ in the
middle decades of the twentieth century. When my parents helped
establish the Carrollton Avenue Church of Christ, it was on the other
end of town from the Garden District, nearer to where we lived in the
Lakeview area. They rented a store building on Navarre Street where
we had our first meeting of eighteen people, several of whom were relatives of ours. Not long afterwards, the congregation purchased a house
on Canal Boulevard, which was just a couple of blocks away from the
original building. It was a two-story structure, and we used the downstairs for the auditorium and the upstairs for classrooms.

We stayed at that location for several years until a building on Carrollton Avenue owned by the Nazarenes became available. It was a very good location, just two blocks off Canal Street, so we purchased it from them and eventually demolished the small building in order to erect a much larger one that seated almost 250 people. It was a nice buff brick building just across the street from the Jesuit high school, and it provided us an opportunity for tremendous growth. In fact, Carrollton Avenue is the mother Church of Christ of New Orleans, as it has helped to launch congregations in other parts of the city, such as Gentilly, Crowder Boulevard, Wyclosky, Hickory Knoll, and DeGaulle Drive across the river. There may have a few others, too. When the oil business was booming, Carrollton Avenue had well over two hundred members, but when that industry declined many people moved back to Houston and Dallas, and membership dropped by nearly a half.

My Sunday School teacher at the Carrollton Avenue Church of Christ was Aubrey Daniel. He had three sons, one of whom attended David Lipscomb, and another who attended Harding. There were not many boys around my age at church, so I enjoyed his family, especially when his boys were home. Mr. Daniel was always encouraging the young men to speak in church, but most of us refused to do so. Personally, I was convinced that if I tried, I would faint and embarrass myself in front of the entire congregation.[5] I wanted to grow up as a young man and a leader in the church, but the public speaking always terrified me.

One day, my cousin George Reagan came down from Memphis to visit us. He was a young teenager and had a nice suit he was going to wear to church. At that time, there were major street repairs happening on Canal Boulevard; they had torn up all the old concrete and were going to replace it. The street was muddy and wet as they were working on it and George accidentally fell in. His clothes were ruined, and he had to borrow some knickers from my brother to wear to church. I remember how disappointed he was that he had to go to church in little boy clothes, but we didn't tease him...at least not too badly.

---

[5] We were a small congregation, but we were close. John Swang, who worked for us, married a young lady from our Sunday School class. His twin brother Axel went to Harding and married a girl I introduced him to at a taffy pull. I liked to joke I got them stuck on each other!

There were several different preachers over the years at Carrollton Avenue, but the one who had the greatest influence on me was Howard White. He had preached in Charleston, Mississippi, and also in Jackson. He was a young man – only twenty-two years old – and recently graduated from David Lipscomb, when my dad invited him to New Orleans to hold a meeting at our congregation. He was to stay with my family during the meeting, and I remember being impressed by the idea that he was only eight years older than I was and already accomplishing so much for the Lord. I was excited to meet him, but wholly unprepared when I came tromping inside in a dirty football uniform to find him having arrived earlier than I expected. I was mortified as to what his first impression of me must have been (and he admitted years later that he figured I was just a typical little city gangster), but we were thankfully able to spend more time together and create a better and more accurate impression on one another. We loved having Howard stay with us; at night, when the service was over, we would come home and play games in the living room, such as pick-up sticks.

My father and the rest of the elders extended an invitation to Howard to come and preach for us full-time. He stayed at Carrollton Avenue for eleven years; and. even though I left during that period to go to college, I always looked forward to spending time with him when I returned home for the holidays and summers.[6]

---

[6]   Eventually, he decided to return to Nashville to teach at David Lipscomb, and he married Maxine Feltman, who was the Dean of Women. I was the best man in their wedding. They moved to California to work with Pepperdine University when it was still located in the old Watts area, before the school moved to Malibu. Howard eventually become president of the university, and I enjoyed visiting him when he lived in the old Brock House on campus. His wife eventually passed away from cancer and he was left with his two sons, Ashley and Elliot. Years later, Howard also got cancer and retired as president; David Davenport succeeded him. He had been like part of our family in New Orleans, and I wanted to have a chance to see Howard before he passed rather than waiting to make the trip to California for his funeral, so I flew out and spent the night talking about the old days and wonderful memories we had shared. Before I left, we had a prayer together. He said, "Help me up," so I did and I held him upright as we stood and prayed together. He died one week later.

I was getting older, but I was still very much a boy. When we lived on Canal Boulevard, I used to go over to the city park where there were a lot of old trees that all seemed to have legends attached to them. There was Suicide Oak, so named because a number of men had allegedly hanged themselves from its branches. Then there were the Dueling Oaks, where a century earlier men used to fire their pistols at one another over matters of honor. Personally, though, I loved the smaller, younger trees that didn't have so much history connected to them – and the reason I loved them was because I would climb up to the very top and then ride them down as they bent over under the weight. One day I climbed to the top of a particularly tall tree and, instead of bending, it snapped. I landed flat on my back with the wind knocked out of me. It jarred me pretty badly but didn't do any permanent damage – to me. The poor tree didn't fare so well, I'm afraid.

One day, when I was visiting a friend of mine from Boy Scouts who lived next to the cemetery I walked through after meetings, I was running barefoot between the graves chasing a rooster. The cemetery wasn't nearly as scary during the daytime and we were having a good time until I stepped on a broken whiskey bottle that cut my foot in almost the exact same shape as the bottle. I hobbled back to the house, but my friend's mother wouldn't let me inside because of how much I was bleeding. Instead, she sat me down on the back steps, got a basin of water, and began cleaning the wound. When she was satisfied that she had scrubbed it as well as she could, she poured salt in it to keep it clean. I thought I was going to die because it hurt so badly, but she wrapped it up and sent me home to my mother. Mother kept an eye on the cut, but she never took me to the doctor and it never got infected, so I guess that salt must have done its job.

With all the water around New Orleans, it was only natural that we had a boat. At first, Dad just had a small one that held six or eight people, but then he found a pre-owned 45-foot Matthews Cruiser that could sleep six and host a whole lot more for the day. It was a wonderful boat for Lake Pontchartrain. We would take it fishing sometimes and once reeled in two hundred pounds of speckled trout, which is wonderful eating. My uncle, Van Pharris, had a smaller boat and would take us out fishing, sometimes fifty or sixty miles south of the city. We would catch redfish and speckled trout, and I would pilot the boat home while he cleaned the fish. By the time we were back home, the fish were ready to cook.

Once we tried pulling a shrimping net behind us, and when we pulled it up to check, it was about half full. We were thrilled – it could almost fill a washtub! Uncle Van put the net back in the water so we could try to fill it all the way, but it caught on something as we were trolling, and the back end ripped out. It was a lucky day for those shrimp, but a sad day for us! We also tried crabbing, using round nets about two and a half feet wide; they would collapse like an accordion, but when you pulled the string the net enlarged, and the crabs couldn't swim out because of the design of the net. We would put a piece of rotten meat in the center of the net, and when the crabs came to get it we would scoop them up. We did this in Lake Pontchartrain and in the bayous nearby. We would boil them up (but fry the softshell crabs) and have good supper. Crabbing and fishing are just a part of life in New Orleans.

I was always sunburned, being as fair and blond as I was. I never did get nicely tanned; I would just burn and peel, burn and peel. My brothers and I joked that we looked like monkeys picking fleas off one another as we pulled little flakes of skin peeling off of our backs and shoulders. Our burns were sometimes very painful in those days before sunscreen, but it was worth it to be out in the sun enjoying nature. Sunburn wasn't the only way I managed to inflict pain on myself while enjoying the great outdoors, however. Once, when I was twelve, I went fishing with a friend named Ralph Williams, whose father was the lighthouse keeper for Lake Pontchartrain. It was 5:00 a.m., and we were eager to get in a full day of fishing. I was tying a hook into a string and I put the string in my mouth to tighten it. The string slipped and the hook flipped up and caught me on the inside of my lip, just like you would catch a fish. It stuck there and I couldn't get it out; neither could Ralph. Finally, we had to wake up Ralph's father. He pushed and twisted and tugged on it until I passed out, but he was finally able to dislodge it. I guess it's a good thing I don't remember any more details than that – but I do know how a fish feels now!

My family also had a small farm on the north shore of Lake Pontchartrain, just outside of Slidell. We raised chickens and calves, and Dad kept his boat in the little canal that ran along our land. When Dad wanted to get away from the business for a bit, he and I would go over to Biloxi and Gulfport to enjoy fishing and crabbing there. Tolbert Vaughan was a business partner of my father's, as they owned a Poor Boy Restaurant together. The Vaughans were also members of the church and would often take trips with us on the boat.

One of the most memorable trips I took when I was young was in 1936, when I was fourteen, and my parents and I sailed down to Guatemala – but not on our family boat. We went on a banana boat. It was mostly intended for cargo, but it took on passengers for extra money. There were only thirty passengers on board, so it was a rather small vessel. We left New Orleans and went a hundred miles down the Mississippi until we reached the Gulf of Mexico, and then sailed to Puerto Barrios, Guatemala. It was smooth sailing on the river, but once we got out into the open water the waves rocked the boat terribly and both my parents stayed in their bunks in our cabin, very seasick. I tried to read the schoolbooks I had brought with me, but I got nauseated. I was fine as long as I stayed up on the deck, but that meant I couldn't go downstairs to eat at the restaurant. Thankfully, the waiters took good care of me and brought me squab with all the trimmings under glass so I could eat it on deck and not get seasick.

When we arrived in Puerto Barrios three days later, we took the train up to Guatemala City, and from there we went by car into the mountains to a small village called Chichicastenango. It was tiny and picturesque, even primitive. A large Catholic church stood in the center of the town, and there was a big market in the square in front of it. Three times a week farmers would bring in their fruits and vegetables and would also butcher cows, goats, and pigs. Up on the roof of the church and other buildings, *zopilotes* – vulture-like, buzzard-like birds – would wait for a piece of meat to fall, and they would swoop down for it. We ordered chicken one night in one of the restaurants, and I wasn't fully convinced it really was chicken and not one of those huge, ugly zopilotes.

We stayed at a hotel, the Mayan Inn, which had a beautiful court-yard with a fountain and flowering trees. The manager had a pretty little girl just my age who I think was named Carmen. She was studying English in her school and I was studying Spanish, so we tried to com-municate with one another. When I got home, I tried to write her a very long letter in Spanish, but I never heard back. I wasn't sure if it was because her parents wouldn't allow her to correspond or because my Spanish was so terrible that she couldn't figure out what I was trying to say![7]

On the voyage back, we sailed right through a pod of orcas, which the captain said was the largest group he had ever seen. We also saw a number of flying fish and some dolphins. That really was a pretty magical trip.

That trip to Guatemala was my first big travel adventure, but we traveled quite a bit after that, too. In 1940 we drove out to California in a car with no air conditioning. We had to improvise, so we bought a block of ice, put it in a pan, and allowed the wind to blow over it. I don't know how much actual good it did, but psychologically it helped a bit. It was an enjoyable trip: we saw parts of Hollywood and even the movie star Edward G. Robinson! I remember seeing snow on the mountains and I excitedly pointed it out, since we had never seen it before.

"That's not snow!" Arvis argued. "It's just white sand."

"No," I insisted, "it's really snow."

He and I bickered about it until we finally reached the top of the mountains and started playing in the snow; then he finally had to admit that I had been right.

---

[7] I went back fifty-four years later and found that not much had changed in either the village or the Mayan Inn. I asked the new manager if he remembered the little girl and he told me that she had moved to Guatemala City, married a man named Rogers, and established a very fine school and tourist agency. When my wife and I got back to Guatemala City, I tracked down Carmen and gave her a call. She remembered me and we made plans to meet so she could show us the school, but then she came down with a bad case of the stomach flu so we never were able to see each other again.

The following year the whole family went to Mexico, and I got as sick as a dog in Mexico City. My parents went to the drug store and got me some medicine, which, according to my reading of the Spanish label, was castor oil. I'd had enough of that as a child, so I initially refused to take any. Eventually, though, I was so sick that I agreed to choke some down. At least it wasn't in orange juice this time. On the drive home, as we were coming out of the hills in northern Mexico, James was feeling so awful that we had to stop and let him out of the car so he could be sick. Finally, he mumbled, "Just go on and leave me here to die." Of course we didn't, and he survived, but he said he really wasn't sure if he was going to or not.

When I finished seventh grade at Beauregard, I entered Warren Easton High School on Canal Street, just three or four blocks from my dad's office and our first restaurant.[8] Dad would take me to school in the morning, and I would carry my roller skates with me. In the afternoon, when school let out, I would skate back home, which was almost four miles away.

I played in the band at Warren Easton all four years – eighth through eleventh grade, which was as high as New Orleans schools went at that time. We had a very good band under the direction of Mr. Marbut, and it kept us in good shape. We met at the very top of the building, which was four stories up with no elevator; we also marched in a lot of parades. New Orleans loves its parades, and some of them were more than a mile long, which is a pretty good distance to tote a heavy instrument. I started out playing the trumpet but changed to E-flat tuba when the band needed a bass horn player. I also played the snare drums for the B Band. It really was a job carrying that horn since I was always very skinny, even after I hit my growth spurt. People didn't make my job any easier by tossing peanuts, rocks, and whatever else

---

[8] I think it's interesting to note that there was another young man who attended both Beauregard and Warren Easton; he was born the same year I graduated – 1939. That young man was infatuated with Cuba and communism and used to hand out literature on the streets of New Orleans about the glory of Fidel Castro. He even traveled to Russia for a period of time. His name was Lee Harvey Oswald.

they could find into the bell of the bass horn while we were marching. Even so, I really loved playing in parades and football games. I was asked to play my tuba for one dance at the high school, too, and I did, but I didn't play for any other dances after that.

My senior year we went as far away as Shreveport to play for the state championship in football. We enjoyed it, even though we lost to Byrd High by the score of 7-0. Warren Easton always had really good football teams. In fact, a few years before I started there, we even played a game against the team from Tulane. High school players were often older back in those days, and some of the guys on our team even went on to the pros. Sure enough, Warren Easton beat Tulane!

I don't remember much about my classes or the students who were with me in high school, though I do remember taking mathematics under a man named Smith, and I did very well. I think I even had a 100 on my report card. But then I was switched to a class with a teacher from France named Bernudi who would say terrible, abusive things to the class, use curse words, and even throw things at the students. This turned me off as far as mathematics were concerned, and I've never revived my interest in it to this day.

Warren Easton was a boys' school, and there were about 1,700 of us; 195 of us graduated in the spring of 1939. John and Axel Swang, Lucian Bagnetto, and Buddy Vaughan were the boys from church who were around my age, and I think most of them also attended Warren Easton. It was not easy for me to make friends with other teenagers, because their ideals, language, habits, and interests were so different from ours. Wine, women, and song were the general themes at Warren Easton, and that just wasn't the world my parents raised me to be a part of.

We would meet for a thirty-minute homeroom every day, and I would finish my homework during that time. I didn't take any books home during the four years I was in high school. I didn't have to. I just got my work done in that short window each morning. In fact, much of the time I think I was reading a comic book or an airplane book called *Wings* or *Flying Aces* or something like that. I liked airplanes a lot. I used to make little model airplanes out of balsa wood, paper, and a homemade glue. I enjoyed reading books, magazines, and anything about airplanes that I could get my hands on – but mine never flew very well, and after a while I would set them on fire and drop them off the garage to let them float down as if they had been shot down in battle.

―――――――――

Our next home was at 6611 Canal Boulevard. It was the last move we made before I went away to college. I was fourteen or fifteen at the time, but that didn't stop me from using bent pins to try to catch the fish in the canal that ran down the middle of the street. For bait we tried everything from worms we'd dug up in the yard to chewing gum. We didn't catch very many, but it was an awful lot of fun trying.

We were quite a distance from the center of town – a little over four miles, I believe. We discovered just how far it was one Mardi Gras, when my cousin Jeanne Sawyer from Dallas was visiting, and we stayed until the end of the parades when the buses had already stopped running, so we had to walk the whole way home!

There were a number of empty lots around us at that time, and, as any Southerner can tell you, wild blackberries have a way of finding untended areas and flourishing there. It is as if they thrive on neglect. We used to pick blackberries by the bucketful, and mother would make excellent cobblers from them. We had a lady working for us at the time named Agnes, and she could also make beautiful pie and cobblers, but she always said she was no good at making chocolate or lemon or pecan pies. Her sister Carrie also worked for us for years, as well as an older man named Sonny. They were almost like family to us.

For a while, we were able to raise chickens in our yard. One time I heard the chickens squawking like crazy, so I went out to see what was the matter, and there was a huge possum trying to get into the hen house to snatch a chick. I ran and got a butcher knife and tied it to a pole, trying to make a kind of spear so I wouldn't have to get too close to the possum and its nasty, sharp teeth. I didn't manage to harpoon the possum, but at least I got him away from the chickens.

The house was tri-level: on the first floor were the living room, dining room, kitchen, and utility room; on the second floor were two bedrooms; and the third floor had one bedroom. My bedroom was one of the ones on the second level. Mother and Dad's bedroom was in the back on the second level, and my brothers were up on the third floor.

Mother always wanted me to be in by midnight; it didn't matter how much before midnight, but when the clock struck twelve, I should be home. One night I was just a little bit late, so I pulled off my shoes downstairs and quietly tiptoed up. When I reached the top of the stairs, I heard Mother say, "Cliff, where are your shoes?"

I dropped them in surprise. "Mother, I was just trying to keep you from waking up," I tried to explain.

"I was not asleep," she replied. That was when I realized she would not go to bed until she knew we were all home and safe.

Mother didn't spank me very often, even when I was very young. Instead, she would make me go to bed. It might have been in the middle of the afternoon, but if I had done something wrong she would say, "Cliff, go to bed." I would beg her to spank me instead, since going to bed seemed like a cruel and unusual punishment, but she would order me to bed and I had to obey.

The last spanking I ever got was when I was around fifteen years old. I don't even remember what I had done, but, whatever it was, it did not agree with my mother. She told my dad and he met me down in the basement. He usually used his hand, not a belt or a switch, and his hands were pretty big; therefore, he covered a good bit of your anatomy. He believed that the hand was best because you could tell exactly how hard the strike was and whether you were applying too much pressure and overdoing it. The point, after all, was punishment and correction, not injury. On this occasion, however, he used a belt. That almost never happened, but it did on this occasion. And it must have worked because I never got spanked again.

———————

When I was sixteen and looking ahead to leaving for whatever was going to come after high school, my mother and father decided to adopt a little girl. They found one at the Protestant Orphanage in the Garden District – a pretty little blonde two-year-old, and Mother and Dad fell in love with her. She sat on my lap when we drove her home from the orphanage, and she immediately became the darling of the family. Mother had a lot of fun dressing little Joy Carlene; she took her to town and bought her all kinds of clothes and toys and had a great time doing it. After three boys who were always getting dirty and messing up their nice clothes, I think she really enjoyed a little girl.

There were more changes coming for my family, too. One day, a man named Dr. George Benson stopped by for a visit. He was the president of a college called Harding and had been traveling in Florida when he visited with Marvin Brooker, who had once served as an elder at the Carrollton Avenue Church of Christ. Dr. Benson was looking for someone who might be interested in helping with the work that Harding did, and Mr. Brooker suggested a restaurant man that he knew in New Orleans. When Dr. Benson went back to Arkansas, he came through New Orleans and met with Mother and Dad. He offered a $100-per-year scholarship if I would come to Harding and play in the band – the only catch was that I would have to provide my own instrument, since they didn't have an E-flat tuba. We agreed and I paid $365 for that tuba, which meant that the scholarship was really only good for less than $100 a year, but I think it all worked out in the end. And after graduation, when I was preaching in Charleston, Mississippi, I managed to sell that bass horn to the local high school for $165, and we ate on that money for a good while.

In September 1939 I packed my suitcases, and we loaded up the family car to drive north to a little town in Arkansas. I didn't know anything about that school except that they didn't have a football team beyond intramurals. But the Lord was guiding my path to Harding, and I have been grateful for that ever since.

CHAPTER 4

STARTING AT HARDING

As my family drove slowly through the campus and up to Godden Hall in our white Cadillac, we saw three young ladies carrying brooms that they were putting into closets in case someone wanted to sweep their rooms. At that time there was a roadway running through the main part of campus, beginning where the west entrance is on Center Street and coming around past Pattie Cobb, Godden Hall, and where the Olen Hendrix Building now stands.

Mother and Dad were in the front seat and I was sitting in the back in my New Orleans best: a white suit, starched shirt and tie, and a white hat. Immediately those three girls – Louise Nicholas, Verle Craver, and Wailana Floyd – decided I was the most stuck-up boy to hit that campus.

We asked the girls where Dr. Benson could be found, and they sent us over to the main academic and administration building – and probably vowed that was the last time they would ever speak to me. Dr. Benson met us and introduced me to a student named Houston Itin, who was to take me over to Godden Hall, where Room 301 would become my new home.

Godden Hall was really a ramshackle old castle of a dorm. It was three stories high, complete with turrets, and it loomed over the rest of campus. The second and third floors were men's dormitories. There was also an auditorium that could seat almost four hundred people, which was where chapel and Monday night meetings were held, along with drama productions and musical programs. Godden Hall also housed the choral studio, the library, and even a post office. Harding Academy High School met there, too; the elementary was in another building roughly where Cathcart stands now. Harding surely did get a lot of use out of that one building!

39

We used to joke that it was just a big fire trap, and that wasn't far from the truth! Once, when I was a junior, I was coming down Park Avenue from town and saw smoke billowing up from the campus. Sure enough, it was Godden Hall on fire. I quickly ran into the building, grabbed all my clothes in one scoop, and brought them down. I laid them on the ground, and then went into the choral studio to help fight the blaze. After it was put out and we were cleared to go back in, I couldn't figure out how I had managed to carry everything down all at once; it took three trips to take it all back upstairs! In that case, an electric organ had caught fire in the choral studio. I remember that Evan Ulrey showed me once where there had been a fire in his closet on the east side of the building. I don't know what caused that fire or some of the other minor fires, but the building certainly seemed to have quite a few. Godden Hall was indestructible, though. We even used to throw ice picks into the doors and there was no damage.

The walls may have been sturdy, but the furniture was another story; it looked like something you would drag down from the attic and question whether it was safe to use. There were old iron bedsteads with springs that would sway downwards and ancient mattresses that were thin and uncomfortable. Yet despite that, we had a great time in the dormitory! There were no screens on the windows – a fact that terrified my mother when they dropped me off, due to my sleep-walking habit and the fact that I was assigned to a third-floor room. I never tumbled out of a window, thankfully, but plenty of other things were launched from them. We would drop balloons or sacks full of water on people below us. We even caught bats that lived in the rafters and would swoop through the hallways, and we would drop them down the stairwell.

Behind Pattie Cobb there was a two-story wooden building called Gray Gables, housing married students and some faculty. There were also a couple of little houses where the American Studies Building is now, occupied by S.A. Bell and B.F. Rhodes and their families. Next to them was a stone house where L.C. Sears lived.[9]

---

[9] Years later it was moved out to Center Street and finally demolished when the education building was erected.

There was also a very small gym – so small that there was only about twenty-four inches of space between the end of the basketball court and the wall itself. There were hot steam pipes that ran around the wall about at knee-height. When we threw in the basketball from out of bounds, we would often hit our legs on those pipes and burn them. We came back on the court faster than the ball did! It was definitely not a regulation-size court, either, because I was able to throw the ball from one end and sink it in the basket at the other end.

When we weren't playing organized games, we might have one of our friends lie in a blanket and then, with three of us on each side, count to three and throw him up in the air. The gym was two stories high, but the ceiling was so low that one day a small freshman named Matt Timmerman was tossed in a blanket and actually hit his head on the ceiling. He was fine, and that didn't stop us from trying to launch the next person almost as high.

The upstairs only had room for about a dozen people to watch a game. That wouldn't have been a problem except that there was no room for anyone to sit and watch a game downstairs, either! The only option was to stand in the small entrance area. Despite all its flaws, we had a lot of fun in that little cracker box gymnasium. We had wrestling and boxing there, too, and there was a large activity room upstairs. That old gym stood until 1950, when it finally was taken down to make room for the Administration Building.

There were only twenty-nine acres in the Harding campus when I arrived in 1939, and only three buildings of any consequence: Godden Hall, Pattie Cobb, and the Administration Building (later completely refurbished to be today's Olen Hendrix building}. There was our tiny gym, a swimming pool, Gray Gables, and a small wooden apartment building, but the other buildings were all pretty inconsequential. The campus was bordered on the south by Park Avenue, which was a gravel road that led from Searcy to Kensett. On the west it ended at Turner Street and on the north at Center Street. On the east, our boundary was Blakeney Street, which is where the Rhodes-Reaves Field House is now. We had a large track and baseball diamond there and a rag-tag football field. We also did a lot on the front lawn. I remember playing football barefoot on the grass as a freshman and jumping up to catch a pass. The defender, Jack Lay, was wearing baseball spikes, and he came down and dug out about a half inch of my heel. It hurt terribly. I just left the flesh there; what else could I do except let it fertilize the front lawn? I like to say that I will always be a part of the Harding campus... even if I am a bit of a heel!

The building that was later converted into the Olen Hendrix building had terribly squeaky floors. There was a center hallway through the building with rooms on both sides, and on the south end there were administrative offices. Dr. Benson had his office in the very last room; next to him was Dean Sears, and next to him was the office of the registrar, W.K. Summit. The science department was on the third floor, so a walk along the creaky corridors was always accompanied by the smell of formaldehyde and other strange scents from chemistry experiments.

We all loved the big trees in the main campus; they made the quadrangle look like a forest. Sadly, we've lost many of those old oaks over the years to windstorms and lightning, and even a few to make room for new buildings. But the ones that have remained have grown mightily!

When I first arrived at Harding, I had been dating a girl in New Orleans named Shirley Vaughn. Her dad was an elder with mine at Carrollton Avenue and our families were very close. But the entire direction of my life changed within ten seconds when we arrived on the Harding campus and I saw those three young ladies putting the brooms away. At dinner than night I spotted one of the girls, and someone introduced her to me as Louise Nicholas from Strawberry, Arkansas. I chuckled a little bit at the name of her town; it just sounded so quaint! That was on a Wednesday, and later that evening I went to a prayer meeting at the Downtown Church of Christ, which was meeting at the intersection of Locust and Vine. I just happened to be sitting in the pew behind her, and, once again, someone introduced me to Louise Nicholas from Strawberry, Arkansas. Then, on Friday evening after dinner, Houston Itin asked if I'd like to go on a walk, and I agreed. He said, "Wait a minute and I'll get a couple of girls to walk with us." The two girls he got were Nancy Fern Vaughn and Louise Nicholas of (where else?) Strawberry, Arkansas. Houston walked with Louise and I walked with Nancy, though I kept wishing we would trade because

Louise was much closer to my age – she was going to be a sophomore that year, but Nancy was about to be a senior. The following night, on Saturday, we walked again, this time with three girls, and I managed to walk with Louise while Houston walked with the other two. I was thrilled but Louise was the one wishing we could trade partners this time. She had no idea how to talk to a city slicker from New Orleans!

On Sunday morning, Houston said, "Cliff, why don't you go over to Pattie Cobb and get Louise to walk to church with you?"

I agreed, but when I got to the top of her dorm steps, I suddenly got cold feet because I didn't know how to ask a girl to go to church with me. I turned around and went back up to Houston's room and said, "I think I'll just go by myself."

He wouldn't hear of it and insisted I go with him and Frances, who was his girlfriend and had just gotten in the night before. I agreed, so we walked over to Pattie Cobb together, and out came Frances... with Louise. The four of us went to church together and then came back to campus for lunch in the dining room. That afternoon, Louise and I, along with a couple of others, walked out to the county farm – near where the fairgrounds are now – to take communion to the elderly folks in the home for the aged there. It was about a mile-and-a-quarter walk, and we passed a little store on the way back that was selling plugs of tobacco twisted around in a funny way so that they looked like oblong circles. I held one up as if I were about to chew and someone took a photo of me. I quickly earned a new nickname: Goofy. I was always pulling pranks and doing silly things.

Classes began the next day, and I was immersed in a whole new world I absolutely loved. One of the greatest influences on me was J.N. Armstrong. I sat at his feet for four years in Bible, Greek, chapel, and Monday night meetings. Other teachers included B.F. Rhodes (history), L.E. Pryor (history), and S.A. Bell (Bible). I also took Sister Rhodes' speech class, but I didn't enjoy her teaching. She talked all the time about her grandchildren, Jack Wood and Kern Sears, so I decided not to enroll for the second quarter, even though it was required. When I was about to start my final semester and was looking to graduate, the registrar realized I had not taken the second half of the speaking course, so they let me take radio speech, taught by Mrs. Armstrong, and I enjoyed it much more. I won first place in the speech contest and received a set of Adam Clarke's commentaries as a prize. If the registrar had not allowed for that substitution, I might still be a student at Harding!

The social clubs on campus meant much to the students because there was little to do in town. Not everyone was in a club, of course, but abstainers were by far the minority. I chose Sub T-16, with TNT as my second choice. I was afraid I wouldn't get into either, but I actually got a bid from both, which was a pleasant surprise. I felt I had a made a good choice with my club; it was only sixteen members large at the time, but they were all fine young men and I enjoyed my association with them. On alternate Monday evenings we would have club meetings, and on alternate Saturdays we could have a date night in the cafeteria, which was in the basement of Pattie Cobb. The Sub Ts had very stringent regulations. If someone had a violation or missed a meeting – or even were just late to one – he would have to endure the beltline. The beltline meant that you had to bend over and hold onto your ankles as the guys ran past, one at a time, and whacked your backside with their belts. Most guys were pretty nice about it, but sometimes someone would be a little less than gentle. I went three and a half years without having to face the beltline even once; then I ended up as skipper (Sub T lingo for president) and getting it seven times, I think, in that last semester of my senior year. It would never be allowed these days, but it certainly had a good effect on efficiency and responsibility!

Part of our meetings also involved selecting an individual and standing him up as we all praised the things in him that were admirable and positive; then, we would kindly share some of the ways we felt he could improve himself. It wasn't much fun to hear those suggestions, but you knew they were made in love and it really was tremendously helpful – much more so than hearing the praise, actually.

I also participated in intramural athletics, and club competition ended up becoming my favorite arena. Our outings were great fun, as well. Sometimes we went to Dripping Skillet or Happy Hollow on the Little Red River, which were both very near to Searcy. None of us had cars or trucks, so if we wanted to have an outing farther away, we would have to borrow or rent vehicles. We also had what we called a "third function," which was a dinner or short-term outing – something that didn't require much time or expense but felt like we were doing something special. Louise was a member of the W.H.C., the Woodson Harding Comrades. They had outings and banquets to which I was invited as her guest. I remember those fried chicken suppers off campus where we would dress up like country people and be farmers for the night. It was a lot of fun!

Once school started, Louise and I didn't have a lot of opportunities to be together; occasionally we would pass on the sidewalk or meet in chapel, and on Sundays we would go to church together. When I began preaching, however, we didn't get to see each other on Sundays because girls were not permitted to go with the boys who were preaching. The college wanted the boys to give their full and undivided attention to the congregation where they were working. We did have an opportunity to go on a date every other Saturday night in the Pattie Cobb cafeteria where we talked and played Rook. She worked at the cafeteria, too, so sometimes I got a chance to see her at the counter when I would go back for seconds just to say hi. We were allowed to go to church on Wednesday night and to go to the theater occasionally when the faculty thought the picture showing would be appropriate. We would all line up at the foot of the steps of Pattie Cobb and would walk together to the Rialto Theater on Race Street. There was always at least one chaperone who went along. Occasionally, both Brother Andy Ritchie and his wife would chaperone, and they would walk one in front of the group and one behind us to make sure everyone was okay in the dark as we walked back after the show. We were also permitted to walk off campus on Sunday afternoons from 3:00 until 5:00, although, we had to have at least three couples walking together. In other words, our dating opportunities were pretty slim, but the regulations didn't deter us from enjoying the time we had together.

Cliff and Louise

I don't remember the first time that I ever held Louise's hand, but it was probably in the first three weeks of meeting her because I was pretty crazy about her right away. I do remember the very first time I kissed her. We had been dating since September, and this was some-time in the following spring – April, I believe. There was a festival that honored the strawberry harvest in Arkansas, and Louise was one of the contestants to be the queen. The selection was made according to whoever raised the most money – it was a penny a vote. It cost me quite a bit that night, but I was determined that Louise was going to be the queen, because I had told her that if she won, I was going to kiss her. She won, and on the way home, when just the two of us were walking back, we stopped in front of one of the two little houses at the western entrance of campus where the American Studies Building is now. I paused just a little bit and then quickly kissed her before we walked on to Pattie Cobb.

After that, I voluntarily worked a bit in the dining hall mopping floors because that way I would get to be near her.[10] We laugh today when we talk about the strict rules and regulations that existed when we were at Harding, but we all loved the school so much that we didn't resent them.

---

[10] Well, that and the fact that I wanted to get in good with Mae Chandler, out dietician; she was the key to the availability of food and portion sizes. Food was always a big motivator for me. I volunteered at the Harding Farm for the same reason. Bob Street, who was in charge of the farm, was a good friend of mine, but his wife, Louise, was an even better cook. She really knew how to make roast beef, mashed potatoes, gravy, and homemade rolls that melted in your mouth. It was worth it to work on the fences or in the potato patches or berry fields just to get to eat with them.

Chapter 5

Behind the Pulpit

I learned how to study in college, since I really hadn't learned how in high school, and I learned how to buckle down and apply myself to my schoolwork instead of just making a minimal effort for decent grades. I even earned a place in our academic honor society. My ultimate goal was to learn business better and then go back to New Orleans to work with my dad, and that's what I set my mind to. But that all changed about three months after I arrived, when Dean L.C. Sears stopped me after chapel one day and said, "Cliff, I want you to speak at Wednesday night prayer meeting for ten minutes." My first impulse was to turn him down, but I didn't know how to say no to the dean, so I told him I would try – and then studied six hours for that ten-minute talk, which I gave in six minutes.

When I stood up to begin speaking, perspiration was rolling down my back and legs, but I didn't faint, so I decided that night I was going to try to preach. When I went home for Christmas, Carrollton Avenue invited me to give the sermon on Sunday and I spoke for twenty-five minutes from a borrowed outline about the need for the church to go, to grow, and to glow. I don't remember from whom I borrowed that outline, but it was the first full sermon I ever delivered, and it was a good feeling.

After I went back to Harding following the holidays, in the spring of 1940, I preached at a small country congregation in DeValls Bluff, fifty-four miles south of Searcy. I was just a beginning preacher boy practicing on the church, but they were very nice to me, and I have a lot of great memories of my semester with the church there. I especially enjoyed going home with the Kerrs for lunch, because they served homemade pickles and buttermilk fudge and ice cream. I had a few more interesting dining experiences during those few months, too. I had heard about "four and twenty blackbirds baked in a pie," but I'd never actually eaten blackbird pie until that spring of 1940. Brother Alexander had gone out to kill a rooster that morning for chicken and dumplings, but he saw a tree full of blackbirds; so he got a shotgun and took down about a dozen of them, which his wife made into a pie. It was actually really good – a lot better than the boiled goat that another brother prepared for lunch on Sunday when his family hosted me. The meat tasted exactly like a goat smells; I think some of the follicles got onto the meat and caused the bad flavor.

Throughout my sophomore year I was an itinerant preacher at different congregations, but at the beginning of my junior year I was invited to preach nine miles west of Batesville at the Bethesda Church of Christ. Dr. Benson wanted to help the congregation, because he had held a meeting up there and they asked him if he could get someone to preach for them regularly. So he asked me if I would be interested and said he could give me $2.50 to help me cover the travel cost. The congregation also gave me $2.50, so I received $5 each Sunday for my expenses. The only challenge was getting there. I didn't have a car, though I had talked to my dad a few times about getting one. He would say, "Cliff, you don't need a car," and that was the end of that conversation. Instead, I caught a bus or a train or hitchhiked or used whatever was available all throughout my college career in order to get where I was preaching.

One week I learned that the townspeople of Bethesda were planning to remove the second story of the community center where the church met to make it a more stable one-story building. I agreed to bring some boys with me to work on the project, so Don Healy, Louis Green, and Sammie Swim went with me – I think there may have been six of us in all. We piled into an old car dressed in our coveralls and bandanas and work caps and drove there. As soon as we arrived, however, I was informed that an elderly man in the community had died and I had to preach his funeral. I had never preached a funeral before and I started to worry, "I don't have a Bible or appropriate clothes," I told them, but they said they could fix all that. They got me a Bible, a suit that was so tight I thought I was choking, and shoes that were so big I could almost turn around in them – and I preached that funeral.

Then I got right back to work on tearing down the second story of the building.

After we finished and had started home on a crooked, narrow, hilly road, the brakes in the car gave out just as we were approaching a sharp curve. I called for the boys to open the doors and drag their feet, so they all dug in their heels as best they could and the car finally slowed to a stop just before we came to the curve, which led to a bridge. We would not have made it if they hadn't all lent their feet. We took one of the bandanas and tied the brake rod together or something like that. I don't remember exactly how we rigged it; I just remember that, somehow, that bandana got us home in one piece. All of the eating adventures and traveling scares were just part of the experience of preaching in those small congregations, and I am glad that I was able to do that.

One Saturday night after Louise and I were engaged, we went up to Strawberry to visit with her family. I loved the country store they owned, selling everything from plowshares and pickles to clothes and crackers. Hardware and food filled the shelves, and farmers would bring in eggs and chickens and milk to swap for tools and seeds. Louise's dad would then sell those things to others who came by. They lived in a shotgun-type portion of the store, straight back, one room after another on one side of the store. They had a well from which they drew all their water with a long cylinder; I was fascinated by it. It was fun for a city boy to see country life in action.

It snowed overnight while we were visiting, which I had not anticipated, and I had to preach in Bethesda in the morning, so I borrowed her dad's car and drove to Cave City, then turned south and headed to Batesville and Bethesda. Just as I was cresting over the top of a hill, I saw two cars struggling up the hill, side by side, and I knew I was going to hit one of them because I couldn't stop on the ice. I imagined losing my fiancée because I had wrecked her daddy's car, and that didn't seem like a very good proposition, so I just turned the wheel and drove into the ditch. There was so much snow that it acted like a cushion and there was not a mark on the car. Neither of the other two cars that had been coming at me were able to make it up the hill, so one of them got off the road and the people came up from the bottom of the hill to help pull me out of the ditch and get me on the way to Bethesda. When I got there, I went to the home of Jewell Latham, one of the members

51

of the church who was a schoolteacher and a cousin to Pearl and Ethel Latham, whom I knew from Searcy. I warmed up at Jewell's house, but when it came time to drive to services, the car wouldn't start, so we ended up having to walk two or three miles from out in the country to the church building in all that snow. We made it, however, and then went back to her house for lunch, after which I managed to get the car started and drove back to Strawberry.

Louise graduated in 1942 at age twenty, one year before I graduated. She got a teaching job in Wynne, and Batsell Baxter asked me to lead singing with him at the congregation there. As much as I loved that congregation at Bethesda, I agreed to go with him because it meant that I would get to see Louise once a week. There was a train that ran the roughly sixty miles from Kensett to Wynne, so Brother Baxter and I could catch it every Sunday morning and be back in the evening; it was very convenient. In the spring, however, he left Searcy to serve as the president of David Lipscomb College – a position he had filled earlier in his career, as well. The congregation in Wynne asked me to stay on and preach there for the remainder of the year, which I did.

I enjoyed going home for holidays and visits, but I was always so glad to get back to Harding. Of course, I couldn't wait to see Louise again, but I know that even if she hadn't been a part of my life, I would have loved Harding just for the friends and teachers who made it such a wonderful place. It was a different experience than I had had in New Orleans with such a limited Christian community. I always came back to campus early in order to be with my friends again.

My life shifted tremendously at Harding because, even though I had always gone to church with my parents, my faith became my own. As I was learning to study more effectively for my classes, I was also learning how to study my Bible better. I had never enjoyed so many godly teachers and friends as I did those who were at Harding with me. Everyone was helpful to me as a new student who was quite a distance from home, and my personal and spiritual life solidified.

CHAPTER 6

CHANGING PLANS

I started out a business major with a plan of going back to work with my dad in the restaurant business, but after three months I changed my mind and become a double major in history and Bible, with minors in business and biology. It seemed, sometimes, like I was taking classes in every single department!

I enjoyed my studies so much that I only recall playing hooky one time in my four years. That happened on one beautiful spring day when several of us boys from Sub T agreed that it was simply too nice to be in a classroom, so we decided to go to Bee Rock instead. We packed a big box of fried chicken and headed up Grand Boulevard and just kept on going straight, cutting through fields until we came to the Little Red River north of Searcy. Obviously, we had not put much thought into this outing, because we suddenly realized there was no way to swim across while keeping the food dry. That's when I had the brilliant idea that Mac Timmerman, a very small freshman, could climb on my back and hold the chicken while I swung across on a vine like Tarzan. The plan worked about as well as you might imagine; about halfway across, my hands slipped, and we both fell into the river. Thankfully, Mac and I were able to swim safely to shore, and someone managed to catch the box of food before it floated away. We ate the chicken even though it was soaking wet, and I like to think that my soggy lunch taught me my lesson never to play hooky again.

While I was a student at Harding, I participated in every sport I could. From horseshoes to badminton to volleyball to tennis – single, doubles, teams – I don't think I missed a single thing in four years, even though I wasn't very fast and wasn't very big. In fact, my first two years I boxed and wrestled at 173 pounds as a light heavyweight. My freshman year I won the championship in boxing, defeating Joe Pryor. He was a large, strong guy, and everybody thought I was going to get clobbered, but I knew a little more about boxing than he did.

I wasn't so fortunate with wrestling. I had never wrestled with the rules whereby you pinned people; I just always wrestled until the other person hollered uncle or gave up. My first year at Harding I wrestled Louis Green, who had been one of the finalists for the Indiana State Championship in high school. We had a very short match; he pinned me in thirteen seconds flat. Apparently, even he was surprised things were over so fast. I learned from experience, though, and the next year when I had to wrestle Louis, I lost by just one point in overtime; and the third year, I finally beat him! That third year, I also had to wrestle Ed Skidmore. We were both heavyweights by then, and he had at least forty pounds on me; I was 185, and he tipped the scale at 225 of solid muscle. He got me on my back one time, and I thought I would never get him off, but I finally did somehow or another.

I had never played basketball before I got to Harding – I'd never even seen a game – but I eventually learned enough to be pretty good at it. I wasn't fast, so track was never a place where I really shone, but the field events were a different story. Shot put, javelin, discus – all of that was easy enough for me. I just didn't have the speed to do much in terms of races. The best I ever finished was fourth in the high hurdles, and I only managed that because my good form in leaping made up a little bit for how slow I was.

Football has always been my favorite, but I enjoyed softball and baseball as well. In short, if there was a game, match, or meet, I was probably right in the thick of it. I was fortunate enough in my freshman year to finish behind Jack Lay for the all-sports trophy. Jack was an outstanding athlete and a senior, so I was delighted to have finished second to him! My sophomore year I again finished in second place. It wasn't until my junior year that I finally came in first – and then I won it again my senior year just to be secure in the title. Those sports really meant a lot to me and allowed me to make a lot of good friendships.

I also wrote for *The Bison*, our student paper, and served as the sports editor my junior year. I figured that if I was going to be at every sporting event anyway, I might as well write up a story on it. We won several statewide awards for college papers; and in 1941, when we earned first place in all of Arkansas, we had a little gathering in front of old Godden Hall and celebrated our victory.

Cliff and Louise celebrating the first-place Bison

Not everything I attempted was a success, however. I played bass horn when I came to Harding and then had to switch to the baritone because that was what they needed at the time to round out the band. I did pretty well on those, but when I tried bass fiddle for one year in the orchestra, it did not go well. A young lady from Little Rock was very good on that instrument and attempted to teach me how to play it, but I was never very good and gave it up as quickly as I could.

———

Those were good times, and they were facilitated by good people. I made good grades and was in the Alpha Honor Society, but I was involved in almost all the activities on campus. I played in the band and orchestra and sang in the chorus and glee club. Leonard Kirk, our choral director, was from Columbia, Tennessee, and he had been quite the horseman growing up. He even headed up the Equestrian Club on campus. Louise and I also enjoyed learning from Florence Fletcher

Jewell. We nicknamed her "Julie," and not only did she teach us, but also our children and our grandchildren.

We all have certain people who stand out in our lives as having tremendous influence, and for me one of those men was J.N. Armstrong. Not only was he the dynamic professor who taught Bible classes and Greek, but he was also an elder in the College Church and president of Harding from 1924 until 1936. Each Monday night the church hosted meetings when young men would make speeches or lead singing or say prayers, and Brother Armstrong and Brother Rhodes would sometimes critique the students. It could be a little painful to hear what they thought about what you had to say, but it certainly was helpful to us as we prepared to go out and lead churches. I have always been deeply thankful for all I learned from Brother Armstrong, both in the classroom and in the pulpit. Brother Armstrong was one of the most dynamic figures on the campus. When I arrived, he was sixty-nine years old; he had a tremendous force about him, despite being a very quiet person by nature. I can still remember his bringing his hand down across his palm when he was emphasizing a point he wanted to drive home to an audience. You forgot about his white hair and the bit of a stoop he had when you watched him preach with such passion. He died in the summer of 1944, while I was preaching in Mississippi. I felt his absence acutely when I returned.

Another giant of Harding to me was L.C. Sears, who had been the Dean of the College since it began in 1924 in Morrilton and continued to serve in that role until June 1, 1960. He was an outstanding teacher and scholar in literature, as well as being a popular preacher. Everyone who sat at his feet said he was one of the greatest teachers they had ever had.

L.E. Pryor and B.F. Rhodes were some of my favorite history professors. Brother Pryor especially was a very loving, calm, and quiet man. He was such a gentleman, in fact, that even during the war when everyone else was cursing Mussolini and Hitler, he, while decrying their actions, referred to them as "Mr. Mussolini" and "Mr. Hitler" in his lectures. As great as these classes were, however, it was sometimes difficult to stay awake after lunch. Once, I was sitting in the back row of one of Brother Pryor's classes and leaned my chair up against the wall. I started to drift off and almost fell flat on my face. I guess it would have been a good time to start talking about Acts 20:9, when Eutychus fell asleep during one of Paul's sermons and fell out a window!

Probably the most influential of all those men for me was Dr. George Benson, and even though he would go on to influence me even more in my teaching career, I was fascinated by him as a student, too. He had spent years preaching and teaching in China, and he had some highly unusual expressions that I can only guess were a result of being steeped in another culture for so long. He also had a unique way of walking, and George Tipps was especially good at imitating him – all in good fun, of course. Dr. Benson was truly the man for the time when he came back to the United States in 1936 to take over Harding's presidency. The board knew they needed someone who had a strong will and a clear sense of where he wanted to take the school. Dr. Benson was able to keep control of the school while also growing it and raising enough money to finally get it in the black. Dr. Armstrong was beloved and deeply respected, but fundraising was not his forte; he showed his great wisdom at his retirement in encouraging the board to invite Dr. Benson back from China to take over the university. Dr. Benson knew how to drum up support, and he certainly put that talent to work for Harding.

He put me to work for Harding, too.

In the summer of 1942, between my junior and senior years, Dr. Benson asked me if I would be willing to do some recruiting for the university in five southern states. He gave me the use of a car – an old, tan Ford, which had a good engine but leaked at the roof and the floorboards. One day in Tennessee, I was dressed in my suit while driving through some heavy rain. Between the rain coming down and the puddles splashing up, I arrived at my destination soaked from head to foot.

I was usually able to keep the car in good running order, but the tires were terrible. Since this was during World War II, we had to use recaps instead of new tires, and some of them were simply awful. One day, in the space of two hundred miles I had three blowouts. Thankfully, I had a trunk full of recaps, so I just threw another one on and kept driving across Arkansas, Louisiana, Mississippi, Alabama, and

Tennessee. I covered five thousand miles that summer – at a top speed of thirty-five miles an hour, because of wartime restrictions. And I had quite a few stories that came out of it!

Once, when I was in Alabama, I was running very low on cash; in fact, I only had two cents left. I had stayed the night with the Weaver family and then drove north to Piedmont, Alabama, on my way to Gadsden. I had written to the school to send me some money to Piedmont, and – sure enough – there was a check from Harding as well as a check from my parents for $25. I was almost out of gas, so I went to the bank to cash the checks, but they refused to cash them since they didn't know me.

My only option, as far as I could see, was to hitchhike the twenty-five miles over to Gadsden, where I had a friend who could vouch for my identity at the local bank. I parked the car in Piedmont and locked it up, preparing to thumb my way to Gadsden, but the key broke in the lock. There was nothing I could do about it just then, so I decided to worry about it after I made it to Gadsden.

I was wearing a tan suit and brown and white shoes, but pretty quickly a blister popped on my big toe, so I had one shoe off and one shoe on as I walked down the highway. I'm sure I cut quite a figure walking down the road, reading a book, and sticking out my thumb when I heard a car coming. One man picked me up and drove me for exactly one mile before stopping at a bar. He bought me a Coke, but then he stayed put and kept drinking, so I figured I'd continue on my way alone. I ended up walking eighteen miles, stopping at farmhouses along the way for water. I bought two penny peanut bars with my last two cents, and they were the only thing I had to eat.

Finally, when I was only about six miles from Gadsden, a man picked me up and offered to drive me the rest of the way into town. As I told him about my day, he shook his head. "You're a preacher, aren't you?"

"Yes, I am," I said with a little surprise. "How do you know?"

He laughed. "Only a preacher would do a dumb stunt like you did."

When we reached Gadsden, I looked up my friend Doyle Earwood, whom I had hoped could vouch for me so I could cash my checks, but it turned out that he had moved so I didn't know any more people in Gadsden than I had in Piedmont. I found a hotel and figured I could spend this night sitting in the lobby if nothing else. I called my parents and told them about my situation, and they offered to wire $25 to me, but the office in Gadsden closed before the wire could come through, so I had no money, no bed, no food. But I did have some old copies of *Life* magazine there in the hotel lobby, and one of the first things I turned to was a beautiful picture of fried chicken fixed five different ways. My stomach was already complaining, and that sure didn't help anything. The clerk at the front desk must have heard it grumbling, because he went to the manager and explained that I'd had money wired that would be there in the morning, and couldn't they give me a room for the night and let me pay the next day? I hadn't even asked for this favor, but they made the offer, and I sure appreciated having a place to lay my head that night, at least. Bright and early the next morning, I got my $25, paid my bill, and went across the street to the bus station where I bought a quart of milk and two fruit pies. I caught the next bus back to Piedmont, so I could retrieve my car, but I would have to have a locksmith take a look at the broken key situation first. The only problem, it turned out, was that the nearest locksmith was in...Gadsden.

I went into the little restaurant where I'd parked the car and ordered a couple of hamburgers and another quart of milk, then took the bus back over to Gadsden, had the key made, took the bus back to Piedmont, opened the car, replenished the gasoline, and drove over to Gadsden, which had been where I was headed in the first place.

I met the preacher at Gadsden, V.P. Black, and then pushed on up into Tennessee as I continued doing my big recruiting circle. While I was in the Volunteer State, I saw brother N.B. Hardeman, who was President of Freed-Hardeman, at a county fair one evening; he was performing on a beautiful black Tennessee Walking Horse, and I recognized him from seeing him at the Freed-Hardeman Lectureship the year before, when I had attended with my dad. At that time, he had invited me over to his home, where we sat on the front porch swing and talked about my plans for the future. He had told me, "You really ought to leave Harding and come over to Freed-Hardeman and study there for a year or two, and then graduate from a public college where your degree will really mean something."

I was surprised at his words, but I replied as respectfully as I could: "Brother Hardeman, I have been at Harding for two years now and I plan to graduate from Harding. That's the school I love and it's great for me."

It made me chuckle a little to see him now, a year later, as I was not only still attending Harding myself but was also working for the school to recruit more students to enroll there, too.

A week or two later, I was in northwestern Tennessee to meet with prospective students, and I encountered Brother E.R. Harper, the preacher from the Fourth and State Congregation in Little Rock. You would think, given our geographical proximity, that he would be a big supporter of Harding, but it was actually the opposite. Somehow, he had gotten the idea that Brother Armstrong and several other faculty members were premillennialists, and he was extremely outspoken against the school as a result.

I went to hear him preach in Union City and introduced myself to him afterwards. He graciously invited me to come back to his hotel so we could talk further, and I was glad to do so. We ended up talking until almost 2:00 in the morning. My dad was serving as Chairman of the Harding board at the time, and Brother Harper wanted me to have my father come by his office in Little Rock to see all the evidence he had amassed that he believed proved Brother Armstrong was a premillennialist. Neither of us wanted to give up on winning over the other, and by the time we realized how long we'd been at it, to was too late for me to head back out into town to find other lodgings, so he invited me to share his room. We were strange bedfellows, but we were determined not to give up our cause nor to leave the other unconvinced.

I did the work I needed to in town that day, and that evening went back to hear Brother Harper preach again, and again we stayed up debating until 2:00 a.m. Finally, I just said, "Brother Harper, I have sat at the feet of Brother Armstrong for two years in his Bible classes and I have never heard anything that would indicate he is a premillennialist." In my view, a person could interpret someone else's words however they wanted to, if they were working from a place of presuppositions and secondhand information. But unless you make the effort to get to know someone on a personal level and really question their teachings one-on-one, it's difficult to say with confidence that you truly understand what their beliefs are. I believed I had a much more accurate under-standing of Brother Armstrong's theology, since I had studied with him and knew him personally.

At the end of the summer, on my way back through Arkansas, I stopped in Beedeville where a certain young schoolmarm named Louise Nicholas happened to be living. She had just graduated that spring, and she and I were planning to be married the following spring. I stayed with some church members and was grateful for the oppor-tunity to get to visit with my sweetheart before I had to get back to Searcy for the start of term.

My senior year, I was editor of the school yearbook, the *Petit Jean*, which was a far more difficult job than I had anticipated when I signed on. For one thing, photographic supplies were greatly limited due to the war, so we had to carefully ration our film and could only afford one shot per club. If someone blinked or a person wasn't posed just right, that was too bad. We couldn't afford to take a second photo. We did the best we could to document campus life that year and sent the proofs off to a printer in Oklahoma, anticipating the annuals would be ready for us with a week or two left at the end of the year so we could all sign them for each other. Then the real challenges began. First, rainstorm after rainstorm in Tulsa left the air so damp that the glue couldn't dry on the books. When they finally were able to be packed up and shipped to us, the Arkansas Railway Express somehow lost them and had to figure out where they'd been left. Finally, when they were on the right train and headed our way, another storm and resulting flood hit eastern Oklahoma and the tracks were underwater. The books finally did arrive, but we were sweating it right up to the day of graduation, May 27!

Getting the annuals on time was actually the least of my concerns, since the commencement exercises in Godden Hall for all thirty-six of us in my graduating class finished at 11:30 a.m., and Louise and I were having our wedding in the same auditorium at 1:00 p.m.! I liked to say I got my bachelor's degree and lost my bachelor status the same day.

Wedding, May 27, 1943

I don't remember much about the wedding itself except that Brother Batsell Baxter, who had left Harding that spring to become the president at Lipscomb, came back to perform the ceremony. I remember who was in the wedding only because we were able to take about six pictures of it. I do remember that in those days almost everyone wrote something in everyone else's yearbook, and I stood outside the auditorium signing annuals while I waited to hear the music that was my cue to enter. Louise had to wait for me after the ceremony because I had not yet packed up my dorm room on the third floor of Godden Hall. In fact, it was evening before we finally got our little one-wheel trailer completely packed and drove to Memphis to visit at the residence of Uncle Guy and Aunt Nora McHand. After midnight we drove to the Peabody Hotel. We spent the first night of our honeymoon at the premier hotel in Memphis for a total bill of $7.25. It is slightly more expensive now!

The next day we started down to New Orleans, but our little trailer broke in northern Mississippi and we lost several hours as we had it repaired. We didn't arrive in New Orleans until after midnight. Nevertheless, we spent a few lovely days visiting my family, and then we continued over to the Buena Vista Hotel in Biloxi. I had spent time fishing and crabbing on the Gulf before, and it was wonderful to take my new wife to the same beaches I had grown up enjoying as a boy.

We had a brand-new Studebaker from my parents as a wedding gift. Despite the fact that I had asked my father for a car for years for my preaching, he had never believed I needed one as a student; after all, I always found a way to get to and from whatever church I was speaking at that week. He changed his stance now that I was a married man. It was quite a treat to have a car at my disposal now.

Later in the summer, I held some gospel meetings in southwestern Louisiana, deep in Catholic Cajun country. It was tough work knocking on doors in that area since they had such a deeply entrenched culture – some folks closed the door in our faces and others said, "Well, I'm sorry I can't come – I'm a Catholic." Nevertheless, we had some good meetings down in that part of the country.

CHAPTER 7

CHARLESTON, MISSISSIPPI

W hen I left Harding, I agreed to go to Charleston, Mississippi, a small town about seventy-five miles south of Memphis just off Highway 51. Charleston had rolling hills in the east and delta land to the west, very flat and good for farming. It was an agricultural community with no industry of any kind except for a few small service areas and buildings for consumer products.

The population was about half-and-half African-American and Caucasian, and the schools were segregated. In fact, back in 1943, pretty much everything was segregated. The African-American community and the white community had their own schools, their own athletic teams, and their own churches. In Charleston, Mississippi, there was no mingling of races except in hospitals.

Louise and I had been married for about three months when we got to Charleston. We had no furniture, so we went to Memphis to Haverty's Furniture Company and bought what we would need for the two rooms in our apartment – a bedroom which was also our living room, and a small kitchen and bath. The kitchen had a kerosene stove, a table, four chairs, a sink, and a pantry. Our apartment was at the home of Mrs. Hutchins, who was a faithful member of the church. She had a couple of daughters, who were married and lived away from home, and a son about twelve years of age named Wiley Carter. Mrs. Hutchins was just like a mother to us. Her husband went to church, but he was not quite as faithful as she was.

We paid Haverty's $25 a month for our furniture, and we paid the Hutchins family $25 for our rent. The old house was a large wooden structure, built by a lumber company some years earlier for their manager. It had a swing on the front porch, and I spent a lot of time in that swing studying, reading, and relaxing. We raised chickens and a pig, and we kept a garden. One year we bought fifty chickens to butcher for meat. I started out plucking them, but got tired of doing that and skinned the rest of them. Louise cut them up, and we took them downtown to a rented freezer. I never did that again. We raised a pig in a little pen out in the back. He was a little black Poland China pig that we called Stinky Inky because we couldn't keep him in the pen; he managed to escape several times, and we would have to catch him and bring him back.

Louise had never cooked much. She worked with her daddy in their store while her sister worked in the home. I, on the other hand, had grown up in the restaurant business and knew a little bit more about cooking at first. Louise was smart and a fast study, though, so she did pretty well and learned to become a very good cook. One time I did get in trouble. Louise cooked rolls for the first time, and when they were warm, the rolls were delicious. I ate three or four of them, and I could tell that made her happy. But when the rolls got cold, they became very hard. I picked one up, dropped it on the floor, just out of curiosity; it made a noise like a rock or maybe plaster of Paris. I never did that again.

When we first arrived in Charleston, the church had a "pounding" for us, where everyone would bring goods to store in our little pantry. One gift was five pounds of coffee. The church members knew that I was from New Orleans and assumed I would love my coffee. It was a reasonable assumption, but I actually didn't drink coffee. Louise liked it though, so she enjoyed their kindness and she didn't have to share that gift with me! The church's hospitality was especially welcomed because we were in the middle of the war, so we had to have coupons to buy meat, coffee, sugar, and gasoline. Many times, we would trade coupons with other families so that we could all end up with what we needed. I had a few extra gas coupons allotted since I was a preacher and traveled to different congregations each week.

The church in Charleston had approximately 100 members with only two elders. One of the elders was a banker named J.H. Caldwell. He was the older, ruling elder of the church. Everyone had a great deal of respect for him, and his word carried a lot of authority.[11] I was the only preacher of the Churches of Christ for the two years I was there, so I preached for ten different congregations in and around Charleston.[12] Those extra gas rations certainly proved helpful as I drove from church to church to church!

For the first Sunday of each month, Louise and I would go up on Saturday night to Sardis, which was about thirty-five miles northeast of Charleston. We would spend the night, usually with the John Langstons or the Bradley family, and I would preach there in the morning and evening. In the afternoon, I would go out to Central, a few miles away. At Sardis, I became acquainted with two families that became very good friends. One was old Doctor House and his wife, and their daughter, Virginia, who married Harold Cogburn. In fact, I performed their wedding ceremony. (He was in the Navy when they married. Later, he became a member of the Board of Trustees at Harding.)[13] The other family that became close to us was the Loden family. Brother Loden was an elder along with Brother House, and they both lived over at Sledge, a few miles from Sardis. Brother Loden owned a drug store and had two sons, Woody and James. They were just little boys in knee

---

[11] The church in Charleston had several people serve there who went on to become outstanding preachers and teachers in the Lord's church, which was very unusual for a small town like that. W.B. West preached there. He ultimately came from Pepperdine to teach at Harding University and then headed up Harding's Graduate Bible Program in Memphis for a number of years. Other preachers of note for Charleston included Jack Dunn, F.B. Sheppard, Howard White, Wyatt Sawyer, and my brother James Ganus.

[12] We enjoyed visiting with the West family in Charleston. He was a worker at the post office. R.L. Peters and his family were also hospitable to us. One of their daughters was in our Sunday School Class when she was five years old. Ultimately, she came to Harding and later sent her daughter Susan to Harding. Susan was an outstanding volleyball player, and on October 27, 2001, she was inducted into the Harding University Athletic Hall of Fame.

[13] Much later, I performed the wedding ceremony for their daughter, Jeanie to Les Wyatt, who became the President of Arkansas State University.

pants when I preached there, but eventually they became good friends of ours. Sardis was a loving and warm congregation, and we enjoyed being there on the first Sunday of the month.

I served and preached at Charleston on the second, third, and fourth Sundays. I would preach in the morning and at night, and in the afternoons I would preach at a congregation in the country and then drive maybe thirty miles more and preach at another one before driving back to Charleston for the evening. Among those congregations were Ford's Well, Tippo, Jackson Grove (the home of the Kiihnl family, some of whom came to Harding), and Sumner-Webb (where the Trannums lived; two of their girls came to Harding). I also preached at Sylvan Knoll, Enid, and Water Valley. These were all small country congregations with no preacher nearby to come to them regularly, so they always received our arrival with joy, which was really quite encouraging. In addition to preaching, I sometimes led singing and often waited on the Lord's table or led the congregation in prayer and taught Sunday School Class in the morning as well as teaching the classes on Wednesday evening and presided at funerals and weddings. Basically, I did whatever those small churches needed doing, and I enjoyed it immensely.

Preaching at all of these places was an interesting experience and took a lot of time, but I didn't mind it at all. In fact, I still have my records of the sermons that I preached and how much money was contributed. My salary at this time was $100 a month from Charleston and $35 a month from Sardis, and then I would get $5-$7 at a time for preaching at the other congregations, even though I had to drive thirty or forty miles in between towns. We usually got about $200 a month total, and that paid all of our expenses, including traveling from place to place. I had to drive a lot, so at only thirty-five miles an hour (the speed limit during the war), I spent a lot of those first years of our marriage on the road.

Two of our best friends in Charleston were Reece Moore and his wife Gertrude. We loved going over to Reece and Gertrude's house because Gertrude was wonderful in the kitchen; we enjoyed her cooking and company. We played card games and blackjack late into the evening. Reece loved to sing, and he led singing at church. I also went on my first duck hunt with Reece.

Reece worked for an oil company and delivered home heating oil. He drove a large oil truck and filled fifty-five-gallon tanks at homes that had pot-bellied stoves. Sometimes I would go with him and help him deliver the oil. One rainy day, I climbed up on a stand about five feet tall and started pouring heating oil into the fifty-five-gallon drum on the stand outside the house. My foot slipped and I fell backward, landing on an oil can in the middle of my back. It is a wonder that I didn't break my back, but since it had rained a good bit and the rain had made everything a little soft, my fall pushed the can a couple of inches into the ground, which helped cushion the blow. The can did leave a mark on my back, but otherwise, I was not hurt.

We kept up our ties with Harding, which was nice. One year our church held a campaign, and some of the students like Buddy Vaughan, Wyatt Sawyer, Rick Harris, and Sammy and Keith Swim came over and worked with us for a period of time, and they did a lot of good in the Lord's work. One day we had a little time off, so we went fishing out at Enid Lake. We caught 102 crappies, but Wyatt Sawyer couldn't catch any. He made up for it, though; he walked down the side of the river near the lake, where there happened to be a catfish swimming lazily across the top of the water. Wyatt walked out into the water up to his chest and grabbed the catfish. Evidently, it had been injured coming down through a pipe or had been hit by a propeller on a boat. The fish was addled, so Wyatt dragged it in. It weighed twenty-seven pounds, which was considerably more than any of our crappies!

In addition to preaching for the area congregations, Louise and I were actively involved in the community. One evening, Louise and I were invited to dinner with a certain popular redheaded movie star. Rita Hayworth was in town visiting her uncle, the editor of the newspaper. He invited a number of people to dinner with them, and Louise and I sat across the table from Ms. Hayworth. We enjoyed talking to her about life in Hollywood. It was so funny to think that we were chatting casually in small-town Mississippi with a woman whose face was famous all over the globe!

I served as a Scoutmaster for the local Boy Scout Troop. The troop needed somebody to take the position, and I accepted. Of course, I had grown up in the Scouts and had served as a Junior Assistant Scoutmaster and was an Eagle Scout, so I was happy to get involved with the organization again. I also ended up coaching at the local high school. The regular coach had to go to the Navy, so when he left Charleston had no one to coach football, basketball, or baseball. Knowing that I loved sports and had played all three, the school asked me if I would be willing to coach. I was delighted to do so. They said they could pay me if I also taught two classes. I said, "Oh, no. I am never going to be caught dead in the classroom. I am not going to teach, but I will be happy to do it for nothing." (Of course, I look back at those words now and laugh.)

The football team went undefeated that season and won a post season game. We beat some very good teams during the year – teams we shouldn't have beaten, but we did. I had a bunch of country boys who loved to play and listened to instructions, so I was able to mold them into a pretty good team. My team used the Notre Dame box formation and a simple wing formation. My blocking back was named Bill Gunn, and he had only one eye; he was a good blocker even though he could not see the entire field. My quarterback was Albert Smith, and he was a member of my church. His brother Charles Robert Smith was a second teamer. My running back was D.V. Smith, who didn't have much in the way of book learning, but he sure knew how to run with the football. I would say, "Now, this is the football. That is the goal line. Take it to the goal line."

Our team had a pretty good offense with fair passing and good running. Defensively, we had a very good team. In the ten games we played, we only permitted thirty-nine points to be scored against us for the entire season. We played Grenada, our chief rival, twice that year. The first time, we beat them by one touchdown. After that game, the Grenada team vowed that they would not shave until they beat us. I guess they are still wearing beards because we beat them the second time by one touchdown as well.

We played a team in Clarksdale, Mississippi, and they were the champions of the Delta Region. We knew going in that the team would be tough because they averaged fifteen pounds per man heavier than we were. They had a bigger school and a better team. During the first quarter, they stymied us completely. At the end of the first quarter, we were down 6-0. Clarksdale had scored on a long pass, and we weren't getting anywhere.

Well, what Clarksdale didn't know was that I had secretly taught my team how to play in the T formation. This was a relatively new technique at that time in college football, and high schools generally didn't use it. I sent word to my quarterback to implement the T formation, and we started running all over the Clarksdale team. They were completely surprised and dumbfounded and didn't know what to do. We beat them 32-6. After the game was over, our team went to eat at a restaurant downtown, and the Clarksdale team came in to see us. They were practically crying, saying, "We just knew we were going to beat you because we had scouted you and knew what your plays were. We just knew we would win, and we were so shocked when you started using a different formation. We couldn't figure it out." I was proud of my boys for being so open to learning a new formation and being willing to test it out against a bigger rival.

We were undefeated and played Sallis in a post-season game. They were the champions of the Big Black District south of Charleston. We beat them 21-0. They were a dirty team in the sense that they would bite and gouge and hold. Some of our boys would come to me and say, "Coach, let me get him. Let me get him."

I would say, "No, you get back in there and you block harder and you tackle harder." They knew if they did something dirty, then I would take them out of the game. They fought hard, and their victory was well worth it. It was a good season, and I guess I am one of the few undefeated coaches in America, but, of course, I only coached one season.

Basketball wasn't quite as successful as football. We won most of our games and had a good record, winning the district championship for the first time in the history of the school. We should have gone a little farther than we did into the playoffs, but during our last game in the regional tournament, our center, who usually averaged fifteen points a game, got only three points that night and just couldn't hit the side of a barn. We lost by three points and did not get to go to the state tournament.

Our baseball team had a pretty good season. I enjoyed getting to be with all of the young men and to be able to coach them as well as to help them to come to worship on Sunday. Several of the team members were also members of my church, and some of the others would go to other churches. They were a really good group of boys who respected my rules and how I felt about life – behaving oneself and not drinking alcoholic beverages. I felt it was important to set a good example for the young men I was entrusted with, and I took the role of coach very seriously.

In fact, I had a little end on my football team who was not very big, but he was a tough little boy and played well. Years later, after I left Charleston, I was walking along Pontchartrain Beach in New Orleans. I looked up and saw some sailors who were cutting up, having a good time, laughing and joking, and I noticed that one of the sailors was that same little end. I walked up to the sailors and stood right behind my former student. He didn't know I was there. Finally, when I was about six feet away, he turned and saw me. As soon as he recognized me, he dropped his head and said, "Oh, no." He turned and walked away because he didn't want me to see him when he had been drinking.

Louise and I stayed in Charleston for two years, until the summer of 1945. I decided to go back to school to get a master's degree at Tulane University in my hometown of New Orleans. I was eager to be near family again, and I will always be grateful we made the move back because I had a chance to learn more about my parents. My dad had built a large home on the lakefront at 24 Swan Street. In retrospect, I guess it was really a small mansion. It was two and a half stories tall and was larger than any place we had ever lived before. Dad loved to entertain, and people always enjoyed visiting with us because my parents were so hospitable. My mother was a wonderful cook, and my father understood how to make people feel at ease. Many people from church would come home with us on Sundays and my parents would welcome them. Years later I heard stories from all sorts of people who were touched by my parents' generosity. One man told me that he and his wife were seventeen-year-old newlyweds, living in Houma, Louisiana, which was about fifty miles from New Orleans. On Sundays they would drive into the city to attend Carrollton Avenue because there was no Church of Christ located closer. My parents would invite them to come over for lunch and to stay the afternoon, and then they would attend Sunday evening services together before driving back to Houma. "They were just like parents to us," he told me. "We were newlyweds and it meant so much to us. We will never forget what they did."

In anticipation of our move back to New Orleans that spring, Louise went down to Louisiana ahead of me to get our home set up while I wrapped up with our churches in and around Charleston. I had been having trouble with my tonsils and had been taking medicine that hadn't helped much, so the doctor agreed to take them out. I figured now was the time for that to happen, since I would be spending a little time out of the pulpit and wouldn't need my voice in the same way. I also didn't want to worry Louise with trying to take care of me during a surgery, so I was glad she was already in Louisiana.

I remember being in bed in my hospital room when the nurses gave me a shot of something. It turned out to be a mixture of morphine and something else to make me drowsy. The hospital staff then put me on a gurney, wheeled me down to the surgery, and placed me on the operating table. However, they failed to strap me down, which was a mistake. I wanted to take ether to put me to sleep, so I had a mask on my face and started to fall asleep. I must have been dreaming and imagined that I was suffocating because I started to panic. I said to the doctor, "Doc, I will take it locally." He didn't pay any attention to me, so I said again, "Doc, I will take it locally." He didn't do anything still, and I felt that I was dying, so I took action. The nurse on one side was holding one arm, and the doctor, who weighed about two hundred pounds, was holding my other arm. Suddenly, I lifted both arms, and the nurse said she almost hit the transom over the door while I picked up the doctor off the floor with my other arm.

I ripped the mask off of my face and said, "Doc, I told you I didn't want any more. I will take it locally."

He replied, "I am going to stick you."

I said, "What? More morphine?"

He said, "Nah, just start counting."

So I did: "One, two, three…"

I couldn't get to ten before I fell asleep. The drug was pentothal, which is a very strong drug for putting a patient to sleep; in fact, it is one of three drugs most commonly used as part of a lethal injection for people on death row. The doctor gave me just enough to get me to sleep and then switched me to gas to keep me asleep so that I wouldn't have more reactions with pentothal. In the end, the tonsils came out. I awakened and had a raspy throat for a while, but by then I was switching back to student mode as I moved to New Orleans to start my master's degree, so I only needed to be able to speak loudly enough to be heard in a classroom and, eventually, to preach at a congregation in Gulfport, Mississippi.

CHAPTER 8

CONTINUING EDUCATION

I n the summer of 1945 I moved back home to New Orleans. My dad owned a big, old two-story white framed house next to A&G Number One at 2621 Canal Street. It adjoined the car lot where the customers would drive in and order food at the restaurant. The house was big enough for Louise and me, as well as Louise's sister and her husband, Ray and Imogene Hawkins, who moved to New Orleans for Ray to practice chiropractic care. At that time in New Orleans, a chiropractor was a "persona non-grata," so he could not advertise his business. As you might imagine, given those circumstances, it didn't go too well, and they eventually moved away from New Orleans. But, for a while, we all lived in the same house.

I wanted to go to Tulane University because it was in New Orleans and would be convenient for me to be at home, so I wrote the dean of the graduate school to ask if I would be admitted. He wrote back an acceptance letter and told me to come on, which I did. When I arrived at the graduate school, I was sent to the head of the Department of History, which was to be my major. Dr. Thornton Terhune, the chairman, talked with me and looked at my record. He said, "Yes, you will be admitted, and you can get the work here at Tulane. We will be glad to have you." Then, he said, "Oh, by the way, Mr. Ganus, where is Harding College located?" I said, "Searcy, Arkansas." He stood up from his seat, grabbed a book from the shelf near him. The book was for the North Central Association on accreditation for schools in Arkansas. He did not find Harding College listed, so he closed the book and said, "I am sorry, Mr. Ganus. You will not be admitted to Tulane University." I said thank you and left.

I thought that encounter was strange since I had been assured of admission from the Dean of the Graduate School, but what else could

I do? I decided to drive up to visit the officials at LSU in Baton Rouge to see if that would be an option for me, instead. LSU was eighty-one miles from New Orleans, but I thought I could commute if necessary. I visited with the Graduate Dean at LSU who said, "Oh, yes, we will be glad to have you." Houston Karnes and Joe Pryor from Harding had already attended there, so they knew about Harding College.

When I drove back home, I began to think about the long drive, eighty-one miles each way, that I would have to make several days a week. I wrote another letter to the Dean of the Graduate School at Tulane, and I told him about the situation with the accreditation book. I asked him in as kind a manner I could manage whether he was the one in charge the graduate school or if it was the chairman of the history department. The dean wrote back and said, "You will be admitted. Please come back to Tulane." So, I did.

I filled out my registration cards, signed them, and brought them to the professor who was to complete my enrollment, Dr. Terhune, that same chairman of the history department. He didn't even look up at me. He took the cards, signed them, and handed them back to me. I was admitted to Tulane.

It was incredibly convenient being a student and living in that house my dad owned, because I could go up to my dad's office at the back of the parking lot. His office was on the second floor of the Mrs. Drake's Sandwich Shop, where his employees made sandwiches all night for sale the next day. I could work late at night after the office personnel were gone, typing until 2:00 or 3:00 in the morning on papers for my classes. This office was a nice place to work, and of course, I could always find food around, too. I didn't have to worry about being interrupted in my studies or typing papers. Sometimes, I would spend the whole night there and then get up in time to make it to my eight o'clock class the next morning.

Since the house was adjacent to the restaurant, we could always hear people talking out in the parking lot. One night, someone parked right next to the window where I was studying at home, and I heard someone say, "Oh, let's go home." Another one said, "No, it's too early to go home. I don't want to go home." Someone else said, "Let's go somewhere else." I could tell by their language that they had been drinking, and they kept talking like that back and forth to each other until finally, I cracked the blinds a little and looked out to see what was happening. They looked up at me and said, "You old peeping Tom." Of course, I was just looking out of my own house, but nevertheless, to them, I was a peeping Tom. It's safe to say that's the only time I've ever been accused of that.

It wasn't all early-morning studying and typing, though. When I first started working on my master's degree, I decided to try to go out for football at Tulane. I went to see the coach, Little Monk Simons, an outstanding football player for Tulane. (In the very first Sugar Bowl game, he ran eighty-five yards for a touchdown. Naturally, he was well known and popular at Tulane.) When I asked about trying out for the team, he said, "Yes, I would be happy for you to come out," so I suited up. I was only a few days late getting started but immediately enjoyed playing.

I also continued preaching. On Sundays, I would drive over to preach at Gulfport, Mississippi, about seventy miles away. The congregation had no church building at the time, so they rented a community building. On Saturday nights, veterans and other groups would have big shrimp parties, so when we arrived on Sunday mornings, we would have to sweep out the beer cans and shrimp heads and clean the building before we could have our service.

The congregation did that for many months and then finally decided to build a church building out of concrete blocks. I contributed by driving over during the week to build the baptistery and the rostrum for the pulpit. The church hired a stone mason to put in the blocks, but the members did most of the rest. The church had a nice little building which would seat about a hundred people, and it was an adequate space for many years in the Gulfport area.

No one seemed to mind that my weekends were divided between the gridiron and the gospel until one Saturday, when I was scrimmaging for the football team and facing a big tackle across from me. I played the right offensive end position, and when I blocked him, the big tackle threw up an elbow and hit me right under the left eye. We didn't have face masks back then, so we had no face protection. My cheek jumped out like a goose egg and turned black. The next morning, I knew I had to preach with that swollen eye. A little embarrassed, I drove over to the church at Gulfport. The congregation didn't notice at first, but when I stood up in the pulpit and turned around, everyone looked at my face and gasped. I said the first thing that came to mind, "I might as well go ahead and confess. She hit me again." Everyone laughed, but then, of course, I told the real story.

After several weeks of practices and participating in scrimmage games for the football team, I would find myself sitting in the library, trying to study but thinking about the 100-plus plays I needed to learn for the game instead. And so, after a while, even though I enjoyed football so much, I decided I should not participate. I had a son on the way; I was preaching every Sunday; and I was studying for a master's degree. Football just didn't fit into those plans.

While I was at Tulane, my first son, Cliff, was born on November 14, 1945, at Touro Hospital. While Louise was in the delivery room, I sat in the waiting room and read about ninety pages of Spanish History. While I was waiting for the nurse to come tell me about the birth, my dad walked in the hospital with a box of cigars with gold bands on them. The bands said, "Compliments of Cliff III and his granddaddy." I told him I thought this was a little presumptuous to have the name already on the cigar bands, and he replied, "Well, he has to be a boy. He wouldn't be a girl." (I'm guessing he had some bands for a girl as well, of course.)

Finally, the elevator door opened, and a nurse walked out with a little baby boy. She said, "This is your son, and he is a healthy boy." I looked at him, and then I went up to see Louise. She had not yet seen the baby because she had an RH factor negative, and I had a positive. With the added risk and potential problems, she was sedated for the delivery.

The first thing Louise said after coming out of the anesthesia was, "Does he have enough fingers and toes?" I assured her that he did and that he was a good-looking boy. The nurses put Cliff in a nursery upstairs, and I would go to stand and look through a big window to see my son and forty other babies in that large room. I liked to watch the other parents, and I would try to match the parents with the different babies, like a dad beaming with pride at his baby with matching thick, black hair.

Towards the end of my master's coursework, I decided to take a class on church history under Dr. Terhune, who seemed to have forgiven me for attending an undergraduate school that did not appear in his accreditation book. He was my advisor for my master's thesis and was quite a character. The class only had three students, so we met in his office, and he would tell us about some of his escapades. For instance, although he was single, he would still receive calls where a salesman would ask to speak to Mrs. Terhune. He would say, "Oh, I'm sorry, but she is just dead drunk, and I can't get her to come to the telephone."

Dr. Terhune's home telephone number was also similar to the number of a local grocery store. People would call his number accidentally and would place an order. He would pretend to take their order and say, "Oh yes! I'll be happy to deliver this to you. I'll be there in a little while." When, of course, the order wouldn't arrive, the customer would call back, and he would say, "Oh, I'm sorry. We got so busy that we couldn't get the order out to you. I tell you what I'm going to do. I am going to deliver them now, and I will throw in an extra chicken just because we mistreated you like this." Well, that was Thornton Terhune.

One of my classmates in Dr. Terhune's small class was Howard White, the preacher for the Carrollton Avenue Church of Christ, who was working on his doctorate at the time. He was a graduate of David Lipscomb College and had been preaching for many years in New Orleans. I had, of course, known him for about a decade, ever since he had stayed with my family while holding a gospel meeting. He was still single at that time and just like a member of our family. The other student in our class was a woman who served as the librarian at Loyola University, a Catholic University just next door to Tulane.

While talking about church history, Dr. Terhune would say something derogatory against the Catholic Church, which would make Dr. White and me smile, but then he would belittle the Protestant

Movement about something else, and the librarian would smile back at us. It was a funny little game we played back and forth during his lectures. Overall, the class was informative, and the three of us learned a lot from it.

For my comprehensive exam for the master's degree, I had to answer seven questions. Dr. Terhune was my advisor, and he put me in a classroom with a pen and paper. He gave me the questions and said, "Take all the time you want on it." Three hours later when I was about halfway through the questions, Dr. Terhune came into the room. He was about to leave for the day and said, "Well, Mr. Ganus, where are you on the test?" I told him, and he said, "Why don't you just take it home with you and finish it at home? I know you wouldn't do anything wrong." I thought that was very nice for him to say, but I decided to leave the test and finish it the next day. I passed that examination, as well as whatever ethical test Dr. Terhune may have been putting to me.

At Dr. Terhune's suggestion, I decided to write about the Tudor Articles of Religion, which had to do with the articles of faith for the Anglican Church, for my master's thesis. Henry VIII established the Anglian Church, and his daughter, Elizabeth I, further developed many of its doctrines, and I was interested in uncovering more about the beginning of the church, its history, and its articles. In order to do this, I not only studied at Tulane but also at the Episcopal Church on St. Charles Avenue, close to the university.

The rector at the Episcopal Church (which is an offshoot of the Anglican Church of England) was very nice to me and helped me with materials. Dr. Terhune had studied in Europe for many years and was directing my thesis, but just before I finished, he hired a new teacher named Dr. Fred Cole to teach history and also assigned him as my advisor instead.

I went in to see Dr. Cole with my completed material. After reading it, he looked at me and said, "I don't know why this topic was ever assigned. I would not have assigned it at all. I just don't think it's really appropriate." He was more interested in American history than European history, but that didn't help me out very much at that point. Thankfully, he agreed to chair my project anyway, and everything went well with the process.

Dr. Cole and I ended up getting along pretty well. He was a good handball player, and he taught me how to play. He wasn't very old at that time, and he didn't wear gloves when he played. He could beat me easily while I was still learning how to play, but I improved, getting better and better with him.[14] Dr. Terhune retired the following year and moved to Kentucky, where I learned years later that he committed suicide. Despite our first meeting, I had grown to really enjoy and respect him, and I was deeply saddened by that news.

When I had just about finished up my master's degree at Tulane, President Pullias from David Lipscomb University invited me to talk about moving to Nashville to head up the history department. I also received a call from Dr. Benson asking me to come back to Harding to teach there. He offered me $150 per month for nine months, and if there was any money left over at the end of the year, it would be divided among the staff.

I knew I loved Harding and decided it would be the right place for me, so I decided to go back to Searcy to teach with my master's degree. Dr. Benson asked me to teach Bible in addition to history and raised my salary to $160 before I arrived. At the end of the school year, I received an additional $225 as my staff share. When I had graduated from Harding just a few years prior, I had a strong desire to preach, and that was what I believed at the time I was called to do. In fact, so strongly did I believe that, I once announced, "There is one thing I will never do: teach." In the end, teaching would become my life's work – but only at Harding.[15]

[14] I went back to Harding, eventually, with a new sport, which many enjoyed. I loved playing handball at Harding through the years as a faculty member, but it all started with one of my professors at Tulane.

[15] I did regret leaving the church in Gulfport, where I enjoyed preaching on the weekends while I studied at Tulane. I liked the H.J. Massie family. They had a young boy, who was only about five years old at the time. Ultimately, he became a medical doctor and moved to Memphis, Tennessee. He had at least three children who came to Harding to study later, and I think our relationship for all of those years contributed to that.

CHAPTER 9

BACK TO SEARCY

W hen I came back to Searcy in 1946, the campus was pretty much as it had been in 1943 when I graduated. Old Godden Hall was still there as the dormitory for both men and women, though they had blocked off the western part of it and called that part East Wing of Pattie Cobb Hall, which housed the women. The remainder of the building was divided by another wall, designating an area for the men. The Administration Building (now the Olen Hendrix Building) also accommodated science classes, and we still had a small gym just south of Godden Hall. The biggest change was that some war surplus buildings had been erected. We now had a health clinic on the southwest corner of the campus near the laundry and swimming pool. There was also a boiler room and other surplus buildings which served as additional classrooms. The campus itself had grown from the original twenty-nine acres, thanks to an adjacent farm that Dr. Benson had been able to acquire when Sterling Morton had given Dr. Benson money for the sixty acres located on the southern side of the campus. Eventually, that farm would become the location of Harding Academy, Harding Place, and the football stadium, but that was still years down the road. An adjacent eleven-acre farm, where the athletic center now stands, was home to L.E. Pryor, a teacher.

When our family first moved to Searcy, Dr. Benson rented a little four-room house to us for $25 a month. It was located on East Market (where the parking lot for the Student Center is now located) near a big house where Myrtle Rowe, a former missionary in Africa, lived.

Our son Cliff was only nine months old when we came back to Searcy, so we built a little playpen for him in our backyard, but he didn't really care for it. Across the street lived the Casey family, and Gerald Casey, a young boy, came over a lot to the backyard when Cliff was outside. He was a few years older than Cliff and teased him a little, but they were good friends anyway. Our rented house was small, and we wanted to get something bigger, so the next year we purchased a small frame house owned by the university, located at 802 East Market near Grand Boulevard.

Through the years, we added to this house and eventually stoned it in. I ordered some limestone, called Carthage Marble, from Carthage, Missouri. It arrived in a railroad car, which was parked near the south side of the campus. These stones were big slabs about twelve feet long, six to seven feet wide, and four to six inches thick. I bought a sledgehammer and broke up them into small pieces before loading them into a truck and hauling them over to our house, where a stonemason placed them on the house. It was quite a job, but it turned out well, and we enjoyed living in that home from 1947 to 1961.

Louise and I did a lot of the updating work on the house ourselves. I nailed in the hardwood floor in the living room area, and we added on a large area with louver windows for a family room and play area. We had a large backyard and built a patio for a barbecue pit and places to sit outdoors. This patio was helpful because we were heavily involved in social club activities. I served as an Admiral (sponsor) for the Sub T Club, and Louise was sponsor for the Tri-Kappas, a girls' club. We had students over from the campus, and many memorable events took place at our home. As our family grew, as well as our involvement in campus social life, that home proved to be very comfortable for us.

Market Street was a great location because it was only about a block from everything we needed. It was a block from the College Church of Christ building. There was a small grocery story just behind us and later a little restaurant called The White House Cafe. The north side of the campus was only a block away. We could go all week and not have to walk more than a quarter mile for anything.

When I left Harding as a student, I had determined only to preach and never teach. However, when Dr. Benson called me to come back to Harding to teach Bible and History, I readily did so. Harding's academic year was organized on the three-term basis, Fall, Winter, and Spring. When I started teaching at Harding, I taught not only American History, but also several Bible classes at Dr. Benson's request. I had one term teaching Matthew, another Acts, and the third Hebrews. I enjoyed teaching those courses as well as my history courses, and I continued to teach them for some time until I was moved entirely into history.

A new teacher

I also taught Conservation of Natural Resources, which was not an easy subject for a city slicker like me because it contained a lot of material pertaining to farming and rural life. I tried to study a day ahead of my students. I remember bringing seafood up from New Orleans and having a dinner for my students in our little gym. One girl, who had never seen a shrimp, put one on her plate and looked at it for thirty minutes. She never ate it.

I decided that I wanted to make my classes interesting and not just provide mere facts to my students. I wanted to make history and the Bible come alive to them in the classroom. I soon found out that teaching was more than just meeting with your class and trying to fill your students with information. It was also helping my students develop appropriate attitudes and skills, and I found that I loved this part of education. In addition to all of this, however, I soon found out that teachers had many other assignments to fulfill as well.

After a few months of teaching, the administration and faculty began to saddle me with committee obligations and assignments. I served for nineteen years on the discipline committee, ten as chairman. That was a rather interesting experience. One young man disagreed so vehemently with the committee's decision that he declared he would like to put his fist in my face. Thankfully, he decided to punch the door instead and probably hurt his hand more than the door. He did get the anger out of his system, though, and several years later he actually apologized to me for that outburst.

My second committee was to weigh probation for failing students, which meant we saw a lot of tears and heard a lot of pleading and promises to do better. In May of 1948 I was appointed to yet another committee for groundbreaking ceremonies for the construction of Armstrong Hall, the first real boys' dormitory on the campus. After that I served on the Public Relations Committee, the Building Program Committee, the Committee for Hospital Insurance, and the Faculty Welfare Committee. I served as chairman of the Division of Business and Social Sciences, the committee to study and improve the Bible curriculum, the Faculty Program Committee, and the Graduate Council. I then served as the faculty sponsor for the Interclub Council. I didn't realize that all of these committees and assignments were preparing me for something bigger and more important in the future.

———

Despite all of the committees, I found that I enjoyed teaching tremendously – so much so that I decided to go ahead and get my doctorate. In the summer of 1948, I went back to Tulane to start working on my Ph.D. Dr. Terhune had retired by then, and Dr. Wendell Holmes Stephenson was the new head of the department. He was an outstanding teacher and a nationally respected historian. Dr. Fred Cole, who had advised me on my master's thesis in 1946, was still teaching, and I was delighted to get to work with him again. My family moved back to New Orleans with me until the summer of 1951 so that I could complete my class work. During this time I also preached in Bogalusa, about eighty miles north of New Orleans.

During this stay in New Orleans we lived in one of the houses my dad owned next to his office and the sandwich shop. It was a shotgun house, a straight, small, narrow structure with one room following the other: the living room, then the bedrooms, then the bath, and finally the kitchen. (Thankfully, the bathroom had a little hall beside it so that you didn't have to walk through the bathroom to get to the kitchen.) The house was about three feet or so off the ground on pillars, which was alright until the weather dropped below freezing. Then the exposed pipes underneath the house would freeze – and in February of 1950 we did get a very hard freeze. The temperature fell to about twenty degrees, which was unheard of in New Orleans. As a result, many of our pipes burst, and when they thawed we had a fountain spraying under the house. We had to cut off the water because we couldn't get any plumbers to come in a timely fashion. All over town the plumbers were having a heyday (or payday) fixing similar situations, so we had to do without water for a little while. We lived in that house for two years and enjoyed being located very close to the A&G Restaurant and Mrs. Drake's Sandwich Shop that were both part of my dad's business, so there was always plenty of good food.

Our best acquisition in New Orleans was certainly the arrival of our second child, Debbie, who was born in 1950 at the same hospital where Cliff had entered the world. It was a delight to have both a boy and a girl in our home now.

At Tulane I played a lot of handball with Dr. Fred Cole and even went fishing on one occasion with another one of my professors. We drove down to Grand Isle, about a hundred miles from New Orleans in the Gulf of Mexico, and in about two hours the two of us caught ninety-nine speckled trout. Just as fast as we could throw the hook in the water, the trout would bite and even swim back up to the boat if they should get off the line. I'm not sure why they were so hungry that day, but it sure was easy to catch them, which was unusual. Speckled trout are very good to eat, so we truly enjoyed it.

Everything went well as far as my work at Tulane was concerned. I wrote my dissertation on the Freedmen's Bureau in Mississippi. This was an organization established under the direction of General Oliver Otis Howard, a federal general after whom Howard University was named. The organization's responsibility was to take care of the freed slaves after the Civil War by helping to protect, educate, feed, and clothe them as well as securing each member some land – the proverbial "forty acres and a mule."

In order to get materials, I had to travel to Baton Rouge to use the library at LSU; to Jackson, Mississippi, for the state archives there; to newspaper offices across both Louisiana and Mississippi; and even to Washington, D.C. It was during one of those research trips in 1950, when I made one of the most interesting acquaintances of my academic career: Alfred H. Stone, Director of the Mississippi State Archives.

Mr. Stone was eighty-two years old at the time and had had a friend who had been a friend of Abraham Lincoln. Mr. Stone told me a story about one of his friend's visits to the White House. Lincoln, who was loved by many, was also heartily disliked by some, including Thaddeus Stevens, Benjamin Wade, and Charles Sumner. Mr. Stone's friend recalled Lincoln looking out the window and remarking, "When I was in school, the students were reading the Bible one verse at a time. We were reading from the book of Daniel, and I looked ahead to see what verse I would have to read. It included different names to pronounce – Shadrach, Meshach, and Abednego – and I thought, 'Oh, no. Here come these three men again.' When I look out this window, I am reminded, 'Here come these three men again.'"

The Civil War seemed so far away to me, living almost ninety years later, but hearing that story about President Lincoln and his three adversaries, Stevens, Wade, and Sumner, made the past seem a whole lot closer. I've always marveled a little at the fact that I shook hands with a man who was a friend of a friend of President Lincoln.

When I traveled to D.C. to study the material on the Freedmen's Bureau at the National Archives, I was shocked to discover that much of the material had never been used. In fact, much of it was stored after the Civil War in big piano boxes, and no one had disturbed it since; I was one of the first to get into some of that material after it was originally stored.

I spent three consecutive summers in Washington, which gave me a lot of material; I personally microfilmed more than two thousand pages and had a stack of five-by-eight notecards about two feet high. Dr. Stephenson, my major professor, had taught me how to take notes, what material we needed to write on each card, and just how to locate it. While I was in the archives one day, I noticed a man, much older than me, who opened up a book, jotted down something on a little piece of paper, and put it in his pocket haphazardly. I wondered who this man was. When he walked out of the room for a moment, I looked at the hat that he had set down nearby and saw his name inside: James G. Randall. Randall was a very famous historian who wrote the book *Civil War and Reconstruction*, which I had used to teach from in my classes at Harding. When I got home, I told Dr. Stephenson how carelessly Mr. Randall handled his notes. Dr. Stephenson looked at me and said, "Mr. Ganus, that may be true, and when you get Mr. Randall's age and have his expertise, you can take notes any way you wish. But in the meantime, you will take them as I have instructed you."

And I did. I brought all of that microfilm and all those notecards back with me to New Orleans, where I would work at the library and also at my dad's office well into the night, sleep for a couple of hours, and then head to class at 8:00 or 9:00 the next morning.

Dr. Stephenson and I had a good relationship, and I enjoyed visiting with him. He was a good teacher and a good man. I also appreciated Dr. Cole, as well as two or three of the other professors. The only real problem came when I was writing my dissertation. Dr. Stephenson and Dr. Cole were my readers and co-directors. Having two was unusual and sometimes unfortunate – it was okay as long as they were friends. Unfortunately for me, I had stumbled into a bit of a political tussle. Dr. Cole had been a student of Dr. Stephenson, and Dr. Stephenson was the chairman of the department with Dr. Cole working under him. That was okay, but then Dr. Cole was made the dean of the graduate school, which meant that he was over Dr. Stephenson as well as teaching under him. They had a falling out with each other, which made my dissertation process rather difficult.

I would take my dissertation to one professor, and he would read what I had written and make suggestions. Then I would take my work to the other one, and he would make suggestions and say, "I don't know why he made the suggestion to do it this way. It should be done this way instead." I felt caught between them. The only saving grace was that I still played handball with Dr. Cole, and he liked me. Dr. Stephenson seemed to like me, too, so I think they generally tried not to let their personal rivalry affect me.

When the time arrived to take my comprehensive exam, I went before a board of five or six professors. Everything went very well except in one area: the professors thought I should read a little more about the History of American Thought. They made some suggestions of books, and I agreed to read them before meeting with them again and, thankfully, that was all there was to that. But I was certainly nervous until I got my approval.

I finished all of my class work in the three years I was gone from Harding, collected a lot of my material for my dissertation, and passed my comprehensive exams. I went back to Harding in 1951 and started teaching a full load, and I also became the head of the History Department after Frank Rhodes left to go to Abilene to teach. I was still preaching almost every Sunday and trying to write my dissertation as well. I spend a lot of time in the library, sometimes until 2:00 or 3:00 in the morning. Fortunately, Annie Mae Alston (later Lewis), an English teacher and our librarian, helped me greatly by reading my manuscript and making corrections when needed.

I completed my dissertation in 1953 and graduated with my Ph.D. in history. Cliff III was almost eight years old at the time, and he and Louise came to see me graduate at Tulane. When I walked across the stage in the auditorium, Cliff got up from his seat and met me as I came off the stage, and he walked back with me to my seat. I loved that a boy so young would do that.

———

I was happy to be settled in Searcy for good, now that I had a terminal degree in my field, but there was one aspect of life in Arkansas to which I could never fully acclimate. Arkansas has always had the threat of tornadoes, and one time I came home to find that Louise had stuffed the children under my desk in my little study just off from our bedroom. On another occasion, she put them behind the sofa. There was a good reason for her concern. On March 21, 1952, at 5:33 in the afternoon, a big tornado hit the nearby areas of Kensett, Judsonia, and

Bald Knob. I was on the sofa at the time working on some papers and heard the tornado pass over us. It sounded like a freight train roaring overhead. It touched down briefly on the east side of Searcy, but it was more destructive later in its track. More than a hundred people died and much of the area was destroyed.

At first, we didn't know about the impact of the tornado until we heard the sirens and watched as the emergency responders began bringing the injured to the Hawkins Clinic across the street from our house. The injured kept coming, and I thought, "My, they must have had a bad wreck out at the Y." I walked over to the hospital to find out what happened, and when I heard, I jumped into my car and drove over to Kensett to check on the tenants of a small farm that I had nearby. The house and the barn were destroyed, but Joe and Mattie Watson, who were living there, had gone into the storm shelter and were not injured.

Crazy things happened in that storm. Even though the house was gone, the table in the kitchen was still standing and had a pan of unbroken eggs in it, just where the Watsons had left them when they ran for the shelter. The cattle were not in the field, and Joe said that he had seen them starting to come up the lane when the tornado hit, but they were gone after the storm moved. We assumed they had been lost to the storm, but a little while later the cattle turned up and made their way back to the remains of the barn.

———————

A more pleasant association with the old Hawkins Clinic than tornado victims was the birth of our third child, Charles, in 1954. Our doctor was Thomas Adrian Formby, and Louise only had to walk across the street to deliver him. While Louise was having the baby, I was at home installing our first air conditioner, a window unit that we put in the living room, along with a fan that blew the cold air into the hall and to the bedrooms. My dad gave us the unit in honor of the new baby, which was a helpful gift since Charles was born on June 26. Searcy is pretty hot in the summertime, and that year was a record hot year.

Unfortunately, the hospital had a round of staph infection, and Charles was inflicted with it. We couldn't bring him home for several days, but he was just across the street from us, which made that difficult period slightly less hard on all of us.

We will always remember the wonderful times we had in that house. I wrestled all three of the children at one time on the living room floor; Louise was always afraid we were going to hurt something, but we never did. The kids found plenty of ways to scare their mother without my help. When Debbie was very young, she was a climber. One day Louise went in the living room and found Debbie – a little bitty thing – on top of the upright piano. Debbie was not afraid, but Louise was scared that Debbie would fall off. Louise got her down safely. And then, when Charles was four years old, I was teaching a class on the second floor of the American Studies Building when I heard a horn honking outside the window. When I looked outside, I saw Louise calling me. She was in the car with Charles, who had jumped on the bed, fallen off, and cut himself right below the eye. The cut looked pretty bad, so we had to take him to the hospital. I dismissed class and carried him into Rodgers Hospital on the west side of town where Dr. Hugh Edwards took care of him. I held Charles while Dr. Edwards cleaned the wound to sew it up. Suddenly, the room got awfully hot, and I got a little dizzy. The doctor said, "You know, Cliff, I think I can handle this by myself. Why don't you go on outside where it's cooler?" I was glad he said that. It had never bothered me whenever I was bleeding, but seeing my young son Charles with a bad cut made me lightheaded.

Those early years as a father and as a teacher were incredibly dear to me. I will forever be grateful to the people who helped me find my way in my career and for the places that were such an essential part in shaping who I was and whom I was going to become. There were big things in store for Harding in the years ahead, and in the early 1950s we were just beginning to see where they were leading.

CHAPTER 10

THE AMERICAN STUDIES INSTITUTE

I n the late 1940s Dr. Benson decided to bring businessmen to the Harding campus for what he called a Freedom Forum. He began to meet annually with outstanding executives and leaders of the business world in Searcy so that they could meet and exchange ideas. Both Dr. Benson and I spoke at the forum, which opened the door for us to be invited to places across the country to speak. The Freedom Forum became an important event for Harding, and Dr. Benson also decided to sponsor Freedom Forums in Michigan, Oklahoma, Texas, and elsewhere. He aimed this educational program toward schools, businesses, and civic clubs all over the country.

Meanwhile, many of the businessmen with whom we met suggested that Dr. Benson begin a program on the campus for Harding students, too. This was the inspiration for the American Studies Program, which was launched in the autumn of 1952. Dr. Benson asked me to be the dean of the new program on the campus, and he asked Dr. Frank L. Holmes to be the director. Frank had spoken on our campus, and he had a great deal of knowledge to offer about the kinds of presentations the program needed. He served in that capacity for Harding for three years.

The American Studies Program grew through the years, offering classes for our college students and educational tours that would take the students to visit prominent businesses, government offices, and historical sites around the mid-South. Whenever I had the opportunity, I would take my family with me on these trips. Traveling with our children was enjoyable but not without some mishaps. My daughter Debbie became carsick easily, and when she yelled, "Daddy, stop!" I knew that I had better do it very quickly or we would have to do a lot of cleaning in the car. One time she managed pretty well on the trip until we got back to Searcy. We were within four blocks of our house when she lost her lunch. At least it was easier to clean up at the house.

I had a lot of fun with those presentations and experimented with different techniques for driving the points home. In some of my presentations for the high school students who visited the Harding campus for the American Studies program, I would be speaking to the students when someone would interrupt and raise a question about what I was saying. We would plant this person in the audience, usually a Harding teacher, and the plant would start by questioning the value of the American free enterprise system. I would answer the question, and then the plant would raise another question, and we would go back and forth. The questions would become increasingly more vocal and more obnoxious. Students had different reactions. Some of the students thought the person arguing with me might be a communist who had infiltrated our meeting. Others wanted to call the police to have the person evicted; some became angry for disrupting the program; others just seemed surprised and confused.

I did not do this in the presentation just to excite the students, although I do think it was exciting. After the presentation was over, I would introduce the plant, who would come up on stage to take over the platform. The students' mouths would hang open in shock. We used this demonstration as a teaching experience to show that we cannot answer arguments with emotions or feelings. We emphasized that we would need to have facts, and in order to arm ourselves with facts, we needed to study and learn to inform our discussions.

Lecturing on the American system

The American Studies Program would also take students out to Camp Tahkodah, about forty miles outside of Searcy. The camp belongs to the school and is a wonderful place for an outing; we would spend the day up there playing ball, swimming, fishing, and hiking, but we would also have educational programs during the day.

Near the camp, there's a big bluff on the other side of Salado Creek, and we had a cable strung from the top of the bluff down to the campfire circle. We would stack wood in the middle of the circle for a fire. After dark, we would call for the spirit of Chief Tahkodah, an Indian chief, to send fire down to light the fire. Someone at the top would send down fire on the cable, and it would hit the campfire and burst into flames. The students loved it. Over the years, many of the high school students from those gatherings went on to attend Harding for college. Moreover, we were able to interest one of the sponsors who came with the students, Dr. Bob Reely, to come to Harding to teach. He was a tremendous addition who worked with the American Studies Program for decades.

The educational tours were always informative and enjoyable. We traveled to places like Cincinnati, Chicago, New Orleans, Dallas, and Washington, D.C. Our groups were always well received by the various businesses we studied. On one trip to Bartlesville, Oklahoma, we met with the president, vice president, and other top administrators of Phillips 66. They explained the nature of the oil business, fed us well, and took us to Willow Rock, a fine museum.

One of the most notable experiences was in Cincinnati, when we visited the Ekaun Sons Meat Packing Facility. After discussing the business aspect of the work, the employees took us to the slaughter pens where workers demonstrated slaughtering the cattle and impressed us with the method of killing a cow to make it kosher. The animal had to be slaughtered by a certain member of the Jewish faith, who hung up the cow by its heels and cut its throat. Blood, of course, gushed everywhere by the bucketful, but that proper procedure of killing and draining was required to earn kosher certification.

After the beef butchering, we went to the hog processing area and observed how they made sausage and put it in the casings. Then we went to lunch, where we were served slices of ham, sausage, and hot dogs. Some of the students had a hard time eating the meat after seeing it slaughtered and processed, but I had worked long enough in the food business with my dad that I didn't mind.

In Cincinnati, we also met with the top officials of the Kroger Company, which at the time was a two-billion-dollar company. We also went to the Cincinnati Milling and Machine Tool Company and watched them build the machines they sent all over the world. These trips were invaluable in showing our students the power of the free enterprise system.

In addition to the business tours across the country, the Distinguished Lecture Program became a vital part of the American Studies Program at Harding. From its beginning, our program hosted outstanding speakers who were knowledgeable about the world in political, economic, and educational affairs. Over the years, Harding hosted a number of distinguished contributors to American society. Wilbur Mills, chairman of the House Ways and Means Committee (and probably the second most powerful man in America after the President of the United States), was one of the earliest speakers. His home was in Kensett, just four miles from Searcy, and he was a very good friend to Dr. Benson. Milton Friedman, who was an economic advisor to Richard Nixon and an outspoken economist, spoke on the campus. Paul Harvey, one of the most noted news commentators in the United States; Sam Walton, a personal friend and Harding supporter; and even President Gerald Ford were all distinguished lecturers.

I probably spent more time with President Ford than any of the other speakers, at least personally. Before the dinner that we gave in his honor, President Ford and I sat together in a small room on the campus and talked for about half an hour about Harding and about his life. Steve, President Ford's son, flew in from California for the speech; I met him in Little Rock and brought him to the campus and to my home. He bathed and took a nap, and then he asked Louise if we minded if he took a walk around campus. He was afraid that since he was the son of the president, he would cause a stir. She told him it was just fine, and I don't think anyone even recognized him, and we were happy that he came to be with us.

Many wonderful people came to speak for Harding throughout the years: President George H.W. Bush, President George W. Bush, Barbara Bush, Laura Bush, Margaret Thatcher, Lech Wałęsa, and many others. Through the years this program brought thousands of people to Harding's campus. The American Studies Program also brought us the

William R. Coe American Studies Building, which is a three-story class-room and office building that is still used today. I had my office in that building from the time it was built until I moved to the Administration Building. When Dr. Benson decided to start the American Studies program on campus, he visited a number of businessmen and told them of his need, and they responded well. The building was named after one of the men who supported our program and provided finances for it because he believed in the importance of what we were doing.

The American Studies Institute partnered with professional animators in California to create a series of short cartoon films. One of them, entitled "Make Mine Freedom," was produced in 1948 and laid out in simple but convincing terms the importance of capitalism as a means of combating the evils of communism. In 1954 Dr. Benson decided that, in addition to those films, he would commission a series of 16mm films to be shown at educational institutions and other gatherings. He asked if I would be willing to be the narrator for the films. The format would be a classroom setting, where I would lecture to the students on varied topics. He envisioned each film to be about twelve minutes in length so it could be shown in any setting. I agreed to narrate the films, and we made the first couple of films on the Harding campus. After those initial projects, we went to Memphis to record at a professional studio, where production was easier and of better quality. We completed the thirteen films by 1955 with the following titles: *The Beginning at Plymouth Colony, Our Two Great Documents, The Structure of the American Way of Life, The Fall of Nations, A Look at Socialism, A Look at Communism, A Look at Capitalism, America's Distribution of Wealth, Spirit of Enterprise, The Secret of American Production, The Profit System, Security and Freedom,* and *The Responsibilities of American Citizenship.* Organizations all over the United States showed this series, and throughout the years we have had requests for them and comments about their use.[16]

---

[16] As late as 2015, I received calls about this series from people who appreciated their content and felt the films did much good.

In 1955, Dr. Benson asked if I would be willing to take off a year of teaching to get a professional diploma in College Administration at Teacher's College, Columbia University, in New York City. I considered the matter, and, even though I already had my doctorate from Tulane University, I agreed to pursue this diploma. I agreed to take the family with me, even though we had three children, and Louise and I made plans to stay on the campus of the university.

My dad had become very ill, and Louise and I decided to detour on our way to New York by way of New Orleans, and I'm thankful we made that decision. The very morning we arrived at New Orleans in September, my dad had to go to the hospital. My brother James and I took turns at the hospital with my dad over the next few days. James was on duty at 5:00 a.m., and I was on my way to the hospital to relieve him when Dad passed away. We held his funeral at the Schoen Funeral Home on Canal Street. People from all over the city came to view his body: government officials, businessmen, church leaders, church members, taxicab drivers, and others who came from off the street. These were all people who had known my dad and appreciated the good he had done in New Orleans.

My father's death was sudden, but it did not come as a surprise; we knew his health was fading. In 1953, when I knew he would not live much longer, I talked to him about the possibility of returning to New Orleans. I had been teaching at Harding for eight years, but I thought I had an obligation to my family and to the business. My father listened to me for a while, and then he replied, "No, Cliff. Harding can't let you go."

I thought his wording was a little strange, but I said, "Well, okay."

Much later, after my father had died, two men told me at separate times that Dad had talked to each of them and said that he knew I could come home and easily run the business, but he also knew I was doing something far more important at Harding. My dad loved Harding and its work. He gave much to the university monetarily, but he also gave Harding his time and abilities, serving on Harding's board of directors beginning in 1940 and then as chairman of the board until his death in 1955.

Dr. Benson told me on different occasions about how wise my father was, how he could work well with people, how he could settle problems, and how he could get along with different personalities. My dad had a knack for natural leadership. Of course, I was happy to hear that because I felt the same way about him; it was just nice to know other people recognized how extraordinary he was, too. Harding bestowed my dad with an honorary doctorate and named the student center in his honor.

My dad learned a lot about Christian education during his time on the Harding board. He became interested in Harding Academy at Searcy and decided he would help start a Christian school in 1950 when my family and I were in New Orleans to work on my doctorate at Tulane. Dad started the school in the classrooms at the Carrollton Avenue Church of Christ. Cliff was in kindergarten at the that time, so his first year of education was at the school my dad started. The school remained at the Carrollton Avenue Church building a few years until Dad was able to purchase a city block of land in Gentilly, in the northeastern section of the city. He paved the streets around the block and slowly built a campus. It was the beginning of the Lake Vista Christian School, which changed its name in 1955 to honor my father as the Clifton L. Ganus School. It became a well-respected school, going all the way through twelfth grade, with a fine campus. The city block of land provided the area for the entire school campus and also for seven building lots for homes. These homes were sold to individual families in order to help build the campus. One of Harding's graduates, Lester Balcom, became the headmaster and served the school for many years. Over the years, I have met many people in New Orleans and across the country who attended that school. It had a good reputation and lasted until 1995, when the city of New Orleans bought the campus. On August 29, 2005, Hurricane Katrina covered the campus with eight feet of water, and so the entire block had to be dozed down. Afterward, New Orleans erected a new multistory classroom facility on the site.

My dad served on boards and committees in addition to running his own business in New Orleans. He was president of the Young

Men's Business Club (YMBC), and he was on the council that developed overpasses and underpasses for the railroads in New Orleans. He served on the mayor's advisory committee as well as the governor's advisory council. He never would run for political office, though many people asked him over the years; instead, he always worked behind the scenes and was liked by everyone.

Dad invested in oil in a partnership with H.L. Hunt. Our family was poor in comparison to Hunt, a Dallas oil tycoon who began his business in Arkansas, but Dad had some good income from oil. My family benefitted from this investment for a while after he died. Dad also served on the board of the United Gas Company. They would meet in different locations throughout the United States, sometimes in Shreveport, their headquarters, but also in New York City. I once flew up with him to New York City on the company plane for a board meeting. As always, we made time for some good food; I remember that we went to the Davey Jones Restaurant. My dad had lobster, I had shrimp, and we enjoyed it very much.

The United Gas Company owned two airplanes, one of which later crashed in Louisiana, killing the dozen people who were on board, including the owner of Braniff Airways. The passengers had been duck hunting in southern Louisiana, and they were flying back north when they hit icing conditions, and the pilots had to find a place to land because the plane's wings had iced up. They flew the plane over a lake, but there were stumps sticking up, so they were afraid to land in the water. They tried to clear a building but didn't make it. When the plane hit, it flipped and burned. Dad, of course, had flown on that plane from time to time, and he knew the pilots and the passengers who lost their lives that day.

The United Gas Company called upon Dad to make many trips, and he occasionally had to make a speech. He wasn't an outstanding speaker, but he would try to speak when requested and did a good job with it. He didn't preach much, but he was an elder in the church until his death. One day, he called my mother and said, "Can you look up some information on Simon Bolivar of South and Central America? I have to speak at the dedication of a statue for him here on Canal Street, and I need to know something about him." Mother gathered the requested information on Simon Bolivar, the champion in the early

1800s for South American countries seeking independence from Spain. Bolivar was a rebel leader and political figure, and Dad quickly educated himself of his legacy. He made the speech as requested, and the statue went up.

———

My mother was not a public figure in any way, but she was an excellent cook and did her share of hospitality for people in and out of the church. She had loved Christian education ever since 1939 when my parents brought me to Harding. Mother and Dad also enjoyed having company, especially when the company was someone like Brother Marshall Keeble, an African-American preacher who would come occasionally to New Orleans to hold a gospel meeting. He would stay with us or visit with us when he was in town. We kept other preachers at our home when they would come to speak for the church at Carrollton Avenue. Our home was like a hotel, but we enjoyed it. Mother had a Cadillac that was big enough to carry as many as ten little children at a time to the Clifton L. Ganus School in the morning and then take them home in the afternoon. The kids loved her, not only for hauling them around, but I'm sure for the candy she always had with her as well. She loved the little children and was glad to see them get a Christian education.

My parents also helped many students go to school. Some students have told me that they would not have been able to come to Harding if my parents had not helped them. Dad never made a fuss, and I will probably never know how many people he helped, since I only learned about it when someone else told me. My dad had been a black and blue graduate from the school of hard knocks, so his life experience heightened his desire to see others get a formal education. Despite his lack of a college degree, Dad learned his lessons well, and he became a wonderful teacher, not only for his family, but also for the church, and the citizens of New Orleans.

Over the years, many people have told me what Dad meant to them and how he could advise them and help them in different ways. I am happy that my dad was so very generous. He never minded giving

$1000 to help someone along, but he hated to be cheated, even out of a dime. I guess I have a similar spirit.

———————

After my father's funeral, my family packed up again and headed to New York City. The trip was a long one for a family with young children, but we enjoyed it. We didn't know much about New York City, but we found the Columbia campus, unloaded everything, and got situated in the apartment. We arrived on a Wednesday, so I planned to attend the midweek service at the Church of Christ located at 48 E. 80th Street in Manhattan.

The church was a good distance away from the campus, but I took the subway and arrived without difficulty. Unfortunately, I took the wrong subway on the way back to the apartment, and I wound up in a rough section of Harlem without many streetlights. I found a policeman and asked him where I was. He told me, and I asked direction to get me back to the Colombia campus. He gave me directions, probably amused that I had ended up so far off target, and I took the next subway available and found my way home.

Our rented New York apartment was on the eighth floor of Bancroft Hall at Columbia University. It had two bedrooms, a living and dining room, a bathroom, and a kitchen that was about the size of a clothes closet with a small stove and a small refrigerator. Only one person could be in the kitchen at a time (and would have to back out if the refrigerator or oven door was opened), and a stairway slanted over the kitchen, so there wasn't much headroom. All of the rooms combined would not be quite as large as the living room in my present home.

One day I almost set that tiny apartment on fire. Our garbage, containing a paper bag, accidentally caught fire. I picked it up to carry it to the bathtub, but the bottom fell out and burning trash fell on the carpet. Fortunately, I was able to extinguish it all out before the floor went up in a blaze, but I was quite worried for a minute that I was about to burn down the entire building.

We didn't have much room for extra furnishings or toys, but we did have a rocking horse for our one-year-old son, Charles. He spent an awful lot of his time rocking on that horse and pretending he was a cowboy. Cliff, my oldest son, turned ten years old during that year and was in the sixth grade. He and Debbie, who was five, walked a half block to their school each morning.

———————

Most of my classes at Columbia focused on education, but I also decided to take a history class. When I looked at the schedule I noticed the name of a famous teacher who had written history textbooks, one of which I used in my classes at Harding. I liked that textbook, so I felt I would have a wonderful opportunity to sit at the feet of a master teacher. I decided to audit the class, but I lasted only two weeks; it was all I could take. He was one of the poorest teachers I ever heard; he read from yellowed sheets of paper with his face partially covered by his hand. Occasionally, he would look up at the ceiling and then back down again, but he never engaged his students. I wasn't learning anything, and I didn't appreciate the class, so I stopped attending. It was a little discouraging to be so let down by a scholar I had admired so much at a distance. Most of my education classes were large, though interesting; and, although I was attending a two-year program, I had enough of the work required through my doctoral program at Tulane that I could complete the entire program in one year. I enjoyed the challenge.

Louise enjoyed being in New York, too. She joined the Columbia Dames, a group of women who were interested in education. Many of these members had husbands who were students at the university, and they liked traveling over New York City to tour historical sites and other places of interest. Louise had a great time on those trips. In addition, she enjoyed going to church in Manhattan. Burton Coffman and his wife, Sissy, worked at the church; he had previously worked on the Harding campus, so we knew him well. I also preached half-time in New Haven, Connecticut, home of Yale University, and we drove over there early every other Sunday morning.

The song leader at the Manhattan church during this time was Pat Boone. He and his wife, Shirley, had a one-year-old baby girl, so Shirley and Louise would sit in the cry room together quite often. Pat would lead singing, and I would often preach to fill in for Burton when he was away at other congregations. We grew to be good friends. Pat was also singing on a television program hosted by Arthur Godfrey, and he invited Louise to go to the studio with him one day; so I stayed home and took care of the children. The television camera panned down the front row where Louise was sitting. I happened to be watching television at that moment. I saw Louise and yelled to the children, "Look! Mother is on television!" We all got a kick out of that, and Louise enjoyed being at the studio.

The trip to New Haven on Sunday mornings would take us two hours, easily following the freeway the entire way with very little traffic. However, coming back on Sunday afternoons was a different story. The freeways would be jammed with traffic, and it sometimes took several hours to get home. The family didn't go with me to New Haven very often, but on one occasion during the winter we decided to go together for Sunday services and then drive up to Boston. We didn't make it that far. We got as far as Providence, Rhode Island, but, due to the heavily falling snow, we had to spend the night there and return to New York City. The snow fell about 18-20 inches deep in the city, and I couldn't even get to the curb to park. I parked out in the middle of the street, since it was as close as I could get, but everyone else was in the same boat.

In New York City, you didn't call for taxis the way you did everywhere else we had lived; you walked out on the street and hailed them down. We did not know that, so the first time Louise tried to call for one, the cab company told her that Cliff III should get out on the street corner to hail a taxi for her. Cliff was willing to give it a try and was pleased when he succeeded, so each Sunday that would be his job – hail a cab so they could get to church. It was much easier than trying to navigate the subway with three children.

My usual avenue of relaxation was to play handball in one of the indoor courts on the campus; we didn't go out much because New York City was so much more expensive that Searcy, and even more than New Orleans. However, for my birthday that year I received a check from my mother for $25, which was a lot of money. For that amount, our whole family watched a movie and ate dinner at one of the automats, where you would put in coins to get sandwiches, salads, and desserts. That $25 covered the entire evening for our whole family.

We enjoyed the stay in New York but were glad to get back to Arkansas at the end of that year to a world of trees and cows. Life was different in our little town of Searcy, with approximately four thousand people compared to the millions in New York. When I returned to Harding after my year away, Dr. Benson appointed me the first vice president for Harding College. He never knew how to take off any hats, however; I still taught classes and spoke at forums and citizenship seminars. I also continued to serve as chairman of the history department and Dean of the School of American Studies. I still preached on occasion, and I enjoyed serving as the faculty sponsor for the Sub T social club and playing with the faculty against the students in rag tag football, basketball, softball, and other sports. My life in Searcy was every bit as busy as life in New York, but it was a kind of busyness I enjoyed immensely and that I knew was helping to shape the lives and futures of young people.

CHAPTER 11

TRAVELS AND TALKS

I didn't do much public speaking during the 1940s, except for the Freedom Forum and the beginnings of the American Studies program on the Harding campus. But the 1950s and 1960s were a different story. Looking back over my calendar for those years, I see that I was gone from the campus quite often. These decades were the most intense period of the Cold War with Russia, and groups all over the United States were wanting to learn more about what made the American way of life so unique as well as the problems our country faced with Russia. As soon as I returned to Harding after studying for my doctorate at Tulane University in the summer of 1951, Dr. Benson asked me to go speak in early September at the Freedom Forum in Detroit, Michigan, with the topic, "History Condemns Socialism." From that time on, I spoke for businesses, civic clubs, schools, and other government and military organizations.

My secretary, Edwina Pace, kept a careful record of the places where I spoke, along with the dates, the organizations, and, often, the topics. I would discuss ideas such as "The Road to America's Future," "George Washington and His Role in American History," "Basic Concepts of Government," "Christian, Ethical, and Moral Values of the American Economic System," "The United States of America – Dr. Jekyll and Mr. Hyde," and "The Secret of American Achievement."

In addition to speaking about free enterprise and economics, I also accompanied Dr. Benson across the country to speak at fundraising dinners to raise money for Harding. One or both of us would speak at a dinner, and then we would go to the offices of the businessmen in the area to see if those companies would help Harding financially. Dr. Benson was a good fundraiser and I enjoyed watching him work.[17]

I enjoyed traveling by planes and trains, but whenever I could I would drive and take my family with me. I had to be away from home so often that I liked having my family join me on the road, and we had a good time together. We would use the hood of the car for a picnic table as we ate at rest areas. Louise and I would unpack our Vienna sausages, pork and beans, soup, and other non-perishable items, sometimes lighting a fire to warm up the food. But we didn't always rely on canned goods. I remember taking the family with me to the Snowshoe Mountains in Wyoming, where we had buffalo burgers for the first time.

I had the opportunity to meet interesting people in my travels, people like H.L. Hunt, the wealthy oil man with whom my father had invested. He was originally from Arkansas, but he lived in Dallas when I met him. He was very frugal with his money, often bringing his peanut butter and jelly sandwiches with him to his office. If he invited people to have lunch with him, they ate what he ate. One day he invited J.D. Bales, one of Harding's professors, to dine with him. Dr. Bales' excitement about the prospect of having lunch with H.L. Hunt was dampened when the peanut butter and jelly sandwiches were served.

I did a little better with trips to Chicago because I would have dinner with John Swearingen, Chairman of the Board and CEO of Standard Oil. His wife at the time was from Arkansas and had attended Harding Academy, so I'm sure this was the reason why I was invited to have dinner in their penthouse on the sixty-second floor of the Standard Oil Building in Chicago.

---

[17] I do remember, however, years later when I became president that he said to me, "you're going to raise a whole lot more money than I ever raised." I laughed and said, "Dr. Benson, that can't be true. You have a done a very good job at it." But he was right in the sense that each subsequent president built on the foundation that Dr. Benson laid. In fact, President David Burks, who succeeded me at Harding, and his group raised far more money than I ever did as president.

I once made a trip to Chicago to eat pheasant. A manufacturer there asked if I would come and speak for his company; if so, he said he would have a big pheasant dinner. I agreed to go and took the train to Chicago. After the program, he had a dinner where he brought out big platters of the breast and legs of pheasant, mashed potatoes, gravy, and thick slices of apple pie. The dinner was wonderful. He raised pheasants as a side business and had a hundred thousand of them. When I finished eating all I could, I rolled down to the train station to come back to Searcy. My big appetite served me well with all those fundraising dinners!

On another occasion, I remember coming home from Chicago, and when I started to board the train the porter said, "Boss, are you with the Brooklyn Dodgers?"

I said, "Oh, no. Are they on the train?"

He said, "They sure are," and showed me where the team was sitting. I went to the club car, and I looked for Preacher Roe, a Dodger player who had pitched for Harding. He was a great pitcher and had struck out twenty-seven batters in a thirteen-inning game at Harding. I found him, and we enjoyed visiting with one another. Later, I had dinner with Clyde Sukeforth and Cookie Lavagetto. The players were all very quiet at first, and when I asked Preacher who had won the game in Chicago that day, he said, "Well, can't you tell?" They had lost 7-0. But they warmed up after a while, and after dinner we went to another club car to play Twenty Questions and other quiz games. I enjoyed visiting with Carl Furillo, Clyde King, Carl Erskine, and other players I had read about over the years. They were traveling down to St. Louis to play the Cardinals.

In 1957, Dr. Benson asked Bud Green, the Director of the National Education Program, Louise, and me to go to Europe to study socialism in seven different nations. We readily agreed to this opportunity. Bud carried his video camera, and I carried a still camera to take pictures in the different countries. We not only traveled to the seven nations for the study, but we also traveled to other countries in Europe and to Great Britain for sightseeing opportunities. It was a wonderful and eye-opening experience. We met with government officials, educators, and businessmen. With the United States and Russia in the midst of the Cold War, the countries in Europe offered an interesting array of government systems.

We first flew to London and on one memorable evening there had dinner on the banks of the Thames River at the House of Parliament. There were several Lords and Ladies present, one of whom was Lady Redding, the first Lady to sit in the House of Lords. While we were eating dinner, a waiter came up behind me and asked, "Sir, what would you like to drink?" I said, "I would like some iced tea." "Iced tea," he said, "Well, it's never been done before, but we accept all challenges." He left and returned a few minutes later with a wine glass with a cube of ice in it and poured hot tea over it. Needless to say, I had tepid tea.

Our group was staying at the Waverly Hotel in London, and one morning I received a call from Bud: "Cliff, be careful if you take a shower. I just fell and broke three ribs." I had just finished taking a shower, and I had also slipped but didn't hurt anything. I guess I just got lucky that my shower wasn't as slippery as Bud's. He couldn't carry any of his bags for the rest of the trip, so I carried his bags as well as mine, but we managed. Bud was able to get through the trip without any further incident, his ribs healing eventually. He could only wrap his chest and endure the pain until then.

Since this was our first trip to England, we traveled around as much as we could and saw many of the important and historical sites. Louise and I went out to the Cambridge Cemetery, which held many American soldiers who had died in World War II. One of those young men was Gorman Wilkes, a good friend and fellow student from Harding with whom I had played quite a bit of tennis. He died in a plane crash near London during the war.

In addition to taking in the sights of England, we took a side trip to Scotland. We first went to Edinburgh, a beautiful and ethereal city, where we enjoyed the antiquities and a monument dedicated to Sir Walter Scott. We also had dinner at 10:00 at night; sunset was very late in the summertime. We loved the mist across the valley as we looked from Princes Street across to the government buildings. We also visited Glasgow, which was more of an industrial city. After Scotland, we visited Ireland, where we enjoyed being out in the emerald green countryside. Our bus driver loved to sing, and he drove us for several hours around Ireland while singing old Irish songs like "Danny Boy." We also made two other side trips to Belgium and Holland, where we were especially enamored with the flowers, the flat countryside filled with lakes and canals, and the windmills that were still in use.

Next we flew to Germany, where we spent time in West and East Berlin as well as Bonn, which was the capital of West Germany at the time. Of course, during the Cold War, West Germany and East Germany and West Berlin and East Berlin had a lot of enmity towards one another. West Berlin was about 110 miles deep in East Germany. It was not under communist control, but the city was completely surrounded by communist rule. You could fly into West Berlin, or you could take a train or bus to get there, but once you were in the city you were enclosed by communism, and the communists were pretty strict. The Berlin Wall was not erected until August 13, 1961, so there was still some intercourse between the residents of East Berlin and West Berlin when we were there, but there was a tremendous difference between the two sectors of the city.

Our group was able to travel by subway from one side of the city to the other. I rode with Louise, Bud, and Crystal Kampfer, a Harding student from Germany. Before the journey, we learned that we needed to dress as plainly as we could. The women were not to wear lipstick, rouge, or flashy clothing. We were also told to not take cameras with us since East Berlin could be dangerous, but Bud and I took our cameras anyway.

East Berlin had not been rebuilt after the war and still contained much rubble. We visited the bunker in which Hitler died. It was blown up out of the ground and left among the weeds as a testimony of the brutality and failure of his regime. In contrast, West Berlin had a tremendous amount of reconstruction. The two cities were as different as day and night. Later, from the footage we collected, we made a movie called *The Two Berlins* that showed this great contrast.

When we started back to our hotel in West Berlin, we were sitting in the subway station in East Berlin when a lady came up to Louise and began asking her questions in German. We thought, "Uh-oh, we are in trouble now."

Crystal translated for us and told us the lady had only said, "Oh, that's a pretty raincoat. Did you buy it in East Berlin or West Berlin?"

"No, tell her I bought it in New York City," Louise said, relieved. Without any serious incident, we were able to go back again into West Berlin.

Early the next morning we were sleeping in the hotel, and at about 5:00 a.m. we were awakened by something that sounded like gunfire – *pow, pow, pow, pow*. Louise whispered urgently, "What's that noise?"

I said, "Oh, I don't know. It sounds a little like gunfire."

"Gunfire?" Louise cried. "Let's get out of here!"

"Where are you going?" I asked. "We're 110 miles deep into communist territory." We had nowhere to go. She insisted that I do something, so I called the manager who said, "Well, I don't think it's gunfire. It sounds like a machine that is trying to start or something, but I really don't think it's gunfire." We went back to sleep since everything was okay and, honestly, there was nothing we could do about it either way.

Leaving Berlin, we made a short visit to Bonn, which was a smaller city than Berlin and, though beautiful, still had a lot of ruins from the war.

After visiting Germany, we traveled to Vienna, where we rode what was then the world's largest Ferris wheel. Each coach held ten or fifteen people, and we could look out over the beautiful city. From Austria we traveled to Italy, where we toured mostly in Florence and Rome. There, of course, we visited with a few business and government leaders, but we were also able to see the main sights, such as the Cathedral, Baptistery, and Pitti Palace in Florence; and the Colosseum and St. Peter's Basilica in Rome. We happened to be in Italy at an unfortunate time of the year because August is a vacation month, with a holiday called *Ferragosto*, and most of the people we saw in Rome and Florence were tourists from America and other countries. They were visiting the cities, but the Italians were all headed for the mountains and the sea for a month of vacation.

From Italy, our team traveled to Belgrade, Yugoslavia. We checked into the hotel, and the hotel staff kept our passports. Louise and I went upstairs, and I looked out over the balcony to see the clerk showing our passports to two men dressed in business suits. They were checking us out. I don't know who they were, but I am guessing that they were some kind of government officials sent to learn more about us. They claimed that the hotel kept the passports as long as you stay in their city. Of course, this procedure is restricting in a sense, because if you don't have a passport when you are out in the city, it's hard to prove who you are if requested to do so. Thankfully, we didn't run into any issues.

When we left the hotel at Belgrade we went out to the countryside to visit a collective farm. Farmers there didn't have personal plots of land as we do here in America. Under communism all of the farms were large, and the government owned and controlled them. The farm we visited consisted of 52,000 acres and raised cattle, pigs, and various kinds of grains. When we arrived that morning, Peter Zecevic, the friendly manager of the farm, greeted us by saying, "You must have some peach brandy."

I spoke for the group and said, "Thank you. We wouldn't care for any."

Peter insisted, "Oh, but you must! It's our national drink."

Bud replied, "Well, thank you, but we wouldn't care for any."

Finally, Peter relented and said, "Well, then you must have some Turkish coffee." Louise, Bud, and I thought that was a good out, so we agreed to take the Turkish coffee. Honestly, we might as well have had the brandy. I don't like coffee and don't drink it, but I have never had anything taste that strong. To make Turkish coffee, you boil it down from one pot to another until you have only the very essence of the coffee left. It was thick and very strong. Fortunately, Peter gave us only a little cup of it, so we choked down our cups and then he took us out to see the farm.

The farm was near a railroad station. We noticed many people waiting for the train, and when it arrived some people entered through the doors. Others, however, climbed in the windows, scrambling for a seat and competing with hundreds of others for a place on the train. Yugoslavia was indeed very different from our experiences in America.

After a good walk around the farm, we returned to the hall for lunch with the workers. The eating hall did not have screens on the windows, and as a result the food had many flies. In fact, I have never seen such a conglomeration of flies as we had at that meal. I had to sweep my hand over my bowl of watery soup to fight off the flies for each bite. Louise was somewhat finicky about eating anything that had contact with flies, but I told her she had to eat some of the meal despite the flies, lest we offend our hosts. She ate some of the soup, and then we were served a plate with greasy meat and potatoes. Again, we had to swat the flies away to eat. Louise ate a little of the meat and potatoes, and by the time our dessert arrived, a pound cake with white icing, Louise looked at me and said very quietly, "I am not going to eat any of that cake."

I asked, "Why? You've had some of the soup and some meat and potatoes. Why not the cake?"

She said, "I saw that cake in the kitchen, and it was just covered with flies. I'm not going to eat it." She stayed true to her word, but she had eaten enough of the other food, so that was okay. I ate everything given to me. Flies weren't going to deprive me.

One day, we went out to see a statue near a beautiful river that commemorated those who had lost their lives in World War II. We decided to have lunch at a restaurant located near the statue. We were sitting out on the open platform by the statue when the waiter came out, and we told him we would like to have soup and sandwiches. He spoke a little English and said, "No. No, we can't do that." We argued that all we wanted was just soup and sandwiches for lunch.

He said, "I know that's not the way Americans eat because I have a brother in New York City working in a restaurant. I know that people don't eat like that." He wouldn't serve us even though we insisted we truly only wanted soup and sandwiches. He went to find his manager who came out to us. We described again what we wanted to eat, and the manager looked at the waiter and said, "Just bring them what they want." And so we finally got our soup and sandwiches and went about our day, but the waiter still felt he knew how Americans ought to eat, and we did not.

From Yugoslavia we went to Switzerland, where I fell sick with the Asian flu, which was spreading across the globe at that time. At first, I could not figure out what was the matter with me, except I knew I was very sick. Switzerland was a beautiful country, and Louise enjoyed visiting parts of it.

From Switzerland we went back to Paris, where we stayed in a very poor hotel. We were, however, able to visit with Maurice Hall and his wife, missionaries living in Ville-d'Avray. While there we visited the palace of Versailles with its beautiful Hall of Mirrors.

I was still very sick with the flu. Louise and Bud visited Mont Blanc, riding a cable car up the mountain. They said it was a lovely view, but I was wasn't able to join them. Back at the hotel, I slept during the night, but awakened the next morning about 5:00 and felt that I might stop breathing – I didn't necessarily mind because I was so sick. Louise stayed up with me the rest of the morning and finally found a doctor to come see me – a physician Maurice knew who was from Hawaii but practicing in France. He treated me with a mustard plaster on my chest and some kind of medicine that tasted like it had alcohol in it. That was supposed to take care of me, and maybe it did help some, but I was ill all the way back to America.

Our flight home was in an old Boeing Stratocruiser, a prop plane that was slow, but comfortable. We had to land at Reykjavik, Iceland, for refueling. I was still very sick, but I wanted to at least touch Iceland. I put my feet on the ground, and then quickly went back to my seat on the plane. We landed in Jacksonville, Florida, and I finally started to feel better. In Jacksonville, we were reunited with Cliff III and Charles, who had stayed with Louise's sister and her husband (Debbie was staying with my mother in New Orleans).

It had been an incredibly eventful and eye-opening trip, but I surely was glad to be home.

CHAPTER 12

SOUTH AMERICA

Following the success of our films about Europe, Dr. Benson and I decided to study communism and socialism in six different countries in South America. We began researching and preparing for the trip, but at the last minute he decided that he ought not to go, since he was considering running for public office in Arkansas and his interest in those countries might be misconstrued. He suggested instead that I go on my own, and I agreed, but I wanted my brother James to accompany me for part of the time.

The itinerary would take us to Ecuador, Columbia, Venezuela (where James would join me), Brazil, Argentina, Uruguay, and Chile to meet with educators, businessmen, and governmental officials as we interviewed them and observed their practices and customs in an attempt to understand how their political philosophies took shape in each country.

My first stop was in Quito, the capital of Ecuador, situated at an altitude of more than eight thousand feet, where it is important that tourists not overeat or overexert themselves for at least the first day upon landing, in order to give their bodies a chance to acclimate. That would have been good to know ahead of time.

I had observed dark clouds gathering as we were flying in, so I was eager to get out a walk around a bit before the storm started. "Oh, it never rains on Sunday," I was assured by a man seated near me on the plane; it seemed like odd advice, but he was a local, so I figured he knew what he was talking about. Once we landed, I decided I should take advantage of the Sunday rain prohibition and see as much as I could on that afternoon. I walked all over the city before the storm started. The man turned out to be partially right, I suppose: It did rain, but not the whole time; the rest of the time, it hailed. The hail looked like snow piled up, it had fallen so thick and fast in marble-sized stones – and I was caught in the middle of it. I had to find shelter until the hail stopped, then I had a long walk back to the hotel where I made my second mistake of the day: I had a huge meal, which I figured I had earned from all that exercise.

That night, my head began to hurt and then I became incredibly sick. It wasn't until I was talking with someone the next day that they explained to me about avoiding exertion and large meals for the first day or two because of the altitude. I made sure to file that information for future travels, but I had to suffer through Quito for the present.

I learned about a communist bookstore in the city that also served as the communist headquarters and decided that it would be quite useful to get some of their literature for studying their writings and propaganda, but I also realized it might be problematic for an American to just walk into the communist headquarters and start asking for their publications. Instead, I asked my cab driver if he would be willing to drive me there and then purchase several copies of the monthly magazine *Mañana* with money I gave him. He was happy to do so and brought a variety of issues of the journal back to the car for me; it was only then that I realized just how anti-American and pro-communist things really were. One of the magazines had a picture of the United States imagined as an octopus with its tentacles reaching down over all the countries of South America. The articles were all in Spanish, of course, and my Spanish was somewhat rudimentary – but it was good enough to get the gist of the message that "Yankee imperialism" was considered the number one threat to the Ecuadorian Communist Party and to their way of life. I put the copies of *Mañana* in my suitcase to bring home and study in greater depth, but all in all it had been an eye-opening first stop – in more ways than one!

My next stop was Bogotá, Columbia. Columbia had never been particularly friendly towards the United States and was already well established as one of the main sources of illicit drugs, but I never felt unsafe while I was in the city. I wished I could have seen some of the Columbian countryside, but I enjoyed what I saw of Bogotá while I was there.

I next flew to Caracas, Venezuela, where an official from the American Embassy met me at the airport. We chatted as the customs officers inspected my luggage and then he opened my bag with the magazines from Ecuador. "*No! Es communisto!*" the officer said in a loud voice.

"*No es communisto,*" the embassy official insisted. "*Es anti-communisto.*"

"*No! Es communisto!*" the officer said again and moved to block me from going any further. Venezuela, at that point, was only socialist; they were not a full-fledged communist government, and they feared anyone (especially foreigners) who may come in and try to rile up the masses.

The embassy official asked the customs official to take us to see the customs chief. The man squared his shoulders and said, "*Yo soy el jefe* (I am the boss)." That settled it. Finally, we compromised that I would just leave my bag with the Venezuelan customs officers at the airport and would retrieve it when I left, so that they could rest assured that I was not bringing communist materials into the country.

James joined me in Venezuela and when I returned to the airport the next day so we could leave for Brazil, the customs officers told me they would retrieve my bag. As we went to board, they assured me it had already been loaded onto the plane.

I should have known better than to blindly accept their word because, as we got off the plane in Rio de Janiero, the first thing I heard was a worker calling "Mr. Ganus! Mr. Ganus!" and beckoning me over to his desk. "Mr. Ganus," he said, when I reached him, "your bag was left in Venezuela. Do you know why?"

I was irritated. "No, I don't know why because I had been told that the bag was on the plane."

Whether the chief was getting revenge on me or they did not trust me not to spread communist propaganda elsewhere or someone had genuinely just messed up, I don't know; but what I did know was that I was suddenly without clean clothes or underwear. My stop in Venezuela had been short, and all of my items for changing had been in the bag that customs had held onto. I was forced to purchase new items in Rio and their sizing was completely different, which resulted in a pretty bad fit. Still, there was nothing I could do so I just had to make the best of it.

We had several receptions in Brazil, which allowed me a number of opportunities to talk with governmental officials and business leaders. I asked one of the lower-level government officials about the president and whether he was a communist. "*Ele não é vermelho* (He is not red)" he assured me. "*Ele é cor-de-rosa.* (He is pink.)" In other words, he was merely a socialist, not a communist.

There were a few little details from Brazil that stayed with me as interesting or humorous experiences. At one reception, there was a huge ball of ice with boiled shrimp stuck on it. Guests just plucked the shrimp off on toothpicks. As a New Orleans boy and a fan of shrimp, that made quite an impression on me! James and I also managed to get stuck in an elevator between floors, and, since James was claustrophobic, I was worried he was going to pass out before someone arrived to help us. Thankfully, he managed to hang on and we made it out safely.

The most interesting thing that happened to us in Brazil, however, was observing the May Day celebrations. In communist and socialist countries, May Day is one of the biggest events of the year with fireworks, speeches, and parades. As it turned out, the president was scheduled to come and speak at the very place where we were staying in Rio, so James and I decided to go down to join the gathering in the street to watch him there. All around us, members of various labor unions from throughout the city were marching with signs against the United States and supporting Castro and Cuba. I was taking pictures and furiously scribbling notes while pointing things out to James, and, inevitably, someone would come up and ask, "Are you with the press?" I would always assure them I was not, and then we would move away from that particular area, so no one got suspicious and tried to cause trouble.

As it turned out, the president did not come and speak; he just gave his address over the radio instead. As the crowd thinned, I noticed that there were some interesting propaganda signs from the platform where he was supposed to have stood, and I decided I would like to have a couple of those signs as souvenirs. The platform was about fifty yards away, so I left James and went up the steps. There was one anti-American sign lying on the ground and another on the well held up just by thumbtacks, so I took them both to bring home with me. Almost everyone was gone by this point but, as I was coming back down the steps, a little old lady came up the stairs towards me and tried to grab the signs out of my hand. One tore a little as we tugged back and forth, but I kept saying "*Obregado, obregado* (Thank you, thank you)" and finally managed to wrestle them away from her and make it back to James.

He had watched the whole thing and was feeling quite nervous, so he said, "Let's get back to the hotel." It was a three-quarter-mile walk, and he was concerned for our safety the entire time. When we finally got back to our room on the eleventh floor, he immediately pulled the window shades so no one could see in. "They might have a gun," he explained when I asked what he was doing.

From Rio we went to Brasilia, about six hundred miles inland. It was a relatively new city that had recently been established as the seat of government of the country, and it was interesting to see a capital city still under construction.

We next visited Argentina where, after all of the usual meetings and receptions, James and I decided to have lunch at an Italian restaurant a block from our hotel. It was an old white-frame structure with a good reputation, and we did our best to order entirely in Spanish, since they spoke no English. James ordered spaghetti and some chicken livers, and I told them I would like a bowl of tomato soup. When they brought out the food, James got his spaghetti alright, but he also got a whole chicken with a row of livers lined up along the breast. I had a tub of tomato soup – literally, a big, big tub of it. We just sat there and laughed because it was such a mountain of food and there was absolutely no way we were going to be able to finish it all. But what really surprised us was when the bill came: I think we each paid just a little over $1.50 for our meal. It was unbelievable how inexpensive it was!

We had a short stop in Montevideo, Uruguay, and did a little sightseeing in the capital before moving on to our final destination, Chile. Chile had been facing a growing influence from communism and socialism recently, and I visited a communist bookstore there, just to see what literature was being distributed. But the most interesting experience I had was with the colonel of the carabinero, sort of a federal police force. This man was a high-ranking officer and talented horseman; he had even competed in the equestrian events at the

Olympics. We met in his office in Santiago and I asked him, "Are you a democratic country?"

"Yes," he answered.

"Suppose the people in Chile voted for communism. Would you permit the communists to take over?"

He stopped for a moment and then said, "Well, it is true that we are a democracy and we believe in democracy and I cannot tell you officially, but if the people voted communism in, there would be no democracy. So I cannot tell you, but no. We would not permit it."

Later, there was an attack on the leader, Salvador Allende, who was a strong leftist. There was a lot of bloodshed, and the colonel was right: The military did not permit a communist or socialist to run the country.

From Chile, James and I flew back home to the United States with an even deeper perspective on the spread of communism across the globe.

CHAPTER 13

A NEW PRESIDENT

D r. George Benson served as president of Harding College from 1936 until June 2, 1965. On that date, he presided at the dedication of the American Heritage Building, which was the crowning jewel of his administration. He served as president for twenty-nine years, and in that time Harding grew considerably in academic rigor, in student numbers, in facilities, and in reputation. Dr. Benson asked me to speak after the dedication on the operation and services of the American Heritage Center, and I was happy to do so. After he retired, Dr. Benson moved to Edmond, Oklahoma, to serve as the chancellor for Oklahoma Christian College. He left Marguerite O'Banion, his secretary, here to work in his office, which he kept in the Heritage Center. She helped him with the National Education Program.

On April 25, 1965, I had signed a contract with the Harding Board of Trustees which contained the following expansions of my responsibilities as I became the third president of Harding College: I would serve as chief executive of the institution and direct the affairs in accordance with the charter, the bylaws of the college, and other directives received from the board from time to time. The board requested that I give special attention to high academic standards and to the development of Christian character. The Board also entrusted me with the finances of the institution. In return for my services, the board agreed to pay me a salary of $15,000 a year and to give me a housing allowance of $150 a month or a house furnished by the college, whichever I desired. In addition, I would have a car furnished with gas, maintenance, and insurance, and I would have no restrictions on its use, noting that this car would save me at least $1,000 a year.

The contract also stated that I would have invitations to speak on various occasions, and the board believed that I should accept these invitations judiciously. The board also said I should agree that the fees I received would accrue directly to the college as college income. The board recommended that when speaking, I should seek gifts for the college rather than personal fees. I agreed to the contract that they suggested. My tenure would begin at noon on June 3, 1965.

In the spring of 1965, I knew I would need all the help I could get when I began to serve as president that coming summer, so I went to Dr. Benson and asked him if I could put together a group of men who would help advise me at Harding. I wanted to call the group the President's Development Council. Dr. Benson gave me permission to start forming my group, and I began to call people whom I thought would be helpful to us. The first person I called was my brother James in New Orleans, who immediately agreed. Then I called other friends and Harding alumni from all over the United States, and I had enough positive responses to ask for a meeting. We designed the President's Development Council to be the eyes and ears of Harding in the community where each participant lived.

In the past, Harding had held a shaky relationship with many members of the Churches of Christ because some people believed that J.N. Armstrong, Harding's first president, was a premillennialist; therefore, many congregations did not have a good feeling about Harding. This accusation was false, but perceptions can often be more important than truth. I was determined to try to improve the relationship with the brethren who did not look favorably upon Harding. The council would be a big asset in this respect. The members would represent Harding in their community and represent their community to Harding. In addition, we hoped the President's Development Council would be helpful financially to Harding as we worked to expand our building goals on campus. We were very pleased with the initial response we received, and through the years the council has grown tremendously and has been very helpful to Harding.

In addition, I wanted to involve more women in the growth of the school, so I helped start the Associated Women for Harding at the same time as the President's Council. The organization became extremely important to Harding. Over the years, the AWH has raised tremendous amounts of money for student scholarships and has been helpful in recruiting new students for Harding as well.

On the morning that I was set to begin serving as president of Harding, June 3, 1965, I awakened to read in the newspaper that I was being sued for one million dollars in the Little Rock Federal District Court by a Harding student, who accused me, as well as Harding's Board of Trustees, of calling him a communist in a board meeting. He claimed to have secured some information about the meeting; but the confounding aspect in all of this was that his name was never mentioned in the meeting. I doubt that anyone even thought of him. We were not frightened by the lawsuit, and, in fact, we laughed about it. The next day, he went to Little Rock and withdrew the suit, and nothing ever came of it. But it was certainly a dramatic note on which to begin my tenure.

Whenever a new president takes office, people want to meet him and hear him speak. I spent much of my time in the summer and fall of 1965 (and for years to come), speaking in church services, civic clubs, commencement exercises, baccalaureate services, and meetings of various kinds. During that summer I worked extensively with members of our faculty and staff in preparation for the inauguration service, which was to occur in September. I also had to present a ten-year development plan for Harding College in September.

A new president

I felt excited about serving as president. I knew that it would be a challenging experience, and I knew I would encounter problems and difficulties, but I had great confidence in the future.

First, I believed that the work of Harding was truly the work of the Lord, and that we, as faculty and staff, were engaged in helping young people to not only prepare for this life, but also to prepare for eternal life in Heaven with our Creator. Second, I had been at Harding for many years as a student and as a teacher and knew the people with whom I would work. I had great confidence in them and knew they would help hold up my hands. Third, I had spent nine years serving as vice president with Dr. George Benson, who was a strong, capable administrator who had helped Harding in many ways. Fourth, I had a good family who loved and supported me and whom I loved and appreciated so very much. Fifth, I knew we had many thousands of Harding alumni and friends who would be of assistance to us, and I trusted they would be behind us and work with us to achieve our goals and purposes. Our people loved God, loved Harding, and loved the students. This is what gave me strength and resolve to accomplish the tasks before us.

Despite being busy during those first few months as president of Harding, I took time off in August for two weeks to travel with my eldest son, Cliff III, who would be entering his senior year as a music major at Harding that fall. On August 13, 1965, Cliff and I flew to Cairo, Egypt, where we stayed at the Hilton Hotel on the Nile River. The banks of the Nile and its tributary canals form a ribbon of lush green in the midst of the Sahara Desert with sand on both sides as far as you can see, and the view from our hotel was breathtaking.

In Cairo, we visited the Museum of Egyptian Antiquities, and its entrance featured a pool of water where some strands of papyrus grew. I had heard about papyrus for many years, but this visit marked the first time that I had ever seen any papyrus actually growing. I liked thinking about how the ancient Egyptian people used these reeds to make paper many years ago and then recorded the history of their people for us to read about them thousands of years later. Once a history student, always a history student.

The museum contained the artifacts from the tomb of King Tutankhamen along with other pharaohs. However, since King Tut's tomb had not been robbed as other tombs had been, his section of the museum contained more than four thousand pieces of material exhumed from his tomb. We saw large pieces of furniture, his throne, and his sepulcher. King Tut's body had three golden coffins, each nesting inside one another, and within the golden coffins rested four large wooden boxes, each stacking inside one another as well. The boxes were gilded and colored with black paint.[18]

In Cairo, a city of seven million people, there were 75,000 mosques, and there were 250,000 mosques in all of Egypt. However, Egypt was restrictive with other religions. During our visit, Cairo had only one small Church of Christ where a handful of members met in the home of Bob Douglas, who was a missionary there. Even though he had members meet in his home, he was not allowed to propagate the faith out in the streets of the city. It was eye-opening to see just how restricted the believers were at that time, but also how faithful they were in their worship.

Our main purpose in visiting Cairo, of course, was to see the Pyramids of Giza, arguably the most important landmarks in all of Egypt. I was all prepared to lecture to Cliff about their history: how Khufu (or, to the Greeks, "Cheops") built the oldest and biggest of the pyramids in about 2560 B.C.; how he was the father and grandfather of the pharaohs who built the other two major pyramids at Giza. Of course, there had been smaller pyramids built before this time, but these two were the largest. They were built about twenty years apart. The first one, the biggest one, stood about 481 feet tall and was the tallest manmade structure in the world for 3,800 years. It contained almost three million stones, weighing an average of three tons each – quite a monument to honor and bury one pharaoh. Nearby, the second pyramid was built by the son, Kefran, and then close to that

---

[18] Later the Egyptian Government allowed King Tut's exhibit to come to the United States, but there were only fifty-seven pieces on display in Memphis, New Orleans, and other cities. Louise got to see it in New Orleans and stood out in the rain for a few hours before she could get into the display.

was another pyramid built by Kefran's son, Mikarinos. But growing up with a history professor dad meant Cliff had known all about the pyramids from the time he was tiny, so I just reviewed the facts in my own mind as we prepared for our adventure.

On a camel, contemplating climbing

After we rode on camels to the pyramids with our tour group, Cliff and I decided to climb the tallest pyramid, which was difficult since there were no steps and no handholds. We crawled up each stone that stood about three feet high, found a little ledge, and from that ledge, we climbed the next stone and the next one and the next one.

We were fortunate to have the world champion pyramid climber to guide us to the top. His name was Hefnawi, and people bowed to him because they knew he was the champion. He had guided Nikita Khrushchev and other notables from other countries and knew how to get up and down the pyramid safely, if not easily. Before we started, I asked him for the price of his guidance, but he said, "Oh, not much, not much." He spoke very good English, but he wouldn't give a specific price.

When the three of us arrived the top, we looked out over a beautiful scene – the green ribbon of the Nile Valley and the hinterland that it supported with vegetation of different kinds. Except for that ribbon of green, the rest as far to the right and left that we could see was sand – no grass and no trees. When we were at the top, Hefnawi began to say, "You are so fortunate to be in the hands of Hefnawi, world champion pyramid climber."

We said, "Oh, yes, we are glad."

He said, "You do want to get down safely, don't you?"

And we said, "Oh, yes, we do want to get down safely."

He still didn't name a price, but we started back down, and he carried my shoes down for me, since I decided to go down barefoot.

Climbing down the pyramids was more difficult than climbing up, because we were generally looking out. As we had gone up, we had looked inward and upward, so the climb was not quite so scary. But coming down, if we made a misstep and started falling, we would fall all the way to the bottom before stopping, so the descent was nerve-racking. In fact, so many people were killed in climbing the pyramids that the government eventually stopped permitting it. They now have guards all around the place to keep people from climbing even on the first level of the pyramid.

When we were down about a third of the way, Hefnawi said again, "You do want to get down safely?"

We replied, "Oh, yes, we do."

Hefnawi said, "Well, you are fortunate to be in the hands of Hefnawi." I could just see the price of this guided tour going up. We climbed down about another third of the way, and he stopped and said, "That will be twelve dollars please." Back in 1965, twelve dollars was a lot more money than it is today, but I was happy to pay Mr. Hefnawi twelve dollars to get down safely. Cliff and I were the only two who would climb the pyramids out of our entire touring group of thirty. When we returned to Searcy, we saw an article in the *Arkansas Gazette* about Hefnawi, describing him as the champion pyramid climber. He had two sons, one of whom he wanted to be a doctor and the other a lawyer – no pyramid climbing for them.

Near the pyramids was the most famous Sphinx in the world, shaped similarly to those of Greek mythology with the body of a lion and the face of a man. In the evenings, there was an informative program with sound and lights that showcased the area and some of its history.

We enjoyed most of the food in Egypt and on one occasion were served a dish called *mansaf*. Mansaf begins with a piece of dough, somewhat like a pizza, layered on top with rice, bits of mutton, yogurt, and butter made from sheep's milk. To eat mansaf, one must reach a hand into the dish, grab a chunk of all that gooey stuff, wad it up into a ball, and then eat it. Mansaf didn't require utensils, and the bread at the bottom served as a sort of plate. We heard a story from a friend about mansaf. This friend had another friend who was eating with a Bedouin sheik who served him mansaf. The friend wore a flowing robe like the Bedouins wore, and he was the guest of honor, whom the sheik always served the best of everything. Sitting next to the sheik, this friend reached out to grab a handful of mansaf in front of him. The sheik reached over and grabbed the eyeball out of the head of the sheep, which was often placed on top of the mansaf. The sheik put the eyeball on the guest of honor's fist, which was full of mansaf. This friend didn't know what in the world to do. He absolutely could not swallow an eyeball, but he also could not insult the sheik. Sheiks could be friendly and hospitable, but they could also get angry easily. The friend decided to put his hand up to his face and discretely rolled the eyeball down inside his flowing Bedouin robe. He put the rest of the mansaf in his mouth and ate it. Luckily, this friend didn't wear a coat and tie because there would have been nowhere to roll the eyeball, and he would have been in trouble. Thankfully, all the mansaf we encountered was eyeball-free.

When Cliff and I left Cairo, we boarded a Russian plane and flew down south to Luxor. It seemed strange to go upriver and yet to be flying south. In the United States, our rivers flow mostly from the north to the south, like the Mississippi River, the Ohio, and others. But the Nile River begin in Uganda at Lake Victoria and then snakes its way up through Uganda and Sudan to Egypt – 4100 miles in total – until it reaches the Mediterranean Sea near Alexandria, one of the great cities of Egypt. While we were flying to Luxor, snow formed inside the plane. Something had happened to the air conditioner, and actual, artificially made snowflakes landed on us in our seats. An already strange trip was made even stranger with indoor snow over the Sahara. Of course, when we arrived at Luxor, we wished for some real snow or even some air conditioning because Luxor was 106 degrees in the shade. When we would put our hands out in the sun, they felt as though they were baking in an oven.

Luxor, which in ancient times served as a governmental seat of Egypt, had two large temples, the Temple of Karnak and the Temple of Luxor, that joined together – encompassing an area over a mile long. Across the river from the hotel in which Cliff and I stayed were the burial grounds, the tombs of pharaohs in the Valley of the Kings and the wives of the pharaohs in the Valley of the Queens. The Valley of the Kings held sixty-two tombs, including King Tut's. We were able to go to both valleys and to walk down into the tomb of King Tut to see where the English archaeologist Howard Carter in 1922 found over four thousand pieces of furniture, jewelry, scepters, and other artifacts that were transported to the Museum of Egyptian Antiquity.

The Valley of the Kings also contained the Mortuary Temple of Queen Hatshepsut, a woman who became pharaoh and ruled for a number of years. After she was gone, her successor obliterated her face from the temple monument in an effort to remove any evidence that a woman had ever ruled Egypt. The Temple was still there, and the figure of her body remained, but her face was taken off of every surface.

We then crossed the Nile in a *felucca*, a small traditional boat quite common on the Nile and its tributaries. Its small triangular sail provided a quick and pleasant journey across the river.

From Egypt we went to Lebanon, which at one time was called the Queen of the Mediterranean. Beirut, the capital city, was the regional center of education, banking, and commerce at the northeastern end of the Mediterranean Sea. We stayed at the beautiful Nautilus Hotel and had dinner on the top floor of the hotel with a wonderful view of the sea. It was sad to me when, just a few years later, much of Beirut was destroyed from fighting between the Arabs and the Israelis.

From Beirut we traveled inland, passing the cedars of Lebanon, which had been important in the days of David and Solomon in the building of the Jewish temple and their kingly palaces. We took pictures of some of the few giant trees that remained, that had been there for ages. They stood tall, spreading out with a diameter of perhaps six or seven feet across the trunk.

Beyond the cedars, in Baalbek, were a few ancient temples. The best preserved was the Temple of Bacchus, a temple to the god of pleasure, where worshippers participated in immoral orgies and revelries. Nearby was a temple to Jupiter, with several large columns standing. A stage for plays and musical performances had been built inside the temple, and hundreds of chairs were provided for spectators. The annual Baalbek Music Festival was taking place, and we saw a performance by Fairuz, the most popular female singer in Lebanon. She happened to also be staying at the Nautilus Hotel, so Cliff and I were able to visit with her in the lobby, and we enjoyed talking with her – especially Cliff, the music major.

From Lebanon, we traveled by bus to Syria and stopped in the city of Damascus, famous to Christians because the Apostle Paul was traveling toward Damascus to arrest Christians and bring them to Jerusalem for jail or execution when he received his calling from Jesus. After being blinded from that encounter, Paul went to the street called Straight in Damascus and was baptized into Christ by Ananias. Before we arrived in the city, our guide on the bus said, "Now, Syria is a very difficult country, and we must be very careful about what we say about the government. Please don't say anything that will get us in any hot water. Just be very careful." We understood that. At least we thought we did.

Our bus arrived at the hotel in Damascus, and while we were still in the lobby, one of the ladies on the tour yelled out, "Oh, Guide! Guide! Why aren't we to say anything about the government in Syria?" Of course, our guide was a little irritated by her outburst, as were the rest of us, but fortunately, nothing came of it.

When we were in Damascus, the guide bought several bottles of liquor and boxes of candy, which he was planning to take with him for personal use, and stored them under the back seat of the bus. When we stopped at the border checkpoint on our way out of the country, I watched the guide go to the back of the bus, get out a bottle of liquor and a box of candy and take them as a bribe to the border guards. Evidently, he thought that was going to be sufficient, but it wasn't. A bit later, he came stomping back on the bus, went to the back, and got some more bottles of liquor and more boxes of candy. From the look on his face, I could tell that he was unhappy, but these extra items allowed us passage across the border and into Jordan.

Jordan, the last of the Arab countries we visited, was a little friendlier to tourists from the United States than Syria was. We were able to visit a large ancient theater that held ten to twelve thousand people, to see other sights east of the Jordan River, and then to visit the West Bank, populated by Palestinians. Once we had toured that area, we passed through the Mandelbaum Gate, after which we could not return to the West Bank or to any of the Arab countries, because they would not permit entry from the Jewish part of Palestine. Therefore, we had to visit all of the Arab nations first and then cross over into Israel. We noticed barbed wire fences, gun emplacements, and armed guards as we crossed the border.

In Jerusalem we went into a restaurant that advertised American food and thought, "Hooray! This will be a welcome break from the food that we have been experiencing." We ordered pizza, and it was probably the worst pizza I have ever tried in my life. We could not finish it. I don't know what the toppings were, but we just could not force it down our throats.

We saw all of the main sights that Jerusalem had to offer from three different faiths. We saw Al Aqsa (the Dome of the Rock), one of the central mosques in the Muslim faith. They believe that Mohammed ascended to heaven from a stone at this mosque. Very near the Dome of the Rock we saw the Wailing Wall, a part of the old Jewish temple, where Jewish men and women gathered to pray, moving their heads backward and forward and moaning. We stood by the wall to watch scores of people as they would come to wail and pray. We also visited a museum that documented some of the atrocities that the Nazis perpetrated upon the Jews in Germany and Poland. One display that seared itself into my memory contained cakes of soap that had been made from human bodies. A German doctor had invented a process to render the flesh of the Jews to get lard. On an earlier trip to the concentration camp in Stutthoff, Poland, I had seen pictures of two large vats in which Nazis placed bodies of Jewish prisoners. Even though the prisoners were almost skeletons due to starvation, the soldiers rendered the bodies to get what little fat remained and used it to make cakes of soap. At this museum in Jerusalem we saw some of this soap. The museum also displayed fingernails that had been made into light switches and lampshades made from the skin of Jewish victims. This was truly a terrible place to visit, but it was a reminder to the Jews of what the Nazis had done to them during the Holocaust.

In contrast to these horrifying sights, there was a beautiful view from Jerusalem looking out across the Kidron Valley to the Mount of Olives, where the Russian Orthodox believers erected a church building. We also saw the Garden of Gethsemane and, not far away, Bethany and Bethpage, all places noted in the Bible. On the Mount of Ascension had been erected a small building over a stone with an embedded footprint. An attendant claimed that this footprint belonged to Jesus, left when he ascended to Heaven. I asked him if he was sure it was the footprint of Jesus, and he replied, with confounding logic, "Well, I am not sure, but it might have been; therefore, it is."

When we left Jerusalem, we decided to go to Jericho and then on to the Dead Sea. The city of Jericho was demolished – not much left but a few small ruins there – but that was what we were expecting, since we knew the story from the book of Joshua. We traveled down the rugged country from Jerusalem to Jericho, down to the plains where the Dead Sea was located about thirteen hundred feet below sea level – the lowest spot on earth. From the Dead Sea we could view Masada, the fortress occupied from A.D. 70 to 72 by Jewish rebels whom Rome was attempting to capture after they had defied the emperor. The Dead Sea, so different from the vibrant Sea of Galilee, had no fish or life because of the concentration of chemicals and minerals of various kinds, including salt. The water is so dense that a person cannot sink in it. I had a picture made with my arms and my legs up out of the water as I lay on top of the water wearing a hat and my sunglasses. If I had wanted, I could have lain on my back in the water and read a newspaper.

We spent some time at the Jordan River, not a very big river, but an important one in the life of Jesus and Jewish history. Standing on its banks, I thought back to the stories in the Bible where the Israelites crossed the Jordan River into the land of Canaan and when Moses went up to Mount Nebo and there was buried by God. Joshua and Caleb also took Israel across the Jordan River, and the river stopped flowing when they put twelve stones in the river, one for each of the twelve tribes. We also saw the place in the Jordan River where, supposedly, Jesus was baptized by John. No one knows for sure about the exact location, but people from all over the world come to be baptized there. In fact, Cliff and I saw several being baptized there, dipped three times into the water.

The Sea of Galilee, about nine miles wide at the widest point and thirteen miles long, was a beautiful lake with mountains around it, but not many towns on its shore. Tiberias was located on the west, and Capernaum, where Jesus spent so much of his time, was at the north shore. Just to the west of Capernaum on the hillside overlooking the Sea of Galilee was the place where Jesus, according to tradition, delivered the Sermon on the Mount. Unfortunately, I lost my footing as we were walking on one of the banks and had to finish the rest of the tour with soggy shoes.

I floated in the Dead Sea. I fell into in the Sea of Galilee. I waded in the Jordan River, and I swam in the Mediterranean. I experienced all of the major waters of historical Palestine in one way or the other.

Our final stop in Israel included the city of Bethlehem, about six miles south of Jerusalem. Then we flew back through Athens to the United States, concluding our trip to the Middle East. It was a wonderful two weeks with my son, and a nice chance to step away before the intense work of running a university began.

My service as president of Harding began in June, but the inaugural ceremony was scheduled for September. It began on Friday evening, September 17, with an inaugural dinner in the John Mabee American Heritage Center. Jim Bill McInteer, an alumnus, member of the Board of Trustees, and very close friend of mine. presided as master of ceremonies. Norval Young, another good friend who was president of Pepperdine College in Los Angeles, led the invocation. The president of the University of Arkansas, Dr. David Mullins, was the speaker for the occasion; his topic was "New Dimensions in Higher Education."

On Saturday morning, September 18, at 10:00 a.m., the inaugural ceremony took place in the Administration Auditorium. The chairman of the board, Dr. Houston Karnes, presided at the occasion, and the Harding A Cappella Chorus under Dr. Kenneth Davis provided the music for the ceremony. Dr. George Benson gave the invocation, and several educators and community leaders offered greetings to the incoming president. Dean L.C. Sears read scripture and Dr. Karnes invested the new president with his responsibility. Then I spoke for a few minutes on the topic, "Pursuit of Excellence." We sang the Alma Mater, and Adlai Croom gave the benediction. He had been president of Arkansas Christian College that merged with Harper College to form Harding College in the fall of 1924.

The auditorium was packed with guests and representatives from other universities that represented the span of American higher education, from Harvard University, founded in 1636, to Crowley's Ridge College, founded in 1964. There were also twenty-four representatives of learned societies and professional organizations. My inauguration was an exciting occasion, but I was also nervous and scared to death at the prospect of appearing before that extremely credentialed group of people. I was deeply honored and humbled by the whole experience; what a tremendous show of support and "great cloud of witnesses" I had to help me find my way! After that incredible weekend, school continued as usual on Monday morning.

Our enrollment that year was very good. I had expected about thirteen hundred students, but it turned out that we had 1,472 from forty-six states and a number of foreign countries. The total cost for tuition fees, room, and board for that year was $1,374.

———————

We would not have been successful during that time of transition if it had not been for the wonderful support and dedicated efforts of several key people, administrators, faculty and staff who gave good advice and support. Joe Pryor was so important to Harding in the area of academics; Lott Tucker played a decisive role in financial management; Floyd Daniel and Billy Ray Cox were extremely important in fundraising and development; Harry Olree played a decisive role in the area of athletics. There were many others, too, of course, who were instrumental in the growth and development of Harding, for which I remain very grateful.

One of the greatest assets that I had was Edwina Pace, my efficient, dedicated, and capable secretary. She had studied business in high school in Magnolia, Arkansas, and in 1954, three months after she was baptized into Christ, Dr. Benson had hired her to work at Harding. She became my secretary in 1956 when I was chosen to be vice president. In 1958, she went home for a while to help her parents, but she came back to Harding in 1959 and remained my secretary for forty-six years, until she retired in 2005. She became and stayed a faithful member of the College Church of Christ.[19]

Harding and I both have been blessed by so many wonderful people who worked together in the spirit of Christ to accomplish his purpose in Christian education.

After the inauguration period, I gave a presentation to Harding's board which detailed the results of our study for the ten-year development program. It was going to cost approximately ten million dollars. Of this amount, $5,935,000 would be spent on building projects in Searcy; $1,850,000 was allocated to the graduate level program in Memphis; $500,000 was set aside for growth at Harding Academy in Memphis; and $1,716,000 was to be used to increase faculty and staff salaries and to provide additional academic training for our staff. The board discussed the proposal and passed it, so we were on our way with regard to raising funds for the growth of Harding College in the next ten years.[20]

On October 15, 1965, we announced the launching of a $500,000 campaign to help build the science building and a new women's dormitory, and Harding also announced the organization of the Harding

---

[19] About 1967, Gertrude Dykes asked Edwina to teach in the cradle roll for the College Church. She agreed to do so and continued to serve in that capacity ever since. She has worked with Carpenter's Kids, a local preschool in Searcy, from 2004 until the present.

[20] It's interesting to note how money has changed value through the years. When I came to Harding as a student in 1939, tuition fees, room, and board came to approximately $400 per year. When I became president in 1965, it was less than $2,000. Now, it is quite a bit higher than that. When we built our first dormitory after I became president, we did so for approximately $500,000. Now, it would take several times that amount to construct one, even knowing that the university tried to be an extremely good steward of all its resources! I guess that's still better than the situation after the American Revolution when inflation ran rampant and George Washington complained that it took "a wagon load of money to buy a pocketbook of provisions."

100 Club. We were asking alumni to give $100 per year to Harding. The faculty members were also asked to make contributions to Harding. At fundraisers we asked everyone to be involved in the building program. The faculty had always helped, not only giving their lives but in financial contributions as well.

My first year as president was a very busy one. I tried to preside in chapel every day that I was on campus, and I enjoyed participating with the students in many of their activities. I especially enjoyed playing in the athletic contests against students. It got a little harder each year as I got older, but playing rag tag football was my most enjoyable experience on the athletic field. I guess basketball, baseball, and softball would be next. The students seemed to enjoy playing against the faculty, and it was amazing how many times we old folks were victorious. It was interesting to see young students just arriving on campus who did not know of the athletic ability of the faculty, as they laughed about playing the old men – and then hung their heads as they found out they still had a lot to learn. Of course, the faculty lost sometimes as well, and we got beat up just as the students did.

Not only was I busy with campus activities and fundraising events, but I also was called upon to speak often during the fall semester, such as speaking for the churches at Gulfport, Mississippi; Gladewater and Longview, Texas; Columbus, Mississippi; Winston-Salem, North Carolina; and others. I also had the privilege of speaking at a number of schools, including Mars Hill Bible School, Fort Worth Christian, Middle Tennessee Christian School, York, Oklahoma Christian, Abilene Christian, and Pepperdine. I had been heavily involved in the youth seminars at Harding and in many parts of the country and continued to participate for several years in these activities.

Each year, the presidents of our Christian colleges would meet for two days on the campus of one of the schools. I always enjoyed meeting with the other presidents and sharing ideas and suggestions about how to improve our work. There was always a good attitude and rapport among the schools and their administrators. For many years I had a busy schedule both on the campus and all over the nation, speaking at church services, commencements, civic clubs, businesses, and citizenship seminars, as well as normal campus events. It took a lot of time, but it was profitable for Harding.

The coming decade would mark a great deal of change for universities across the country, and it was exciting to see Harding continue to grow and expand, too, while staying true to her core values.

CHAPTER 14

A TRIP TO ASIA

In 1967, from October 31 to November 10, I made a trip to Japan to visit Ibaraki Christian College, about one hundred miles east of Tokyo. The college chose me to serve on its financial board, and several of the other board members living in the United States, including Clarence Daily, Mr. and Mrs. James Cone, Elmer Morgan, Richard Powell, and Winston Atkinson, went over to view the operation as well. The school began after World War II, when General Douglas MacArthur realized the United States was going to have a great hand in trying to reconstruct Japan. He asked President Truman for one thousand American missionaries to come to Japan to help teach the people. Japan's emperor had been dethroned as a god, and people needed something religious to replace him.

This program invited Dr. Benson to send some young people over to be missionaries, and one day during Harding's morning chapel service he asked for students who would volunteer to go to Japan to teach and preach. Several students accepted the offer: Virgil Lawyer, Joe Betts, Joe Cannon, Harry Robert Fox, and others decided to move to Japan. Some of the men left fairly soon, and some left a little later. Not only did this group preach and help establish congregations in Japan, but they also started Ibaraki Christian College, supported by a group of Americans led by E.W. McMillan, who also made the trip with us in 1967.

Clarence Daily, who was preaching for the Union Avenue Church of Christ in Memphis at the time, was my roommate for the trip, but I was not going to join the group until they arrived in Hawaii. When I arrived at the hotel in Hawaii, I checked in at the front desk, saying I would be Clarence's roommate. Later that night, he came into our room, sometime around midnight. I don't remember much except that

I awakened enough to say, "Hello, Clarence," when he walked in, and then went back to sleep.

The next morning at breakfast, our group (a bunch of preachers) sat at the table, and a waitress came by, put her arm around Clarence's shoulder as she refilled our coffee cups, and said, "How's your hangover this morning, honey?" Her question startled all of us, especially Clarence.

When he looked up at her, she realized he was a different man than she thought, and exclaimed, "Oh! I'm sorry. I made a mistake."

We could not stop laughing about this, and for the rest of the trip, we kept asking Clarence at the most inappropriate of times, "How's your hangover, honey?" Clarence was a fine man, and I enjoyed rooming with him on the entire trip.

When we arrived in Japan, our hosts had a dinner for us at 7:00 in the evening. Our entire group had been up all night and were suffering from tremendous jet lag. We all enjoyed the dinner, except none of us who had just arrived could stay awake; we all kept falling into our plates. After a while, Bill Smith, the President of Ibaraki Christian, said, "Dr. Ganus, why don't you and Clarence go up to your room to sleep? We've made this trip before, and we know what it does to you. You will be fine if you go on up to bed."

We thanked him for his understanding, left the table, walked up to our room, climbed into bed, and fell asleep immediately. At 2:00 in the morning, I awakened to hear a muffled sound over by Clarence's bed. Softly, I said, "Clarence, are you awake?"

He replied, "Yes," with a loud voice. We started talking and did so until daylight, unable to go back to sleep. That jetlag was terrible!

At another dinner for us, our hosts seated us around a tabletop just one foot from the floor. We were supposed to sit on cushions in the style of the Japanese, who bend their legs under them to sit on the cushions, but I could not do this comfortably at all. I couldn't shove my feet under the table, and I had no back to lean against. I couldn't sit with my legs out in front of me for any length of time, so I put my legs to the right of me, and then I would switch to the other side. I was shifting and moving that entire meal, trying to figure out how to honor their customs but also sit in a way that my legs could comfortably bend and not fall asleep. Despite all the sitting issues, though, I enjoyed the dinner, and the food was good. Our hosts served us sukiyaki, which was a meal of vegetables and meat, thinly sliced, and dipped in a brazier on the table full of hot soy sauce. We would put what items we wanted into the brazier and then take the food out when sufficiently cooked. We had a common brazier, but each of us had a plate.

I was enjoying the food until they brought us each a bowl with a raw egg in it. It looked like the egg had been prepared for scrambling, but it wasn't cooked. I learned that for this dish, you were supposed to take the food hot from the brazier, dip the meat or vegetables into the raw egg, and then eat it. I looked over at Joe Cannon who had egg dripping off of his chin. I said, "Joe, do you like that stuff with the raw egg?"

He said, "Nope, but I have learned to eat it," and he continued eating.

Joe Betts, sitting on my left side, poured his raw egg into the brazier and cooked it. I sighed with relief and said, "Oh, thank you, Joe." I followed his lead, cooking the egg as well as the rest of the sukiyaki, and it was all very good.

Eating was definitely the biggest adventure in Japan; the visits to the school were quite calm and uneventful. Our team enjoyed meeting the professors and many of the students. We attended chapel and had an opportunity to study the organization we were helping to support by raising funds in the United States, which made us all feel better equipped to continue our support of its great work after we returned home.

Even though we planned the trip primarily as a way to visit the Christian school in Japan, we also took advantage of the opportunity to take some extra excursions around the Far East. After visiting in Japan, we flew through Taipei, Taiwan, where we hoped to be able to see a little bit of the capital city while there on our six-hour layover; unfortunately, we were not allowed to leave the airport. From Taipei, we flew down to Manila. When we arrived in Manila, the thick clouds gave a promise of heavy rain. We landed safely at the airport and drove to the hotel near a bay. That evening, a terrible typhoon hit the area. The storm tore up a railroad line to the south of us, and sixty-three people died on a train knocked off the track by the wind. A ship sank out in the harbor just in front of the hotel during the night. It was terrible to witness so much devastation to such a lovely country and friendly people.

That was one of the things that struck me most about the country – how hospitable the people were and how very eager to accommodate any requests. I had heard that a favorite dish in the Philippines was *balut*, an egg that has been incubated for two weeks and then cooked with the fully formed bird (chicken or duck) within. I had been told that you then take a spoon, chip off the top of the egg, cut off the head of the bird, and eat the entire thing. At dinner that first night in Manila, I asked the waiter, "By the way, do you have balut here?"

He said, "No, we don't, but they have it at the restaurant just up the street. I can get you some if you would like."

"Thank you very much," I replied quickly. "I wouldn't care for any."

Another special Filipino dish I had heard talked about was roasted dog. Bill Smith mentioned that when he had traveled in the Philippines before, he was the guest of honor at a meal where both a roasted pig and a roasted dog were on the menu. The hosts wanted him to slice off the first cuts of the dog and eat it. He wanted to go over to the pig badly, but they insisted on the dog. Of course, the roasted dog of the Philippines was not a common cur; the dog lived a good life and was fattened up and prepared for slaughter, like cattle or pigs in the States. After slaughter, the dog would be prepared with rice and seasonings inside the cavity, roasted, and eaten. But still, it had been quite a shock to Bill's American sensibilities. Given how eager the waiter was to track down balut for me, I decided not to even ask him about roasted dog.

From Manila, our group traveled to visit a church located in a small town outside the capital. When we drove around to the back of the church building to park, I exclaimed, "How in the world did *that* get here?" There, in the middle of a parking lot in the Philippine Islands, sat a Harding swing just like the white, stand-alone wooden swings that dot the Harding campus in Arkansas. After my initial shock, I remembered that the missionary who lived and worked at that church was a classmate, Douglas Gunselman, who graduated with me in 1943. He and his wife decided to have a little piece of Harding with them, so they got the plans for the swings and built one over there.

While we visited the church outside of Manila, we had the chance to ride a water buffalo. As long as the path stayed smooth, it was not a difficult animal to ride. Unfortunately, Elmer Morgan was riding a water buffalo that started going too fast and bucked him off. He was injured in the fall, but not severely. He recovered in a few days.

When we left the Philippine Islands, we traveled to Bangkok, the capital city of Thailand, which is surrounded by little canals called *klongs* that crisscross the area, serving as streets for small boats to transport things to and from the city. Some of the boats serve only for public transportation while others are for produce, hauling goods back and forth. Some boats sell fruits, vegetables, or flowers, serving as a marketplace on the water. The klongs were colorful and beautiful, but the water was dirty because it was used for everything. For instance, I saw men using the water as a toilet, and then I watched a woman sweep a dead dog into the water with her broom and then use the same water to wash her dishes.

The streets of Bangkok were busy, but the river through the city was just as congested. We saw beautiful colored boats, richly decorated, used for royalty and religious purposes. Up and down the river, we saw Buddhist temples that were so different from Christian church buildings in the United States. I wished Louise could have seen these beautiful sights, so I bought some souvenirs: several silver napkin holders with different animal impressions on each one, an entire set of bronze silverware with rosewood handles, and a pretty little chest in which I could bring those things home. We treasure these things in our home and still use them on occasion.

From Thailand we traveled to Seoul, South Korea, which rested close to the 38th parallel that divides South Korea from North Korea. I remember the time in Seoul as very cold, since we were there in November. I stayed at a home used by students of a preacher-training program; the students slept on pallets on the floor in a room next to the kitchen. Since the students had to sleep on the floor, I felt sorry for them at first because I had a bedroom with a nice bed, on which I noticed piles of blankets and quilts. During the night, the temperature dropped to about thirty degrees, and I learned that the house had no heat, except for a little heater in the bathroom. The kitchen stove, however, had a fire burning in it all night, and pipes running under the floor that passed the heated air from the stove, keeping the men warm at night. I almost wished I could sleep on the floor, too.

From Korea we flew to Hong Kong, beautiful and mountainous, and at the time still under British control – China claimed they had given Hong Kong to Great Britain as a hundred-year lease. Water surrounded the island-city of Hong Kong, and one American plane trying to land at the Hong Kong airport had touched down too soon and fell in the water. One of our preachers from the church was on that plane. The water was shallow, so no one was injured; but, of course, the landing dampened their baggage at the bottom of the plane.

Hong Kong was a wealthy city, serving as the window of trade between Eastern and Western markets. I first noticed the taxis because they were all Mercedes; walking down the streets, I began to notice Rolls-Royces lined up – each handmade and costing about $100,000. We enjoyed the seafood of Hong Kong, especially on a floating restaurant. After visiting for a short while and doing some shopping in the city, we headed back to the United States. I enjoyed the experience of this trip with fellow Christians who wanted to serve Ibaraki Christian College in an effective way, and I loved getting to see more of the world and the way people lived outside the United States. But there were pressing matters back home that needed to be attended to, and I wanted to make sure that I was preparing Harding for the next major stages in her growth.

CHAPTER 15

CHANGES FOR HARDING

The last years of the 1960s turned out to be a time of exploding growth for the Harding campus, but those years also mirrored the civil unrest happening in the rest of the country. In the United States, our citizens faced divisions due to racism and the escalating Vietnam War, with much of the violence and backlash of these movements occurring on college campuses. Meanwhile, the United States and the Soviet Union continued the Cold War, pitting against one another the ideas of capitalism and communism, comparing these systems of government through technological advances, economic growth, and, most notably, the race to the moon. I witnessed all of it.

As its student body continued to grow, Harding found an urgent need to add more facilities on campus for housing and classroom accommodations. We completed the Joseph E. Pryor Science building in 1967 and constructed Stephens Hall for a female dormitory in 1968.

In 1969 Harding constructed the Stevens Art Center and built Keller Hall, a dormitory for male students, which was named in honor of May Keller and her Uncle Albert. We also renovated the Claude Rogers Lee music building, adding a large area for recording. The year 1969 was a huge year for growth on our campus, but it was also one of my most difficult years as president of Harding.

———

Throughout 1969 there were an increased number of demonstrations and conflicts on college campuses concerning the Vietnam War as well as escalating racial tensions between black and white citizens in the United States. It seemed as if a malaise had settled over our entire country during that year. There were bombings, riots, burnings, and other forms of violent protest. And then, just a year later in May of 1970, two shootings on the college campuses of Kent State and Jackson State University occurred within eleven days of each other. At Harding we worked towards racial integration while emphasizing kindness and respect.

Nevertheless, there were some who felt we were not doing enough. I attended a meeting of about 120 students and a few faculty members in the American Studies Auditorium one evening in February. The meeting was designed to make public the feelings of some of our African-American students and the demands that they and some of the teachers were making. I sat quietly at the back of the auditorium and did not participate in any way.

Earlier, I had received from this group a list of changes they would like to see. The list included:

1. A Negro social club should be allowed
2. More social life for Negroes should be provided
3. That better relations between Negroes and faculty be encouraged
4. That the playing of "Dixie" at athletic events should be eliminated
5. That there be a better relationship between Negro students and the president of Harding College

They continued to expand the list over the next few weeks. Some of these requests we worked on and improved the situation. Others did not seem best at the time. In a chapel speech in March, I responded to the requests, and several students left the room when I spoke.

On the next Saturday, I received a telephone call at my home from a staff member who told me that a reporter from the *Arkansas Gazette* was on campus and a number of students were following him around like chicks following their hen. The caller filled me in on the reporter's questions and asked me to come to the campus. As I passed the library, I saw the group gathered together. The reporter approached me with a pad and pencil in his hands, asking: "Dr. Ganus, what do you think about what has happened?"

"Oh, what has happened?" I said, as if I didn't know what it was.

Three of our African-American students had gone over to the Heritage Center where the Freedom Forum was being held, had picked up some literature from the table out in the foyer, and had brought the brochures over to the Lily Pool, where they burned them and threw them into the water.

When the reporter told me what had happened, I said, "That's nothing." And that was true. I added, "The flyers were there for anyone who wanted them. If those students wanted to burn them, then that was their privilege to do."

The reporter was disappointed that I did not make some great pronouncement about it, and the event quickly passed.

Later, I called in the three young men and told them that we did not want to have any problems that would require us to send them home. Thankfully, we had no difficulties with those students, and the racial problems on our campus began to die down. We were fortunate in not having any conflicts on the campus as significant as those in other parts of the United States. Despite the violent incidents happening all over the country, our campus did not lose a single windowpane or have any serious difficulties with our students. I appreciated their attitudes, as most of them really wanted to do what was right.

I did receive a telephone call from Texas, however, that was disturbing. A father who had a freshman son at Harding called me. When I answered, he said, "Dr. Ganus, what's the matter with you bunch of n—— lovers at Harding?"

I replied, "Sir, I don't think you have all the information that you need."

"My son is not a liar," he said.

"I did not say your son was a liar," I responded. "I just said you probably don't have the information that you need." He continued ranting for several minutes, and I couldn't get a word in until he finally said, "I'll tell you what I am going to do: I'm going to send my son a gun."

"Sir, the day you send your son a gun, I send your son home to you."

He hesitated for a moment, and then he said, "Dr. Ganus, I'm a fool. You guys at Harding are doing a great job, and I appreciate it."

I was happy that nothing more came from the call. We were trying to do the best that we could in a very difficult time for our nation.

On April 7, which is my birthday, our Harding board met on the campus to discuss a situation. After an investigation, the board asked me to request a particular professor's resignation because the board felt his religious beliefs were not in agreement with Harding's beliefs. I liked this professor personally, and, in fact, we had socialized together on many occasions. However, I somewhat agreed with the board and was concerned about some of his beliefs.

I talked with the professor about the situation, and he stated that he wanted to be dismissed by the administration rather than resigning. I told him that was his prerogative and that the proper procedure would be followed. But later, he came to me and stated that another Christian university would hire him if he resigned from his position, but they would not hire him if he was dismissed. So, he changed his mind about being dismissed. Naturally, our faculty was concerned and wanted everything to be handled in an appropriate and proper way, with which I agreed. The professor continued to teach at the other school for a number of years.

While this was going on, the Christian college presidents met on the Harding campus. On April 10, I had just finished with this meeting when I received a midnight telephone call informing me that my mother had just died at 11:55 p.m. Immediately, I planned to leave for New Orleans for the funeral.

My mother had a very calm spirit. She didn't like for people to fuss and fight in her presence; she couldn't take it. After her death, we not only found a will, but we also found a list of items that were to be distributed among her children. These were household items like furniture, rugs, automobiles, etc. On the list, she put her desires as to who should receive certain items, mentioning things she wanted each of us to have; she also wrote, "Don't bother me." When we read that, our family all laughed because we knew exactly what she meant. She didn't want anyone fussing or questioning what we should receive, and we didn't. We divided things out according to her instructions, and everyone was happy. I know she was pleased also.

To lose my mother at the same time that all of these things were happening on campus was very sad for me. My family and I weathered the storm, and we continued to appreciate the opportunity to serve the institution we loved. And, fortunately, 1969 happened only once.

The beginning of the 1970s saw the continued growth of Harding College and the strengthening of the academic and athletic programs. On May 1, 1970, Dr. Jimmy Carr was made the Assistant Academic Dean, which was a great move for Harding. He was valuable to us because of his wonderful experience in the Florida educational system and because of his Christian demeanor. He may have been short in stature, but he was long in accomplishment and value to Harding and to the College Church.

On June 19, 1970, Louise and I, along with our children Charles and Debbie, flew to New York City where we joined a group to tour Russia and the Eastern European capitals. Louise and I had been in some of the Eastern European nations in the past, but we had not yet traveled to the Soviet Union. When we arrived in New York City, other couples joined our group who were from the Big Apple, and they added a lot of spice to the trip. We knew it was going to be an interesting experience in cultural difference both with our host nations and our traveling companions.

One of the couples from New York City made our trip especially interesting. They just had to be the first in line for everything, first to their seats on the bus, and provided the best rooms in the hotel. One time I went down to the desk to ask a question, and there they were, standing and fussing to the staff about how inadequate their room was. They wanted to be shown better rooms, but they were told that there were no better rooms. They didn't believe it, so the hotel staff finally showed them that it was true. I guess they finally accepted it.

There were two couples, both from New York, who started out the trip as great friends but then had a falling out – and both couples took it out on the rest of us. They began to curse one another and yell across the bus to one another. Finally, all of the rest of us just said to them, "Shut up. Just be quiet." We got tired of hearing their wrangling when we were on the bus. The worst thing happened later in the trip, when we were in Warsaw at the ghetto where some 300,000 Jews had been killed by Hitler and his henchmen. One couple, which was Gentile, pointed to the Jewish couple they had been fighting with and said, "There's a couple of Jews that Hitler didn't get" loud enough for everyone to hear. It was a horrible, shocking moment to see people be so hateful towards people they had counted as friends just a few days earlier.

There was another Jewish couple on the trip that was very kind, and we became friends. We talked together about Harding and about their lives in New York City. His name was Charles, and he owned a hotel in New York's theater district. "Cliff," he said, "whenever you come to New York City, I want you to stay at my hotel. I will give you a suite any time that you come up."

"Oh, no," I laughed. "I wouldn't want a suite. If I come, a room would be sufficient."

It turned out that before we parted at the end of the tour, he gave me a check for Harding written in the amount of $500. Later, I did go to New York City for a meeting, and I called him. He said, "I'll have a suite for you," and sure enough, when I got there, he had a suite ready and invited me to go to dinner with him at Dinty Moore's, a famous restaurant around the corner from his hotel. He turned out to be a good friend.

When we arrived in Russia, we found most of the people to be friendly and accommodating. We stayed at the Metropole Hotel in Moscow, a sparsely equipped hotel with one bed, one table, a couple of chairs, and a lamp in each room. We felt sure that there were also some surveillance bugs placed in the room so that the hotel could learn what information they could gather from their guests. We passed some of the other hotels that seemed to be more lavishly outfitted, at least from the outside, like the Hotel Rossiya, one of the biggest hotels in the world at the time with roughly three thousand rooms. We didn't go in farther than the front entrance. We learned this hotel was also the headquarters of the government's bugging system, which permitted them to keep up with what happened in each room of the hotel. Knowing the Russians at that time, I was not at all surprised by any of these facts.

The meals in Russia were adequate – nothing fancy, pretty plain – but I could never really get used to the sour cream blintzes that we had in the mornings for breakfast. I liked the borscht soup, made from cabbage and beets. For drinks, we tried what they called *boda*. They sold it out on the streets in large machines, similar to any drink machine, except that each machine had a glass on top that everyone used. You would just put your kopeks in the machine, put the glass under the spigot, catch the boda, drink it, and then put the glass back. I really couldn't do that, though I really wanted to taste the drink. I figured my hands were probably just as clean or cleaner than the public glass, so I put in my kopeks, cupped my hands under the spigot, got some boda, and drank it. It tasted like a lemony drink, but not quite the same as lemonade. There was also one beer-like drink made out of barley or some other grain which vendors would sell it on the street. As we walked along the streets, we would see big containers of that drink, and the people would stop by and purchase a cup. We did not try that one.

The international airport at Moscow was really pitiful in 1970, small and inadequate. In fact, it would have been too small and inadequate for Little Rock, let alone a major city.[21] The airport was divided into separate terminals for international and domestic passengers; however, there weren't many people flying into the country internationally at that time.

We enjoyed visiting the Kremlin, the old fortress center of the capital city and the headquarters for the Soviet Union government. We were allowed to go in to see the old churches in the Kremlin as well as the parliament building, with the big hammer and sickle emblem everywhere. These days were at the very height of the Cold War. As a history major, I had studied Russia and knew a good bit about their life and what occurred in the history of the nation. I had several good discussions with our guides, most of whom were young women named either Natasha or Svetlana. They were all well versed in their role as guide and really believed, or at least indicated that they did, in the

---

[21] I returned to Russia in 1981, and I saw their new airport, built by the Germans. It was much, much better.

communist system; they thought the capitalism system was decadent. They believed that Russia was really going to win out in the long run.

Once, when we were on a bus with the entire group, I looked up and saw big electric lights with Russian words. "Svetlana," I asked, "What does that say?"

"It says, 'Communism will take the world' and we will, too. You just wait and see." She was very positive in how she felt. She tried to tell me that there had been no inflation in Russia. I tried to assure her that I knew there was inflation because I knew prices from previous times I had been to communist countries in Eastern Europe, but now the prices were higher. She insisted that the price of bread was the same as it had always been, and since bread was the same price, there was no inflation. I knew that the government deliberately kept the price of bread low. They subsidized it, because if they let the price of bread go up very much there might have been a revolution. Other prices had increased greatly, but Svetlana held out for the fact that capitalism had inflation and communism did not; therefore, communism was better. She was sure that they were going to take over the entire world.

One evening, Louise and I were in our room at the Metropole when Debbie and Charles came running in, excited. We had purchased Debbie a set of dolls nested inside one another, which usually came in sets of four or five. Debbie came rushing in and took her dolls apart. There were eight dolls – seven within the biggest one, each one smaller than the other until a little tiny doll was the last one. She was excited about finding out that her set had "bonus" dolls.

Those dolls were not the only place we encountered more than we expected. The most important things to Soviets were the government, the military, and the subways, so all of the government and military buildings were of good construction. The subways were beautiful and deep below ground, probably a hundred and fifty feet or so beneath the surface. They would have made good bomb shelters for the entire city of Moscow. White marble statues and shops were everywhere along the subway system. Russia also focused their efforts to build planes and space technology. In 1957 Sputnik initiated the space race, in which Russia led for some time, until the Apollo program put Americans on the moon in 1969.

As far as most other construction was concerned, however, Russian projects were inferior to those in the United States. In fact, we saw buildings literally falling apart; stones and tiles were falling off before the building was ever occupied. At one place, big nets were placed over the sidewalks near the KGB headquarters, catching bricks and items falling from upper stories of the building. The government officials did not seem interested in creature comforts or the citizens' well-being. For instance, they had failed to make any private air conditioners that year because someone at the top had made a mistake and didn't have the needed components, so air conditioning simply was not available. The Russians were aiming for world power but certainly did not have the wherewithal to accomplish it.

When we were going through Gorky Park we saw a wooden fence, and I went over and looked to see what was happening behind the fence. There were women with pickaxes and shovels working on the ground, and some of them were dressed in bikinis. It was quite a sight to see big, husky women in bikinis working with pickaxes. I told Louise I was going to try to take a picture of such an absurd sight, and I put my camera up to the crack in the fence to snap a photo. Just as I did, one of the women happened to look up and saw me take the picture through the crack in the wall, and she was very unhappy and let out a yell in Russian. I don't know what she said, but I'm sure it wasn't very friendly. I was so happy that there was a fence there. She didn't come through the fence, and we got out of there pretty quickly.

We left Moscow and flew to Bucharest, Romania. When we got up in the air, all of the people began to applaud. Many times I have seen people applaud when we *landed* safely in an airplane, but this was one time when people applauded when *leaving*. It's strange, but even though the Russian people were mostly kind and welcoming, and even though we had freedom to move about, everywhere we went there was still a feeling of suppression and control that is very stifling. As we flew out of the USSR, we were all excited to see Pepsi Cola being served on the plane, and since we had not had any soda for several days we were all looking forward to a cold Pepsi. The flight attendant served until she got right in front of me and then ran out of it. I didn't get one, but when got to Bucharest to the hotel, we made up for it.

We were sitting in the hotel dining room, and not only did we have Charles and Debbie with us, but we had two or three other children of couples at our table. We all had a lot of fun drinking a lot of Pepsi – several bottles of it. Finally, the waitress went to our guide and said, "Would you please ask the gentleman over there to pay for the Pepsi? They have drunk a square meter of Pepsi." It turned out that wine was free with the meal, but you had to pay for Pepsi, and we had gone through an awful lot of it!

We enjoyed visiting in Bucharest and also taking a bus ride over to Constanta. From there we flew to Warsaw, Poland. Warsaw was a beautiful city, especially the area downtown, which had recently been rebuilt. Hitler didn't want to leave it whole, so when the Nazis pulled out he had downtown Warsaw dynamited. The restored Polish government had rebuilt the city almost exactly as it had been before the war.

We also flew to Budapest, Hungary. Budapest is a beautiful city on the Danube River; one side of the river is Buda and the other side is Pest. They have a number of parks and a lot of trees, and a large parliament building was on the Pest side of the river. We stayed in a ship that functioned as a hotel on the Danube. (Again, the difficult couple from New York City had to have the biggest room available – and it turned out they were on the riverbank side of the ship so they couldn't see anything. They complained about it but to no avail.)

We next went to Vienna, Austria, which is also on the Danube River, and from there we went to Prague, Czechoslovakia, which looks like a city in a storybook. I enjoyed seeing the old statue of John Hus, a religious leader who was martyred for standing up to the Catholic Church. We went to Berlin as well and saw the two Berlins, just as we had seen them in 1957, when Louise and I were there. The Berlin Wall, of course, now completely separated the west from the east. West Berlin had really been rebuilt from the war by that point, but East Berlin still had a long, long way to go. There was not only a wall that prevented people from crossing from one side to the other, but there was also barbed wire and a cleared area patrolled by dogs, motorcycles, and men with guns.

On the west side of the wall was a platform for tourists and spectators to stand and look over into the east side. Our guides took our group to this spot one evening. I was standing down at the foot of the ladder for the platform, which was probably twenty feet tall, while Louise climbed up to the top of it to look out over East Berlin. I was working with my camera when one of the girls in our group who spoke Russian yelled out, "You Communist pig!" in Russian. Immediately, a searchlight from the East Berlin side shown directly onto the stand, and Louise came scurrying down the steps in a hurry. I said, "Why did you come down?"

She tilted her head towards the woman who had yelled. "I was afraid they were going to start shooting!"

At that time, there was a battle going on. The East Berlin government was very unhappy because West Berlin had erected a big flashing sign (like Times Square in New York) that sent messages for the people on the east side to read. The East Berlin authorities retaliated by blaring music very loudly all night long, so that the West Berliners couldn't sleep. This strategy worked, and West Berlin stopped using the sign – a little tit-for-tat between the East and the West.

Altogether, our family's visit behind the Iron Curtain was a great experience. We were able to see the Soviet Union, the Eastern European countries that the Soviet Union still controlled, and the effect of their communist system of government and economics. Austria, of course, was an independent nation, and Hungary was working to gain its independence. Czechoslovakia was wanting freedom from control of the Soviet Union but did not have it at this time. As we toured each country in a different phase of freedom, the comparisons were powerful and humbling and reminded me of the importance of the work we were doing at Harding to keep the free enterprise system and limited government the law of the land in the United States. We returned home with a renewed appreciation for our own country.

On Saturday, July 17, 1970, I went up to Camp Tahkodah to participate in activities with our students and campers, as I so often did. While I was there, I received a telephone call that Harry Risinger, our pilot at Harding, had died from a heart attack. It was a very sad occasion because Harry was not only an excellent pilot but a fine Christian gentleman and a great friend. We had flown many times together and had many wonderful experiences. On one occasion, when we flew in our single-engine plane to New Orleans, my mother came out to the plane as we were getting ready to take off and said, "Harry, you be careful. You have my son in that plane."

"Mrs. Ganus," he replied, "I'm in that plane also."

She smiled. "I hadn't thought about it like that."

The morning after Harry's death, we were scheduled to leave for two days of flying. It would have been even more serious if the heart attack had come while we were in the air, though Harry had actually taught me the rudiments of how to fly the plane, just in case something had happened to him.

CHAPTER 16

A TRIP TO AFRICA

I n May 1972, Louise and I flew to Africa by way of Brazil. We spent
a few days enjoying Rio de Janeiro, a beautiful city bordered to the
east by the sea and to the west with mountains, where the famous the
Christ the Redeemer statue stands, overlooking the city. From there
we flew to Johannesburg, South Africa.

Louise and I were most impressed with the gold and diamond
mines throughout South Africa. We saw mounds of soil where the
miners dug deep into the earth to extract the precious metal and minerals. We also had a chance to visit one of the diamond-cutting establishments; for the first time in our lives, Louise and I saw rough, uncut
diamonds. To me, these diamonds just looked like stones or little pieces
of glass or crystal, but people who have been trained to spot them could
easily pick them out of a pile of regular stones. We watched as the diamond cutters would start with rough cuts, then polish, and then add
the diamond facets or sides – first four, then eight, then sixteen and
so on. Every time they cut another facet, the diamonds became more
dazzling and more beautiful.

While we were in South Africa, apartheid governed the South
African culture and economy. Black people had their place and white
people had theirs, even on railroad stations. When disembarking from
a train, black people had to go one way, and white people went another.
I didn't know about this rule, so when I went down to the train station, I walked in an area where only black people were leaving. I had
no idea I was in the wrong place; however, no one said anything to me
at that time.

Louise and I were able to visit Soweto, an area of Johannesburg
which had been reserved only for black people. It was here that the
inequality was especially apparent: Soweto was a ramshackle part of

the city, occupied by the poorer class of citizens, as evidenced by the quality of homes in which they lived. Some of the members of the Church of Christ lived there, and we met a preacher who had built a baptistery in his backyard.

Louise and I also visited the capital city of Pretoria, where a missionary named John hosted us. John took us around to several neighboring cities, one of which was Benoni, where the school of preaching was located.[22] There were some English-speaking missionaries in Benoni, and one missionary couple was from England. They invited us to have dinner at their home, and I still remember the good roast beef, mashed potatoes, and gravy we had for dinner. In addition, we met John Reese there, who was also serving as a missionary. Years later, his children attended Harding, and John Reese served on Harding's Board of Trustees.

When we left South Africa we went to Southern Rhodesia (now Zimbabwe), where we were able to visit with more missionaries. We went to Nowhe Mission, which housed a school for children, a grade school, and a high school. Visitors to Nowhe Mission stayed in a hut with a thatched, circular roof. Louise and I spent much of the night looking up at the ceiling, watching large spiders playing around in the thatch. We wondered when one would drop in bed with us, but, fortunately, all the spiders stayed up high.

We visited another mission station where Loy Mitchell was serving, and from there we traveled to Bulawayo, where the Shorts lived. These families had been serving in those areas for a number of years – missionary pioneers in that part of Africa. We also met the Flynn family, missionaries with a young son named Dorian, who was determined to follow in his parents' footsteps as a missionary.[23]

---

[22] A couple of years after this visit, I received a telephone call from John asking, "Do you think it would be possible for me to come to Harding to get a degree and then teach in a preacher-training program?" He was sixty-nine years old when he called me and seventy-one by the time he finally arrived at Harding. John decided to stay on at Searcy and remained there for a number of years after completing his work.

[23] Later, Dorian attended Harding and then after graduating, served as a preacher in Antigua in the Caribbean. While there, he invited me to come down and speak at the first Caribbean Lectureship that I attended in 1983.

From Southern Rhodesia we went on to Northern Rhodesia (now Zambia), where we visited Victoria Falls, one of the great waterfalls in the world. When the water flows rapidly over the falls a mist rises up in the air, resembling smoke, and we could see that mist from quite a distance away as the great Zambezi River thundered down to the plains below.

We also traveled to Namwianga, a school associated with the Church of Christ in Zambia. Located in the little town of Kalomo, the school was established by Brother J.D. "Dow" Merritt in the late 1920s to help people to learn how to farm, to teach, and to live, as well as how to become Christians. Brother Merritt performed a tremendous service in his work there. Brother A.B. Reese and his wife also served in that area, as did other people from the United States, including Alvin Hobby and his wife. Alvin was there in 1972, teaching science, and he had just constructed the largest telescope in the country of Zambia. Alvin ground the lens himself and built the entire thing on his own, so he was well known in Zambia for the remarkable work he was doing.[24]

Ken and Iris Elder also lived in Zambia and were close friends with us, going back to our time together as students at Harding. They lived and worked at Kabanga, a small town about fifty miles from Kalomo, which was the nearest city of any notable size. Ken and Iris had chickens and a garden and raised a lot of their own food.

We were there about six days and traveled with them into the countryside to visit churches. One of the congregations was way out in the bush country – not even in a town. The members made a small hut where they met, and they had logs on the ground to sit on. Ken was scheduled to preach that day, and we arrived early for the service, just as they were getting ready to call in the other members. A member took an iron rod and beat the rod against an old iron rim. This made a sound that traveled all over the countryside. We could look out and see people coming in because they heard the rod and rim and knew church was about to start. While we were waiting, the members gave us something to eat, which turned out to be a boiled egg each, and we were happy with that because we had not been sure how food would be out in the bush country.

---

[24] Alvin's son Ken eventually became a professor at Harding.

During our stay, Ken and his family took Louise and me over to a game park, and we were able to observe different kinds of animals. A giant male ostrich came up to the Land Rover and put his head in the window. I hadn't seen him at all until I looked up to see an ostrich head right by mine. Startled, I rolled up the window up very quickly because I didn't know what might happen with an ostrich so close to my face. We wanted to see elephants close up, but we only caught a few glimpses of some in the distance; then, just as we were leaving the park, we got our chance. The bull elephant was big, at least eleven feet tall, with tusks that weighed about ninety pounds, and he was unhappy about something. He was standing at the edge of the road, shaking a tree with his trunk when Ken saw him. Ken jammed on his brakes and announced, "Elephant!" Immediately, I opened the door and started taking pictures with my camera. "Get back in here!" Ken yelled. He was frightened and shaking.

Iris began to put their two children under the seat as Ken backed up the Land Rover far enough to be out of the angry elephant's eyesight. Louise and I were confused by the panic, but we waited quietly a good while, sitting in the Land Rover out of the elephant's view.

Finally, the elephant crossed the road and disappeared in the woods on the right. Ken took a deep breath: "Well, okay, we can make it." We slowly started up the road but, almost immediately, saw the elephant re-emerge from the woods. He started running parallel to the Land Rover, so Ken hurriedly stepped on the gas and shot us out of that area with the elephant running beside us. Later, when we drove out of trouble, Ken told me he had seen people killed by elephants, and he had been charged by one himself. He told me that elephants could run about forty miles an hour and were strong enough to crush the Land Rover with us in it. I hadn't known enough to be afraid.

One of the most interesting people we met on our trip was a farmer and preacher who had established at least eleven congregations in Zambia. His name was Bicycle Sianjina. We visited his compound and had a good talk with him. He was a fine Christian man who had been a friend of Dr. Benson, and he was passionate about teaching others how to preach the gospel. He was a model farmer with a tractor; in fact, the government used Bicycle as an example to try to teach other farmers how to farm. He had several children, one of whom was called Rayton and another Bornwell. Both of them eventually came to Harding as students. Bicycle was tremendously kind, and when we started to leave he had one of his sons run out to catch a chicken, which he then gave us as a present to take home. I didn't realize how important gifts are in that culture, so I had not brought anything special to give Bicycle in return. Thankfully, I remembered I had a good ballpoint pen with me, so I gave him that as a parting gift from Louise and me. And since we could not bring the chicken on an airplane back to America, of course, we put it in the pen at Ken's house.

Louise and I flew on through Kinshasa, the capital city of Zaire, now the Democratic Republic of the Congo. Throughout its history, the Congo has seen much death and destruction, especially in the last few years. In fact, it's estimated that about 2.5 million people in the Congo have died, most often at the hands of rival tribes or disease and accident. It is heartbreaking to think of the suffering to which the people of that beautiful country have been subjected.

Next, Louise and I went to Nigeria, where we were planning to spend a good bit of time. We landed at the airport in Lagos, which was then the capital city. (The capital moved to Abuja in 1991.) We have never seen anything quite like it; the airport overflowed with more people in one small space that I could have imagined possible. Nigeria has the largest population in Africa, well over fifty million people at that time, and I believed it from the crowds in the Lagos airport.

When Louise and I arrived, we were alone in a crowd. We were supposed to be met by a couple who were both teachers; unfortunately, they were not able to get to the airport. I telephoned the family and told them we had arrived, and they suggested that we just take a taxi to their home. It would take less than forty minutes to get there, they explained, and should cost no more than eight pounds. (A pound was the equivalent of three American dollars at that time.) We told them that we would be happy to do that.

When I walked back to Louise from the telephone, I immediately saw she was overwhelmed because there were a number of people standing around her, with each one having a finger on our suitcases. Putting a finger on the luggage meant that they were going to help us carry them, and therefore would get a tip, which they called a *dash*. Louise didn't know what to think about that many people calling dibs on carrying her luggage, so we grabbed our bags ourselves and went out to a taxi stand in front of the airport. The starter, the man who sent the taxis off with their loads, told me the trip would cost me eight pounds and no more. "Okay. I'll take it," I told him, since this price matched what the teacher had told me on the phone.

Louise and I climbed into the cab, and the driver started off. We drove only a couple of blocks when the driver stopped at a service station, took out a pad of paper and a pencil, and asked, "And what is your name?" I told him. He then asked, "What is madam's name?" I explained that she was my wife. I was wondering why he was asking when he said, "It will cost you eight pounds per person."

I said, "No, it's eight pounds per trip. This is what I was told and agreed upon. That's what it will be."

"Oh, no, you are tying up my taxicab. I can't pick up any other people," he insisted. "Therefore, it will have to be eight pounds per person."

"No, it was eight pounds per trip," I replied.

He drove us a few more blocks, then he stopped again said, "I'll tell you what I will do: Since you are both going to the same place, I will knock off ten percent."

I was fed up. "No, it's eight pounds per trip. Take me back to the airport."

So the driver took us back to the airport, and I told the starter what happened. He really lit into the taxi driver. He was speaking another language, so I don't know what he said, but it seemed that he was reading the riot act to him. Finally, the driver humbly started off again and didn't say anything else as he took us all the way to our friends' home in less than forty minutes, even with all of the delays. When we arrived, I gave him the agreed-upon eight pounds, and he held his hand out for me to give him a dash. I shook my head. I would have tipped if he had not treated me as he did, but I refuse to reward dishonesty.

After our stay in Lagos, we visited in Aba, where we stayed at the hospital complex that Henry and Grace Farrar had helped start. Glenn Boyd, a friend from Searcy, also worked with African Christian Hospitals. Though he spent a great deal of time in Aba, Glenn was not there during our visit. We stayed almost a week at the hospital compound with the Farrar family. Their daughter Samantha had a pet monkey who would follow her around; I got to feeling a bit like that monkey as I followed Henry as he did his daytime work. And at night and on the weekends, Henry would go out to preach. Henry was the only American doctor there at the time, and he had a tremendously heavy load. He would operate on three people in a day's time and then see another hundred people during rounds. The amount of work he had to do before he could go home each night continually amazed me.

The man serving as an administrator of the hospital was Moses Oparah, who previously had been a witch doctor in one of the villages. When he put a hex on people, they usually died; needless, to say, he was not a very kind person. Then one day, Jimmy Massey, a Harding alumnus, was preaching about Jesus in the village. Moses heard him and later explained, "I quaked when I heard him talk about Jesus." Moses went to Jimmy and asked if he could learn more about Jesus. Moses became a Christian and a preacher of the gospel.

Moses faced difficult life circumstances. Once, he was preaching in northern Nigeria, in a region that was heavily Muslim. Some local men broke in the back door of the building where the Christians were gathered, and cried out, "Is Allah known here?"

Moses replied, "No, Jesus Christ is known here."

The men shouted, "Kill them, kill them!" and started beating on the people. One of them picked up his infant daughter and dashed her head against the ground until she died.

Moses was able to escape to go back to his own part of the country, but the Biafran War took place and he was caught in the middle of it. He and his family, surrounded by fighting and unable to travel, completely ran out of food and were forced to eat toads, frogs, snakes, and anything else they could find. Finally, they were reduced to eating grass. Some of his children died of malnutrition. After the war was over he took in some young orphan children he raised as his own. His family lived in a house very close to the one we stayed in at the hospital compound.

He had several children living with him when we were there. In the morning, at daybreak, we would hear singing at their home. They were having their morning devotional before he would go to work. Then we would see the children head out to the river nearby, carrying cans and pots and pans of various kinds on their heads to bring water back to use during the day. Moses would work as an administrator at the hospital, and then in the evenings and on the weekend he would go out and preach. Despite his life's struggles, Moses had done a lot for the Lord in that community.

Louise and I also had an opportunity to visit the school at Ukpom, where they were training young men to be preachers, as well as several other vocational schools in the area. I remember eating a meal at one of these schools with the headmaster and his wife where I was quite excited, as a New Orleans boy, to hear she had fixed us a crayfish stew. It was tasty...except that she left the shells of the crayfish on, as was traditional in that part of the country, and we were supposed to eat them whole. It was hard to chew those hard shells of crayfish, but when you are a guest and people serve you their best, you eat whatever is put before you. Our jaws got a workout that day.

We also experienced some pretty intense weather. Louise and I were in Nigeria during storm season, and rain fell often and hard at night. The houses had sheet iron roofs, which made the sound almost deafening; the Nigerian people called this "thief weather" because the rain was so loud that thieves could come into your house and rob you, and you wouldn't even know that they were there. Thankfully, there were night watchmen who walked around outside of the hospital grounds and the homes of the workers, making sure no thieves took advantage of the downpours.

That first trip to Africa gave me a thirst for going back. I was continually amazed by the tremendous work being done by the African people as well as by the missionaries who were living there. It was quite humbling to see how much they were able to accomplish with what most of us in America would have considered spare resources and insurmountable conditions. As a result of that visit, I resolved to return to Africa and visit even more countries to learn about the tremendous work being done for the Lord there – and I have.

———————

The rest of the summer was quiet, as was most of the 1972-1973 school year, but there were more big trips and more adventures on the horizon.

CHAPTER 17

TRAVELING THE GLOBE

F or a number of years it seemed like the end of each school year
was marked by my taking a major trip. On May 14, 1973, I left
to visit several cities in the southeastern part of Russia, in regions that
have since become the independent nations of Uzbekistan, Tajikistan,
and Kyrgyzstan, as well as a few other important places in central Asia.

My first stop was the city of Samarkand, Uzbekistan, one of the
oldest continually occupied cities in central Asia. Surrounded by dry
countryside and irrigated cotton, the ancient city has a large number of
distinctive and grand mosques. One of the great heroes of Samarkand is
the fifteenth-century king Tamarlane (or Timur the Lame), who ruled
with a brutal hand, killing an estimated hundred thousand people
during his reign. I sat on the stone where he placed his throne and
marveled at his brutality, which not only dominated central Asia but
also captivated the imagination of many European artists and writers
from the Renaissance onward. Tamerlane's tombstone epithet inscrip-
tion succinctly summarized his life: "If I were alive today, the world
would tremble."

In Samarkand I also saw astronomical artifacts from medieval
times. One of the city's rulers developed an instrument by which
he could study the stars and the heavens – a large device built into
the ground and many feet across. After marveling at these incredible
advances of centuries-old technology, I had a bit of a frightening experience with some of the more modern sort: I got stuck in an elevator by
myself between floors. The elevator would not budge, and I got scared.
Thankfully, the only Russian word I could remember – *pomogite* (help) –
was appropriate, so I yelled out for help over and over. Finally, someone
heard me and found a man to climb on top of the elevator from the

outside. He had a key that he used to slowly open one of the half-doors, so that I could crawl up to the floor above to escape.

After Samarkand, I visited Tbilisi, Georgia, which was the original home of Joseph Stalin. I don't remember much about this pretty little city, except that it had the only statue of Stalin still standing. Since Stalin was a native son to Tbilisi, his statue remained, even though other citizens throughout Russia had torn down his other statues. At this time, Stalin's contemporary and predecessor, Vladimir Lenin, was still in vogue, and his statues remained standing. I had to crane my neck to look up to the top of the building where Stalin's statue sat, but trees blocked most of the view. I didn't really mind; I wasn't exactly a big fan of Stalin myself.

Next, I visited Yerevan, the capital of Armenia, a Christian country adjoining Turkey. Turkey and Armenia were bitter foes during World War I, and the Turks killed approximately a million Armenians in what is now known as the Armenian Genocide. It was a tragic chapter in world history, and I saw many memorials to it while in the country. In the city of Yerevan, I saw the remains of an ancient church building dating all the way back to the second century and with an immersive baptistery in the middle of the floor. As a member of a church that still practices immersion, I enjoyed seeing the link to my faith history from that far back.

After Armenia I traveled to Kiev, located on the Dnieper River in what is now Ukraine. The entire city was surrounded by a large forest of trees and verdant green vegetation and was one of the loveliest places I had ever visited. Kiev had many monuments to commemorate the soldiers who fought in World War II, and, like many other places throughout Russia, Kiev featured museums with memorabilia pertaining to the war.

A phenomenon I discovered while traveling in the Soviet Union during that time was that even though Stalin's statues had been taken down everywhere but Tbilisi, communist supporters were more than willing to downplay the terrible atrocities he orchestrated as he ruled Russia from 1924 to 1951. It was as if they all knew Stalin served as a brutal dictator who would ensure that his opponents died (figures in

Ukraine alone range from three to six million deaths), but they still defended his actions as if they were Stalin apologists.[25]

While in Kiev, my tour guide's name was Igor (we called him "Igor the Beaver"), and Igor served as a member of the *Komsomol*, the Communist Party youth section. Igor wanted to be a member of the Communist Party but was not quite old enough, so he served with the youth section and was well trained in the Communist doctrine. When my touring group visited the different monuments, Igor would say, "Now this is a monument to the forty-five Russian officers who were killed in a certain battle, and this monument was dedicated to the people who died in another battle" and so on.

After several of these monuments, I finally said, "Igor, tell me something. Is there a monument to the three million peasants who were killed under Joseph Stalin?"

He became very unhappy with my question. "Of course not. They were murderers. Those people formed bands and killed people."

The truth was actually that they were trying to defend their land and their lives, protecting themselves against the communist government of Russia. Nevertheless, Igor's answer was the party line and he spouted it out like a good communist. I don't think Igor was happy with me because of the questions I asked.

Other chapters of Russian history weren't nearly so bleak. For example, we visited the storybook city of Leningrad (now St. Petersburg), which was built upon many islands, so water surrounded the city and was a feature throughout the city as well. At one time Leningrad was the capital of Russia, home to the Winter Palace of the czars and a house of government for Russia. When the Communists took over under Lenin in October 1917, the Winter Palace remained the government seat for a while until the capital was moved to Moscow, and the palace, with well over one hundred rooms, was converted to a museum with art and artifacts from different time periods in Russian history.

---

[25] When I visited Russia and surrounding areas many years later, the numbers had been escalated to almost thirty million who died under Stalin's rule. Many of those who died were simply peasant farmers who didn't want to give up their land to Joseph Stalin, so he starved them to death or killed them in some other fashion. If ever there were an object lesson that absolute power corrupts absolutely, Joseph Stalin would be it.

I also enjoyed visiting the palace of Petrodvorets, on the Gulf of Finland near Leningrad, constructed by Peter the Great in the early 1700s as the summer palace for the czars. Petrodvorets had also been converted into a museum with notable gardens, a canal, statues, fountains, and flowing water scattered throughout the palace grounds. I particularly enjoyed an area of the Petrodvorets garden where water would suddenly squirt up and douse whoever happened to be in the area. Apparently, Peter the Great enjoyed a good joke, so he had the architect design the garden to spray any person who stepped on a particular stone when walking along the garden path. I liked watching the children (and some of us older children, too) trying to get through the path without getting sprayed.

That trip to the Soviet Union and Armenia allowed me to see a different aspect of life under communism and to discover some glimpses of very early Christian life. As a historian and administrator, I found these lessons to be extremely valuable in helping me to appreciate more and more the work that Harding was doing both to educate and equip the next generation of Christian leaders and also to educate people about the dangers of a communist system of government.

———

Six months after that trip, on November 5, 1973, Louise and I traveled to Mexico City so that I could speak at the Pan-American Lectureship. I remember Mexico City as big and sprawling, with one of the largest populations of any city in the world. When Hernando Cortez captured it in 1521, he and his men set about expanding the city around Lake Tenochtitlan, originally as a measure of defense. The many waterways and canals are still an important part of the city's layout and topography. Louise and I enjoyed a great deal of history on that trip, taking in many of the museums and sights, like the city square, the cathedral, and the Pyramid of the Sun.

———

That was my last trip for almost eighteen months, though, because we were busy preparing for and celebrating the fiftieth birthday of

Harding College in 1974. The college commissioned Kay Gowen to produce a large magazine for the events of the year, and she did a wonderful job. Even today, I enjoy looking back through the magazine to see all the events that occurred and reading about the growth and accomplishments that Harding made in its first fifty years. We brought in a lineup of speakers during that year, including Arkansas Governor Dale Bumpers; Milton Friedman, a noted economist; Wilbur D. Mills, from Kensett, Arkansas, who served as the Speaker of the U.S. House of Representatives; Howard K. Smith, a famous news reporter; Mark Rafferty, an educator with national acclaim; Dr. Walter Judd, a news commentator, contributor, and editor of *Reader's Digest*; and Roger Staubach, quarterback for the Dallas Cowboys.

It was a wonderful year of celebration for Harding and for those who loved and served the institution. To commemorate the year, we produced a medallion with the images of the three presidents on one side and the Administration Building on the other. Each member of the faculty received a medallion and a copy of the commemorative magazine.

In 1974, Harding also traded in our old Cessna 411 plane for a Piper Navajo, which was a good move on the part of Harding's board because the new plane was faster, larger, and nicer. We were flying a lot as the college continued to expand its reach, and the new plane helped quite a bit.

We also started the Christian Communication Program in 1974, with thirty-three students whose ages spanned from twenty-one to forty-three years of age. Ed Sanders served as the first director of this program that would be very effective for decades to come as it trained many men to fill the pulpits of the church of the Lord, both in this country and abroad.

We had developed the Mission Prepare program in 1968 to help young people become interested in being long-term missionaries and to prepare them for that responsibility. Missionaries who had served well in the field came each year to teach and mentor the young people. Mission Prepare was effective, and many of our students became foreign missionaries because of it. Dr. Joe Hacker, the chairman of the department, oversaw Mission Prepare and headed up the required fundraising to keep it going. With the addition of the Christian Communication

Program and Mission Prepare, Harding increased its ability to serve the church and to spread the word of the Lord in more effective ways.

When I think about marking a half-century of Christian education, I am always impressed that we found a way to honor our past without resting on our laurels; Harding had built itself up greatly from humble beginnings, but we were also fixing our eyes on the future and how we could continue to grow in our mission.

After a full year of celebrating Harding's latest milestone, Louise and I traveled to Spain, Portugal, and Morocco from May 24 to June 8, 1975. We started in Madrid and had a wonderful visit with Juan Monroy, who preached there. He was scheduled to perform a wedding for some members of his congregation, and he invited us to attend so we could witness some of their traditions. At the ceremony, which was in a banquet room in a restaurant, Juan asked the boy and girl to sit down in chairs in front of him, and then he preached a gospel sermon for about forty-five minutes in Spanish. When Juan finished, he asked the couple to stand, and then he helped them repeat their vows, which only took about five minutes, and then Juan proclaimed the couple to be man and wife. When I asked Juan afterwards about the length of the ceremony he replied, "Yes, the ceremony took a long time, but I knew that I would never have another chance to preach to this family again after the ceremony."

Louise and I took a bus from Madrid to Granada, an old city with a famous castle called the Alhambra. One of the rooms, where the rulers of Spain would meet with state dignitaries, had a dining area set up for a state dinner, so we had a chance to see the table heavy with beautiful china with silver and gold dishes. It was quite a sight.

Louise and I then traveled to the southern coast of Spain, near the famous peninsula of Gibraltar, where the sun baked us and the hot sand burned our feet, even though the Mediterranean Sea was still too cold for swimming. We decided to take a ship over to Morocco, past the Rock of Gibraltar, which I found interesting because of its historical connections – Spain and Britain struggled over control of the Rock of Gibraltar for centuries because it was the gateway to the Mediterranean Sea.

In Morocco we visited Casablanca and the capital city of Rabat before going on to Fes, one of the other important cities. We saw a few towns and oases, but most of the country was sand, desert, camels, and goats; it was like traveling hundreds of years back in time. We visited a carpet factory to see the workers create the beautiful rugs for which Morocco is so famous. Most of the artisans were young ladies who started work at an early age to learn the secrets behind all of the intricate designs that make each rug unique. Of course, vendors tried to sell us carpets everywhere we went, but I preferred watching the artistry of how they were made to walking on them.

From Morocco we traveled to Portugal. I have long been amazed that this small country, only 320 miles long and 125 miles wide, with a small population, became such a dominant force in the history of exploration. During the sixteenth through eighteenth centuries, adventurers like Vasco de Gama, Pedro Cabral, and others explored around Africa, islands in the east Atlantic, and South America, claiming much larger countries and territories for Portugal.

Unfortunately, in the twentieth century, Portugal's main exploration had more to do with political ideas. In Lisbon, Louise and I had an unusual experience that involved a parade celebrating communism. The marchers were ardent and loud, chanting pro-communist and anti-American sayings. I had seen similar parades in other communist-controlled cities, and this situation was equally frightening, but I also wanted to get pictures of it. I took photos from a hill looking down on the parade, and then I ran over to the parade's ending point to get pictures from the side street. I carefully avoided getting involved with any of the people marching, though. I had a feeling an ardently anti-communist American would not be particularly well received.

I kept up my tradition of marking the end of the school year with a major trip, so the following May, in 1976, my son Charles and I left for a trip to Norway, Sweden, and Denmark. We first visited Bergen, a small fishing town on the west coast of Norway, and the home of Edvard Grieg, who wrote the *Peer Gynt Suite*, a piece of music my family enjoyed. Charles and I visited his home, a lovely place in the woods, with a little building separated from the main house, where Grieg would go to be alone and to compose his music. We could almost hear his music as we walked through the woods at his home.

In the town we visited one of the cafes and had a real *smörgåsbord*. I had eaten what Americans called a smorgasbord many times, but this was a real Norwegian one with various kinds of fish and other meats as well as several different vegetables. One of the most unusual items on the smörgåsbord was a baked eel. They served the eel upright for the patrons to carve off pieces to put on their plates. Naturally, I tried the baked eel since I enjoy being adventurous with food, but I didn't really like it. It tasted a little bit like fish, but I guess the sight of an eel on display made eating the meat a little difficult for me.

Charles and I visited Oslo, the capital city and a beautiful seaport. There, we were privileged to see the *Kon-tiki*, a large raft preserved in Oslo, which Thor Heyerdahl built in 1974 to prove he could cross the Pacific Ocean in a ship built of reeds. Next, we boarded a ship and traveled for a day in the fjords. I enjoyed touring the beautiful fjords, great ravines, waterways, and mountains of Norway.

Our next stop was Stockholm, Sweden, also a seaport. We saw one of His Majesty's royal ships that had a remarkable story attached to it. It sank the day it launched in the sixteenth century because a large crowd of civilians had been invited to board; when something of interest happened on one side of the ship, every rushed over to see, but the ship didn't have enough ballast in it yet to keep it from turning over. The ship was rediscovered and restored in the 1860s, many years after the incident.

We also visited some of the great cathedrals in Stockholm, as well as the Stockholm Concert Hall, which hosts the Nobel Prize ceremonies. From there we toured the University at Uppsala, one of the oldest universities in Sweden, established in 1477. Sweden's governmental structure was much more socialistic than America's and provided a lot of help for its citizens; however, the taxes were also extremely high in order for the government to provide these services.

Interestingly, while in Sweden, Charles and I happened to stay at the same hotel as Kiss, the popular rock band from America. Charles went to their concert, and when he came back to the hotel, he said, "Dad, they really had the audience eating out of their hand. In fact, they could have started a revolution if they had wanted to." The band wore bizarre makeup and clothing to perform, but when we saw them in the hotel, they looked like ordinary men. We had a chance to talk with them at the hotel without all their makeup and equipment, and they seemed just like quiet gentlemen, very different from their stage personas.

We took a quick side trip across the North Sea from Sweden to Copenhagen, Denmark, and visited the home of Hans Christian Andersen. We saw his homestead and the famous Little Mermaid statue, commemorating one of his most beloved stories. The trip was short, but we enjoyed seeing the home of a famous author.

———

My May trip the following year was especially interesting, as Louise and I spent eight days in Cuba. I had always been curious to visit the country, since my parents had gone years before, and my Dad had helped organize a campaign to send some students there. That was prior to Fidel Castro's revolution in 1959, though, and I was sure things had certainly changed quite a bit.

Louise and I decided that a visit to the island was in order. There were members of the Carrollton Avenue Church in New Orleans who had relatives in Cuba, and they offered to share with us their names and addresses and let us visit with them. We were excited to meet with members of the Churches of Christ there, but before we left, our friends got cold feet and said it would be too dangerous for their relatives to have Americans visit them.

At that time, there were no direct flights from the United States to Cuba because of the political situation between the two countries. Instead, Americans who wanted to visit Cuba had to fly through Montreal, Canada, or through Mexico City, and then to Cuba. We decided to fly to Montreal where S. F. and Maxine Timmerman, Harding alumni and our schoolmates, lived and served as missionaries.

From Montreal, we flew directly to Havana's Martine Airport; then we went to our motel, just a few miles out of Havana, where water was heated by the sun in big, plastic barrels on the roof.

Louise and I enjoyed walking along the coast where we could see the "pill boxes," gun emplacements that had been built when Cuba was afraid of an invasion from the United States. The food at the hotel was good, and there was plenty of it, but it was clear it was only for visitors who would pay with foreign dollars. The automobiles in Cuba were all from the 1950s, and the Cuban citizens had to keep them running because they didn't have any new vehicles to replace them. The stores had very few articles for sale; a general air of poverty existed everywhere outside of the main tourist stops. Many of the buildings were in pretty bad shape, but the Cubans didn't have the money to repair them. At this time, the communist powers in the USSR were still very strong, and they were helping Cuba with more than two billion dollars a year. But the corruption in the government ensured that very little was actually passed on to the people who needed it. The Soviets were also giving Cuba armament and war material.

One day, when I was walking in downtown Havana, I came to one of the government buildings. When I tried to cross the street to take a closer look, a man with an automatic weapon came up to me and herded me back to the other side of the street. He would not let me cross, so I figured that somebody important must be in that building – maybe even Castro himself, given the urgency with which the man waved his gun.

The people of Cuba were friendly enough to us, but the government was officially very much opposed to the United States. One evening I was in the lobby of the motel, watching a documentary on television about Salvador Allende of Santiago, Chile. He had been the President of Chile, but he was overthrown and killed. This documentary blamed the United States government for his death and also claimed companies like IBM, General Motors, and others joined to oppose Allende as well. I felt very funny sitting in that audience, the only American among a group of Cubans, watching something so strongly against the United States. No one said anything to me, but it was certainly a little uncomfortable.

Louise and I took a bus ride out through the Cuban countryside and saw the sugar cane fields, tobacco fields, and villages with modern school buildings. For all the corruption, the government was spending a lot of money trying to educate the young citizens; unfortunately, much of that education centered around communist indoctrination.

When we were ready to come home, we had to go back to Montreal. We almost flew over Arkansas to go back to Montreal and then had to fly south to Arkansas.

Finally, in 1978 I had a chance to make my first trip to China, a place I had wanted to visit for many years. When Dwight Eisenhower was president, he created an organization called "People to People," a civilian ambassador group that sent representatives to many nations to improve relations with their citizens. I was invited to go with a group of university and college presidents in July 1978 to visit Pakistan, China, and France. I was excited about the trip, but I was distracted for the first few days. Cliff and his wife, Debbie, were expecting our granddaughter Sherrill, and she was due to arrive before I left but decided to stay put. I called when I got to New York City; still no Sherrill. I called when I got to Karachi, Pakistan; still no Sherrill. Finally, I got to Beijing and called from there, and Sherrill was waiting. I was absolutely thrilled she had finally arrived, and mother and baby were doing well!

This trip to China was especially outstanding. I only knew one man in the entire group, who happened to be president of Armstrong State University in Savannah, Georgia. He was a Baptist who had visited the Harding Graduate School as part of an accreditation committee. I had met him there and liked him, so I asked if I could room with him. I had been assigned to room with a man from New York whom I didn't know, but the organization was kind enough to swap roommates for us.

Our group met up in New York City, then flew first to Karachi. There we met with education leaders, government officials, and businessmen, which we did later in China and France, as well. We also visited Islamabad. I think one of the most interesting things that I saw while in Pakistan was a building that had been erected by the architect of the Taj Mahal with the same type of architecture. It was much smaller, but beautifully impressive, and I had no idea that there were any "sister" buildings to the Taj Mahal!

After finishing our work in Pakistan, we went on to Beijing. China had not been open very long to the United States – only about six years at that point. It was in 1972 that President Richard Nixon had gone to China and helped open it for western travelers, so Americans were an oddity almost everywhere in China at that time. In Beijing, we stayed at the Friendship Hotel, which would accommodate about five thousand people. Actually, it was built as a dormitory for Russian technicians during the days when Russia and China were good friends after World War II. But in 1961 they had almost had a war over a common boundary line, and China decided to send all the Russian technicians home. The building was then converted into a hotel.

One evening, when I looked up in the sky and saw a big full moon, I thought that it would not be long until that same moon would be coming over Searcy. My roommate and I decided to celebrate my new granddaughter and our families in general. He had brought Gatorade, and I had brought Dr Peppers. We had purchased a watermelon – a small, round one – that day, so we went out on our balcony, burst open the melon, drank Dr Pepper and Gatorade, and celebrated our blessings.

Everywhere we went in Beijing and in other cities there were red slogans on the light poles – Mao's sayings and images of Mao's little red book. In 1978 he was still very much the man of the hour. His slogans were usually in red, so they were easy to spot. I didn't see any commercial advertising of products or goods of any kind, just images of Mao's book and his expressions. Despite the prevalence of communist propaganda, the people were very interested in the Americans. Our group traveled mostly by train, and whenever we arrived at a station there would be several hundred people standing in a crowd outside the station, just waiting for the Americans to come out. They would quietly wait as the police stood by, watching and waiting. They showed little emotion at first – they just looked at us. But when we said, "*ni hao ma*," which is one way of saying "Hello, how are you?" in Mandarin, they would answer back and make friendly gestures.

Whenever we went into a store, people would follow us – great crowds of people. I remember trying to buy a handkerchief in a store, and people crowded all around me just to see what I was doing. They watched me take out my pocketbook and take out the money and pay the clerk. Their eyes were glued on us Americans. They hadn't really seen many foreigners and were very curious. One young man said that he had not seen a person from outside of China until he was nineteen years old, and he had never seen an American until he was twenty-five years old.

We went as far north as Manchuria, or Manchukuo, as it was called by the Japanese. There we saw the Japanese Imperial Palace. In 1931, Japan invaded this area of China, and the Imperial Palace was used as their headquarters in the region. Later, in the city of Harbin, several young boys started following me as I was walked down the street. They would follow about twenty-five feet behind me, and when I stopped, they stopped. When I went, they went. I kept trying to get them to come up to me and I would say, *"ni hao ma"* in Chinese, but they wouldn't come. Finally, one young boy plucked up the courage to get close to me, and I shook hands with him. Then he ran back and showed his hand to the other boys who were with him. I don't know how long he waited to wash that hand. Americans were an oddity to the Chinese people at the time.

One of the most interesting eating experiences we had was at a restaurant in the city of Kirin, where three chefs prepared the meal for us. It was a twenty-one-course extravaganza, beginning with ice cream and ending with watermelon, a treat for the eyes as well as the tongue. One dish looked like a whole chicken on a plate, but it was made with different types of vegetables. It was very interesting and very tasty. Then they served us a whole fish with a head on it, which is the way they ate fish. (Actually, they would eat the shrimp heads as well, but I never got used to that. They would suck on them, but I assured them that I liked the tails much better.) When we finished the meal, the three chefs came out and we applauded them. They took a bow and seemed to be well pleased with what they had done. We certainly were.

After Kirin we went to Changsha, which, surprisingly, looked like a major city in America. The countryside had more of the flavor of the nation itself, and we enjoyed getting out into the rural areas. Still, the cities did offer a few interesting cultural insights. For example, every-where we looked there were bicycles. In Beijing, a city of eleven million people at the time, there were at least two or three million bicycles, and it seemed like they were out on the street all at once. There were far more bicycles than there were automobiles.

One of the most interesting places that we visited was the Great Wall of China, which was begun in the third century B.C. and designed to keep invaders out. It is twenty-one feet tall and several thousand kilometers long, and I have heard it is the only manmade structure in the world that can be seen from the satellites in space. The scope was staggering.

From China we flew to France, stopping in Paris, where we were to spend four days. Even though all the expenses were covered in the cost of the trip, I decided I wanted to bypass Paris and get home to see my new little granddaughter. I got permission to stay on the plane and just continued straight back to New York and home again.

CHAPTER 18

THE DECADE OF DEVELOPMENT

T he last years of the 1970s and the beginning of the 1980s saw a dramatic rise in student numbers as well as in new facilities for Harding's campus. Beginning in 1965, Harding ushered in the Decade of Development, focusing on growing the campus and increasing student and faculty numbers. The original decade for which we had planned extended as the numbers kept climbing. In 1976 the athletic center was constructed, designed for student activity and basketball competitions. In 1978 we added more apartments for married students. In 1980 we completed the construction of the Benson Auditorium, which was the largest auditorium in the state of Arkansas. That same year, we also added the Harding Academy building on Park Avenue, just down the road from the main Harding campus. In 1982 Harding erected the J.C. Mabee Business Building, and in 1985 Harding purchased the Stafford Apartments on Park Avenue. That's six buildings in nine years.

The enrollment for the Searcy campus in 1964-1965 was 1,274 students from forty-one states and four foreign countries. There were ninety-three teachers. The total annual cost was $1,374. In 1970 there were 1,916 students from forty-six states and six foreign countries; our faculty had grown to 121 professors. The cost for attendance was the same. Five years later, in 1975, the attendance had skyrocketed to 2,520 students from forty-eight states and seventeen countries. The cost for attendance that year had climbed a bit to $1,827. By 1980 the student body had risen to 3,002 students. I remember very well stating that Harding had more than three thousand students – it may have been by the skin of our teeth, but we did top that number!

As the student body and campus grew, so did the faculty and the academic programs, both in the graduate and undergraduate level.

When Dr. Jimmy Carr joined Harding in 1970 from the educational system of Florida, he encouraged us to begin the process of building a program to train nurses. We agreed to do this, and I am happy that we did so.[26] To start the nursing program, the Board needed to find a director who had the right qualifications and who was a member of our church fellowship. This was not an easy task. I flew to Detroit, Michigan, to talk with a lady named Mickey Warren who was married to a preacher. Fortunately, we were able to get her to come to Harding, and, in addition, we got a good Bible teacher with her husband, Will Ed Warren. The only catch was that Mickey agreed to come only for a few years to get us started while we looked for someone else to take over.

We continued our search for Mickey's permanent replacement, and I flew to Atlanta, Georgia, to talk with Cathy Smith, who was at Mercer University. Cathy agreed to come to Harding when Mickey left, and we were on our way. The nursing program developed wonderfully and provided good training for thousands of young people.

On February 18, 1978, we lost another of our pilots. Don Smith had flown with us since the death of Harry Risinger, but he decided to work on his own business in Newport in a crop-dusting enterprise. His replacement was an alumnus named Jerry Moore, whom Don was training personally, and they were practicing taking off and landing in challenging conditions. There were two passengers in the plane who were sitting in the back.

It was a cold and snowy Saturday morning, so I was at home when someone called to tell us about the crash. There was concern that I had been onboard, too, since it was the school plane. I rushed to the hospital and was waiting at the door when Don's wife, Ann, arrived. She looked at my face and saw the answer but said, "No, no, don't tell me." I had to break the news that Don died, and Jerry, too. The passengers were injured but survived. I'll never forget what a deeply sad day that was.

---

[26] I got a daughter-in-law because of that program

———

But life went on the Harding campus, and there were much happier times that spring. For example, on April 1, 1978, Harding assembled the largest pizza that probably has ever been assembled. It was laid on the floor of our athletic center and was almost eighty feet across. We sold the pizza by the square foot, and I bought several of them to take home and freeze. It was quite a picture to look down from above and to see a pizza that size.

On September 1, 1978, the Harding Board of Trustees approved Harding Academy of Memphis to become a separate entity and have its own board of trustees and administration rather than falling under the jurisdiction of Harding College.

———

I had the opportunity to do more traveling, as well. Towards the end of June in 1979, Dr. Ken Davis, a music professor at Harding, took the A Cappella Chorus to Poland, Russia, and Germany. Dr. Davis invited Louise and me to go with them, and we decided that it would be an interesting trip. There was a choral festival to be held in Sopot, Gdańsk and Gdynia, the tri-cities, as they were called, on the Baltic Sea. This location held a very important place in history because this was the area where World War II began on September 1, 1939, when the Germans shelled the shipyards at Gdańsk.

The choral competition included choruses from Russia, France, the United States, and other countries, and the singing was outstanding across the board. The festival happened to fall on July 4, and the Polish people, who were under the influence of communism at that time, liked the United States very much but were not very friendly to the Russians. Therefore, our Polish hosts played up that it was America's birthday. They provided cake and a big sign that said, "Happy Birthday, United States!" The Russians had to sing on the stage with that sign showing. We might have gloated a little bit.

Louise and I stayed in the dormitory on the university campus with the rest of our group. Honestly, it was not very fancy, but it was adequate. The only real problem was that everyone from all of the different nations who were performing there had to use the same showers and the same bathroom – both men and women. When we arrived, we were the only ones in our wing of the dorm, so we thought we could work out a plan: when men were in the bathroom, there would be a triangle placed on the door, which would signal that only men should go in. When women were in the bathroom, we would place a placard with a circle, and only women were to go in. If no one was in, then the placards would be taken down. I decided I wasn't going to take any chance, so I didn't even go to the restroom until about midnight, thinking that it would be a safe time. So, I put the triangle up, went in the bathroom, and sat down in my little stall. While I was sitting there, someone knocked on the door of the stall, and I looked down to see women's shoes on the feet in front of me. I said, "Yes," in a very deep voice, so that she would know that I was there. Well, the door on the stall next to me opened, and she went in and sat down right next to me. I could see her feet, and I had a funny feeling. In Europe this happened all the time, but we weren't quite used to that in the United States.

The preacher of the church at Sopot was Walenty Dawidow, and we decided to go to the church, which met at his apartment. We took the train out to an area near where he lived in a small three-room apartment, about the size of my living room in Searcy. There were about forty-two members of the church who were meeting there, and there were forty-five of us from the chorus. We walked to the apartment in twos, trying not to bring attention to ourselves because it was against the law to have unapproved worship services in Sopot. At Walenty's apartment we had to stand up for the worship service because there were about eighty people stacked in those three little rooms. We couldn't sit down, so we sang and prayed and studied and took the Lord's supper all while standing up. They worshipped in their Polish language, and we worshipped in our own language. It was a good experience, and we enjoyed it. After worship, I glanced at the dresser in the room where we were standing and was surprised to see a picture of Louise and me. Then I remembered that our son Charles had done mission work in Vienna, Austria, with Brother Otis Gatewood, and Charles's roommate in Vienna was Mike Dawidow, who was the son of Walenty. The family must have been praying for our work with Harding as we trained preachers of the gospel.

I had a good visit with Brother Dawidow and tried to get as much information from him as I could about the church and the problems they faced. He explained that the government was taking away the ration coupons that they had to use to buy food in an effort to dissuade the believers from worshipping God; the government would also take away their songbooks and Bibles. Brother Dawidow said that the church members would go down to the police station to sing and pray until the police would get so tired of them; they would say, "Take your songbooks and take your Bibles and get out of here."

I knew that brother Dawidow had been in jail on many occasions for preaching, so I asked him how many times total. He shrugged, "Oh, ten or eleven times." One time he was imprisoned for six months, and his wife didn't even know where he was. "But, Brother Ganus," he said, "I had a wonderful time. Those communists put doctors and lawyers and businessmen in jail, and I taught them about Jesus. I had a great time." That's the kind of man he was. He had already baptized approximately 165 people and had pictures of them there in the white robes that they used for baptizing in Sopot, right in the Baltic Sea.

While we were on that trip, we also traveled over to Kaliningrad in Russia. When we got to the border of Russia late at night, all the traffic had been stopped. The people were not permitted to cross over the border, so Mike Dawidow went out to see the guards and talked with them. Finally, he came back and took a cassette tape from one of the students; he also grabbed a two-liter bottle of Coke from me and some shaving lotion. "Bribes," he said.

We were fortunate; the bribes worked. Otherwise, we would have had to spend the night on the bus there at the Russian border.

We finally arrived in Kaliningrad, where we found a statue of Lenin. The chorus all joined together at the feet of the Lenin statue and sang American songs, including our national anthem. It was a small act of defiance, but it felt important for us to do, nonetheless. We stayed in another dormitory, which was also subpar by American standards. Thankfully, this one had separate facilities for men and women, but they were so separate that Louise and I had to stay in different wings. We spent the night in Kaliningrad, sang, looked around the town, and then went over to Warsaw.

During this trip, I also made a quick trip over to Florence, Italy. Don Shackelford had been trying to get me to start an academic program for Harding in Florence, so I told him that I would go from Poland to Italy to look around and see what I thought about it. So when they went on to Warsaw, I flew to Florence and quickly decided that Harding should start a program there, as Don had suggested.

I flew back to Warsaw and met our group at the new lodging place, where Louise said she was glad to see me. They had put the group in a dormitory with other men, and our girls, including Louise, had to have the men from our group escort the girls to the restrooms because of the harassment the women were receiving.

From there we went on to Berlin, Germany, and back to the United States in time to start preparing campus for the 1979-1980 academic year.

By 1979, we felt we had enough professional programs and training to move to a university status, so our Board of Trustees and administration made the preparations necessary for Harding College to become Harding University. As part of the festivities to celebrate this new university moniker, we buried a time capsule – a black cylinder about three feet long and eighteen inches in diameter. In the capsule we placed a number of documents and other information from that year and decreed that it would be opened at the school's hundredth anniversary in 2024. I told the audience that I expected to witness this opening. I would be 102 years old, but they should be listening for me as I would be circling overhead. We buried the time capsule six feet deep about thirty-five feet south of the Olen Hendrix building. I was afraid that some boys' club might decide to be a little mischievous and try to dig up the capsule as a prank, so I covered it with three tons of concrete.

Burying a time capsule on University Day in 1979, with Lott Tucker

Softball with the faculty at Camp Tahkodah

187

In the fall of 1979, the faculty met at Camp Tahkodah, as it usually did before each school year. This time allowed the faculty a few days off and away from the campus, where they could enjoy the company of one another and in a sense, let their hair down. At the same time, we could have our necessary meetings.[27] The year 1979 seemed to be occupied by a government decree entitled Title IX, which dealt with requirements for support of women's athletics at the university level. There were several faculty meetings concerning requirements, the necessity for Harding to implement them, and how we could go about developing more programs so we could be in compliance. The school desired a temporary exception from Title IX while we worked to grow our women's athletics, but it took several months for the government to reply to our application and we were scrambling in the meantime. Finally, we received word that we had been granted a partial exemption, so we were able to take a more measured approach to how we grew our women's athletic programs until we were in full compliance with the new mandates.

As a fan of athletics myself, this was an interesting time with athletics dominating the news. First, there was the implementation of Title IX in colleges and universities across the country, then there was 1980 boycott of the Moscow Olympics. In protest of the Soviet invasion of Afghanistan, the United States did not participate.

I was interested in seeing all of the new facilities that had been erected for the event, however, so in 1981 I decided to go to Russia and then on to Siberia and Mongolia. I had always been intrigued by Mongolia and thought it would be a good time to go. For the Olympics, Moscow had built a brand-new airport (rather, the Germans built it for them). On previous trips, I remember the airport being really terrible, but the new one was very nice. The Russians had also commissioned French builders to construct a new hotel called The Odessa, and that

---

[27] We did this for several years until the faculty grew too large to house everyone, and it became more difficult to have that many people on the road. Therefore, we moved the session back to campus. Many of us, however, missed the good times that we had together at Camp Tahkodah.

was where I stayed in Moscow. It did not disappoint. For the meals, the hotel served buffet style, which I enjoyed very much. The food was good, and the hotel was beautiful – so much better than the Russian hotels that I had stayed in previously.

While staying at The Odessa, I attended a meeting to which tourists were invited. There were two speakers: a lady who was teaching at the Academy and a man who was a newspaper reporter. The Academy in Russia is a post-graduate school, and this teacher spoke English very, very well. In fact, I would not have known that she was Russian just from listening to her speak. Twice during the presentation, she took the Lord's name in vain, and I thought that was a little unusual for one who was a communist and an atheist; after all, weren't they trying to eliminate any references to God at all? We were told that we would be given a chance to ask questions after the presentation, so when she finished speaking, I raised my hand.

I made the comment that she had used the Lord's name (I didn't say, "in vain") on a couple of occasions, and I thought that was unusual in view of her politics. "Oh, but many of the communists are believers," she said as she opened her purse and took out a crucifix. "See? I carry a crucifix, and when my poor husband and my son died, I lit candles for them." It seemed to me she was somewhat playing both ends of the fence, but I wasn't going to press the point.

The matter where I did push back was with regards to the beginning of World War II. This teacher had made the statement that the war began on June 22, 1942, and I knew that was not correct because the universally acknowledged start date is September 1, 1939, when Germany invaded Poland and set everything else into motion. About two weeks before the German invasion, in August of 1939, Hitler and Stalin had met and agreed to divide Poland: forty-nine percent to the Germans and fifty-one percent to the Russians. What amazed me was that the teacher had lost a husband and a son in the conflict, but she kept insisting that they were not in a war, even though the Russians had been part of the invasion and had taken their half of it. She did not consider the invasion of Poland as a part of the war; as far as the Soviets were concerned, the war didn't begin until June of 1942. No matter what facts I pointed to, I could not get either the teacher from the Academy or the newspaper reporter to agree publicly that the war actually started on September 1, 1939 – when the rest of the world says it began.

When we were finished with the meeting in the auditorium, I went out into the lobby and met the newspaper reporter. He was talking with a young lady, and when he finished, he turned to me, took hold of my arm, and said quietly, "It was a dark day when Adolph Hitler forced Joseph Stalin to make that agreement to divide Poland." Personally, I don't think Hitler had much trouble forcing Stalin.

When I left Moscow, I flew to Siberia to the little town of Irkutsk, located on Lake Baikal, the deepest freshwater lake in the world. It's about five thousand feet deep, and the water was so clear that I could see down roughly 110 feet. I would walk along by the wharf to see the ships, but then I would also walk along the banks of the lake, where there were no ships, and could look straight down to see various objects on the bottom.

Siberia, of course, got very cold in the wintertime. In fact, the citizens I met said the temperature could go down as low as sixty-three degrees below zero – cold enough that if someone threw a glass of water up in the air, the water would crystallize before hitting the ground. I also learned that in the winter the lake would be covered by a layer of ice a meter thick. In fact, a small railroad track would be laid across the ice for people to ride a train over the lake.

Most of the homes in Siberia were wooden homes. There was a lot of timber in Siberia, and I guess the wooden homes were cheaper and perhaps stayed warm more easily. All of those wooden homes gave everything an antiquated appearance, as if we were still in the nineteenth century. The conditions were harsh and modern conveniences scarce; the Russian government sent many exiles to this area as punishment. Many of the people in Irkutsk had Polish ancestry because 21,000 Poles were exiled to this area by one of the Russian czars.

I was surprised one morning at my hotel as I was coming down to breakfast. I heard someone say, "Dr. Ganus?" and I turned around to see Bill Searcy. Bill, a Harding graduate, had been to Russia many times. He had been forbidden to come back because he had been smuggling Bibles into Russia and was teaching Jesus to the people. This trip, he came into Siberia with a German group. I didn't know that he was making this trip, and I admired his tenacity. We had a chance to visit that morning in the hotel, and that afternoon I was out at one of the parks just seeing some of the sights when I met Bill again as he and his group happened to be in the park at the same time.

After my trip to Siberia, I flew on a Russian plane to the city of Ulaanbaatar, the capital city of Outer Mongolia. Outer Mongolia had a close relationship with Russia at that time; the communists controlled the country.[28]

I found a group of ten people, most of them from Germany, who were making the same trip, and I flew with them. One of them, a young man about sixteen years old, was an obvious show-off and always misbehaving, but he got a lesson he would never forget when we were waiting for our plane at the Irkutsk airport, where tourists were forbidden to take pictures.[29] This young man decided that, despite the ban, he wanted to get a picture of the airplanes on the tarmac, so he quietly walked up to the window, took out his camera, and pointed it toward the planes. There was nothing secret about it, but he thought no one saw him. What he didn't know was that in the little kiosk nearby, an airport employee saw him take the picture. She told the authorities who came and got both him and the director of our tour group and took them away for a long time. When they returned, the young man was very quiet and subdued, and we had no more trouble from him. The airport security must have really read the riot act to him – probably telling him that they could very well put him in prison for doing what he did. Instead they just took his camera, ripped out the film, and reprimanded him. We were all concerned as we were waiting for their return, but we were also kind of happy that it had happened in order to subdue that young man a little.

Ulaanbaatar was a city of about 400,000 people, half of whom lived in yurts, which were round tents made from camel's hair with a hole in the top for smoke to escape. The city had large suburbs filled with yurts. There were many camels, some domesticated and some roaming wild from the desert, and many mares, horses, sheep, and goats. Many

---

[28] Inner Mongolia, next to Outer Mongolia, was a separate country with ties to China.

[29] The same was true of bridges and subways, and anywhere else the government felt there might be a possibility of some attack.

of the people made their living raising animals. I think there were about four times as many animals as there were people.

Our group visited one of the temples, where the priests used prayer wheels. They would insert a note or prayer request of some kind, such as a prayer for rain, in a cylinder and then twirl the wheel. Every rotation represented a prayer going up to heaven; if a person twirled the note one hundred times on the prayer wheel, it was as if he or she offered one hundred prayers from the one note. We also visited a monastery where the monks from the temple lived, and we watched them serving yak milk in bowls and saying their prayers.

I decided that I wanted to travel more deeply into the Gobi Desert, so I again boarded a Russian plane, which didn't have much in the way of safety measures; I observed workers smoking and refueling the plane at the same time. The plane didn't have many people on board, fewer than a dozen of us, so they used the unoccupied seats for cargo. The airplane crew didn't buckle down the boxes; they were just loose. If we had hit rough weather, the boxes would have flown all over the plane, but we made it okay, thankfully. The plane landed in the desert where there was no airstrip, just pure sand. Then it flew off with the promise to come back and pick us up in a few days.

I stayed in a yurt by myself with a bed, some rugs on the sand, and a fire in a stove because it was cool at night. That was my home in the Gobi Desert. The restaurant near where I stayed was also a big yurt, and the food was okay. I ate cheese made of camel's milk and cooked over camel dung, the most popular fuel there. I also drank the milk from camels as well as milk from mares, which was used especially for people with tuberculosis and other respiratory diseases. The locals kept their mares tied up in little folds nearby and milked them seven times a day. The horses were not big, but they were very strong. Many of the horses were used for racing, but the races were not for a mere mile, like most American horse races. Mongolian races were thirty miles long; the endurance of those little horses was amazing.

The people were very hospitable and took us out into the wildest parts of the desert to see the great sand dunes. We also saw what was called a glacier, which might sound strange, but it got so cold there in the wintertime that this glacier formed each year and then would melt during the warm months. We could see the glacier was melting from the water running underneath it, a stream about a quarter of a mile long.

One of the most interesting places that I saw while I was staying in the yurt was Karakorum, the city of Genghis Khan. Karakorum was Khan's capital from which he looted, pilfered, burned, destroyed, and captured people all the way to the Danube River in Europe. He was one of the most ruthless men in history, with his motto: "If they stand taller than a wagon wheel, cut off their heads." That was his philosophy of how to treat people when they were captured: let the children live but kill the adults. In the early thirteenth century Marco Polo made a trip to the Far East, stopping in Karakorum for a while in 1206. In his record of the trip, he mentioned four great stone turtles, one at each corner of the city. One of those stone turtles remains – a very large turtle keeping watch over the dunes and mounds that cover a lot of artifacts. The area still hasn't been excavated extensively because the government doesn't have the resources and they don't want anyone else to do the excavations. Someday, more of Karakorum will be excavated, and the world will know more about life in the times of Genghis Khan.

After my time in the Gobi, I flew back into southern Russia and visited Bukhara, a Muslim city with very strict rules concerning alcoholic beverages. Even in 1981, a person who was caught drinking alcohol would have his head cut off and then that head would be nailed into a wall by the ear. Then the city officials would send the body home to the parents or wife. It was a brutal way to respond to the use of alcoholic beverages, but that was their creed.

I enjoyed that trip a great deal, since it allowed me a chance to see parts of Russia and Central Asia that I had never visited before. It also allowed me to witness the continued change of facilities and structures within the Soviet Union, even as certain modes of thinking seemed to be hopelessly locked in the past, committed to a system that had already proved a failure. I could think back to the days at the height of the Cold War, when it seemed that the Soviets might pose a real threat to the American way of life. But cracks were starting to show in the Iron Curtain, and I felt optimistic about what the coming decade would bring.

CHAPTER 19

CHRIST BEHIND THE IRON CURTAIN AND THE GREAT WALL

I n April 1982 I flew to Poland, where the Church of Christ had not yet been recognized. Approximately ninety-five percent of the people in Poland were members of the Roman Catholic Church, at least nominally, and Catholicism was permitted by the communist Polish government, so that was pretty much all there was of recognized Christianity. Churches of Christ were not allowed to advertise over the radio, on television, or in newspapers because the Polish government did not recognize the church. Members of the Churches of Christ were persecuted in that their ration cards to buy meat, gas, and other items were sometimes confiscated; the government also confiscated their Bibles and songbooks. A few members were even imprisoned.

However, Poland faced severe political unrest in the early 1980s, and there was a major food shortage at the same time. The Churches of Christ in the United States and other countries came to Poland's rescue by sending a convoy of more than thirty trucks that delivered clothing, food, and medicines to different affected areas. Because of our benevolence work, the communist government decided to recognize the Church of Christ in 1982. The Polish government invited some leaders of our membership in the United States to represent our country in the recognition ceremony. I attended along with John Gipson from Sixth and Izard in Little Rock; Alton Howard from White's Ferry Road in Monroe, Louisiana; and Jerry Harris and Bill Stokes from Shreveport, Louisiana.

Our group was to fly through Atlanta to Vienna. While we were in the Atlanta airport, the airline officials called my name and beckoned me over to the desk. "Sir, we are sorry," the attendant began, and

I braced myself for the worst, "but we have overbooked in the economy class. We wonder if you would mind sitting in first class on the trip overseas." I told them I would be very happy to accommodate them. Being 6'2", I welcomed that extra space on such a long flight.

So I flew upstairs in the first-class area of a 747 for the first time in my life. The airline asked me not to say anything to anybody about it, so I didn't. When I went back to where my buddies were sitting, they all began to tease me and say, "Uh-huh, you got in trouble. You got called on the carpet." But I didn't say anything. Then, when we boarded the plane, all of my friends turned right to join the peons, and I turned to the left and went upstairs to first class. It wasn't until after the flight, when we were waiting to go through customs together that I told them what had taken place.

When we arrived in Vienna, Mike Dawidow, whose father preached in the Polish city of Sopot, was waiting for us with two cars for our trip to Warsaw, where the ceremony was to take place. He drove a little red Peugeot, and he asked me to drive his big Buick, which had a license plate on the front that said "USA-1" and looked diplomatic and official. While the soldiers inspected our cars at the Polish border, I stepped out to go to the restroom. When I was gone, the soldiers told Mike they wanted to talk with me. They asked my friends in the car, "Where is your chauffeur?" From then on, my friends teased me about being the chauffeur.

After roadblocks – Poland was full of them at the time – and delays, our group finally arrived in Warsaw at 2:00 a.m. As we drove to our hotel, we approached a traffic light. Mike, who was leading us, drove right through, but I was stopped by a red light. When I did, a nearby soldier saw the USA-1 plate, came up to our car, looked in the window, assumed we were people of importance – and he saluted me. After that, I teased my friends about being the only one to be saluted by the military in Warsaw.

We checked into the hotel and early the next morning prepared to go to the Radziwill Palace, where our ceremony of recognition would take place at 2:00 in the afternoon. The Radziwill Palace served as the meeting place for the signing of the Warsaw Pact in 1955, where the Soviet Union and seven satellite Soviet nations signed a treaty to control Eastern Europe, counteract NATO, and promote the spread of communism. In 1982, in the very same room and at the very same table under the very same double eagle symbol of Poland, the Polish government recognized the Church of Christ as an official religion.

During that ceremony, I spoke as a representative of the United States and the Churches of Christ in the United States. Brother Walenty Dawidow represented the Churches of Christ in Poland. Two leaders of the Polish government also spoke. One of them, Jerzy Kurbersky, served as head over all religions in Poland. The other man, named Mr. Dusik, was over just the Protestant religions; therefore, he had worked with Walenty Dawidow throughout this process. After we all spoke, Mr. Kurbersky presented the Article of Recognition, signed by Walenty Dawidow and the government officials. Later, we were allowed to take pictures, but not in that particular room.

After the ceremony we left for the hotel, where we were to have a dinner together with our group and the two officials from Poland. I sat right across from Mr. Dusik and next to Brother Dawidow. After the dinner, Mr. Dusik said, "Mr. Dawidow, you are the head of the Church of Christ in Poland. We expect you to be benevolent as you have been in the past, and we expect you to be ecumenical." He went on with other expectations.

After Mr. Dusik had finished, Walenty Dawidow rose and said, "Mr. Dusik, you have been very kind to us, and you have been very helpful to us." (He really had been helpful in securing the recognition for the church.) He went on to say how much they appreciated what he had done, but in a loud voice he said, "But you have offended me. I am not the head of the Church of Christ in Poland. Jesus Christ is the head of the church in Poland." And he preached a sermon right there. I was amazed that he would speak so boldly toward communist leaders in his own country, but Brother Dawidow got away with it.

After our Church of Christ group finished the dinner with the Polish officials, Mike took us to eat a second meal with the patriarch of one of the other large denominations, which had about a million members in Poland. We ate at his personal residence and enjoyed visiting with him. After the day was over, we flew back to America, and I had to fly economy class once again. All my hopes that I could get bumped up as I did on the way over came to nothing.

———————

Two months later, on June 28, 1982, Louise and I flew to China and stayed until July 17. We flew first to Beijing, which I had visited four years earlier with People to People. In just those few years, I found a tremendous difference. Whereas previously there had been no advertising except Chairman Mao's sayings and his Little Red Book, this time there were different kinds of advertisements everywhere, even in English – and not just about Chairman Mao or his book. The people explained to Louise and me that the English advertisements were necessary because of so many visitors coming from the United States and other English-speaking countries. The Chinese businesses wanted to advertise in English to sell the tourists products produced there in China. Louise had never seen such a concentration of bicycles as there were in Beijing. There were still bicycles everywhere. But there were a few more cars on the road. Hotels had been built and new businesses had been opened. China had undergone a remarkable change in only four years.

Louise and I visited The Great Wall as well as Tiananmen Square and the Forbidden City. The most interesting cultural items for us, though, were the markets, which were really the center of life for the people. Each market was a social place as well as a destination for daily shopping. Many of the citizens didn't have refrigerators or freezers at home, so they had to buy their food almost daily. We especially enjoyed observing the difference between the two types of markets, similar to those we had seen in Russia. There were free markets, which were open areas where people could bring products they had produced and sell them. That type of market was always full of people and of good produce brought by farmers and growers. We saw snakes and toads and all kinds of little animals that Louise and I wouldn't think about eating, but the other shoppers did. Then, we would walk across the street to a state-run market, which was not nearly so nice. The fruits and vegetables didn't look as good as they did in the free market, because people tended put more care into their work when they owned those things themselves rather than having to give them to the state.

We also traveled to the city of Xian, where the authorities had unearthed approximately six thousand terracotta soldiers that had been preserved for more than two thousand years. They were made to stand as soldiers to protect the emperor in the other world when he died. Each figure was distinctive from the others, as if they were representative of all the different tribes in China. Louise and I, as well as other tourists, stood above this sea of soldier statues, seeing them all lined up as a great army, prepared to protect their emperor.

We visited Changsha, where the Changsha Railway University was located. A young student named Paul Bao came to the hotel to visit us. He was interested in coming to the United States to study education. Due to visa regulations, he couldn't bring his wife or his baby son, but he wanted to come to Harding. I helped him make the arrangements, and he eventually graduated from Harding and got his master's and doctoral degrees from Ole Miss. He was later able to bring his wife and son, Joe, over, and he secured a teaching job in the United States. My family became good friends of the Baos, and they would occasionally come back to Searcy to visit us as well as one of our local dentists, who had provided financial assistance to Paul when he was at Harding.

From Changsha, Louise and I took a train to Guilin, and that trip was one of the hottest I have ever experienced. When we left Changsha, the weather was very warm, and the train had come down from Wuhan, nicknamed "the furnace of China." When Louise and I boarded the train, we noticed a western-looking man standing in the hall in his shorts – that is, his underwear. We couldn't believe that a man would disrobe like that in public, but he started to chat with us and we discovered he was from Memphis, Tennessee. We even knew some of the same people! After a little while, I came to understand why this man had disrobed: The train was unimaginably hot. Thankfully, Louise and I had purchased a compartment to ourselves, and I eventually stripped down to my shorts, as well. Louise took off almost everything she could, too. Even after doing so, we were still very hot. To make matters worse, we didn't have anything to drink. We put our clothes back on and ventured out of our private compartment to the dining car to find something to eat since it was an overnight trip, and we hadn't had any dinner. We were able to get a meal, but all they had to drink was beer – no water, no juices, no sodas. I had a little can of 7 Up I had stashed in my luggage, and Louise and I split it. That was all we had to drink on the whole hot, sweaty, miserable trip.

Early in the morning, we arrived in Guilin, and we went to the hotel to deposit our luggage and to drink a lot of water. Then, we immediately left to ride on a boat up a river to see some unusual mountains shaped like upside down ice cream cones. On the trip, we saw cormorants that fishermen were using to fish in the river. The birds would dive, catch fish in their mouths and bring them back to their owners. A ring around the birds' necks kept them from swallowing their catch. We watched these birds as they performed, and we marveled at their efficiency. We also watched the cooks as they prepared the meal for us at lunch. They had fresh vegetables, which they washed by dipping them in the river just before cooking them for us.

From Guilin, Louise and I traveled south to Canton, where Dr. George Benson had worked and taught when he was a missionary in China. He taught at Sun Yat-sen University and started a Bible school, which also offered English language lessons. Teaching English opened doors for him in his work in the schools because the Chinese really wanted to learn English. The communists forced Dr. Benson out of country in 1936; he was fortunate to escape with his life. Dr. Benson tried for a number of years to get back there; however, when communism took over all of China and the government took over the church property, it became clear that the plan would never succeed. Louise and I visited the old Bible school building Dr. Benson had established to see what had taken place after the government took it over; it had been converted to a military facility.

After leaving the school site, Louise and I went to the home of one of Dr. Benson's close Christian friends, who was about eighty years old and almost blind. This friend remembered Dr. Benson very well, and he talked with us about him and his work in China.

Hong Kong, our next stop, was still under the control of the British; their lease for ninety-nine years did not end until 1997. Hong Kong was a lovely and lonely city surrounded by water and many islands, right on the periphery of China. Unlike mainland China, Hong Kong was not nearly as full of bicycles. In fact, Hong Kong displayed a tremendous amount of wealth. As I had seen on my previous trip, most of the taxis were made by Mercedes-Benz, and there were Rolls-Royces for sale behind large shop windows. A number of people who lived there told us they dreaded the day when the Chinese government would take over the city again. Many of them were getting ready by sending much of their money out of the country and sending relatives along with it.

Watching many parts of the world stumble through communism made me wonder how much longer it could last. I was sure there were many places where I felt confident it would fall within a decade or two, but elsewhere I feared communism would stay deeply rooted for generations. All we could do was continue to preach and pray to support those people who were working to bring freedom to everyone.

CHAPTER 20

MORE CHANGES FOR HARDING

I n 1980, Harding started a program in Florence, Italy, that we dubbed HUF (Harding University in Florence). The plan was for roughly forty students to live and study in Florence each semester, spending their free time traveling all over Europe. When we first started the program, we rented space from the Italian Bible school, and the students had a wonderful experience. We quickly saw that the program would be successful, so we decided to explore purchasing a villa in Florence in order to have a permanent location for our group to meet.

In 1984, I asked Don Shackelford, who was in charge of the program, as well as our staff and friends in Florence, to look at about thirty different villas that were for sale. I told them to pick out the top three, and then I would come over to look at each of them. The most promising one was a villa in Fiesole, on the eastern side of Florence, which would have been a good fit except that it needed roughly $150,000 worth of repairs and upgrades. As we mulled over the idea of buying it, an Italian restaurant owner we knew who owned a villa on the west side of Florence told us about a friend of his who also owned a villa in that area, near Scandicci. "He may be willing to sell it," he told us. "He is a very wealthy man and this is his summer home, but he is not using it much anymore. His kids are gone, and he is afraid of vandalism. Would you be interested in seeing it?" Of course we told him we would love to!

The restaurant owner took us out to the countryside in Scandicci to see this villa, and we were immediately impressed. It sat in a beautiful location, overlooking the city of Florence. We could look in every direction and see other villas dotting the rolling acres of olive trees and grape vineyards. It was an old structure, although it looked very new. It had twenty-three rooms and nine modern baths, and there was a large wine cellar that could be converted to a student center. The property had a number of apple and apricot trees as well as many olive trees; tall poplars lined the way up to the house. The entire villa was made of masonry, even the window frames. The door frames were stone, so that they would not wear out. About every forty years or so, stucco would need to be applied to the outside, and then the building would then be good as new again. As I was talking with the owner, a Count, I remarked, "By the way, how old are these roof tiles? Are they about fifty years old?"

He said, "Oh, no, they are about two hundred years old."

The Count who owned it was an orthodontist and a professor at the University at Florence, and his brother was the ambassador to France from Italy. The family was a prominent one, and the house had history. The main portion of the building dated back to the early 1500s, and the latest addition, an appendage to the west of the original house, was added in 1734. During World War II, twelve or thirteen families stayed in this villa, and they used the wine cellar as a bomb shelter. In fact, during the war, a German tank fell off into the ditch and was trapped. The people in the villa were afraid of being bombed by the British or American militaries, so they helped camouflage the tank until they could pull it out of the ditch and send it on its way again.

We had already put a great deal of prayer and preparation into the decision, including selling some property Harding owned in Memphis in order to have the finances necessary to make the purchase, and after touring the property in Scandicci we felt confident this was the place the Lord had set aside for us.

Despite the excellent condition of the villa, it would still need a little work. One of the greatest changes we anticipated was to convert a little chapel on the northeastern side of the building into a kitchen – and this was almost a big mistake. When the Count learned of our plans, he nearly backed out because he feared it would ruin the building, even though he had already made that chapel into a junk room. We were able to convince him of the need for a large kitchen to feed forty students and our staff, and we showed him our plans to make the changes with quality equipment and to hire excellent local cooks and housekeepers to feed the students and help care for the property. He agreed to the plan, and we proceeded with the remodeling.

At the time of purchase, we also bought much of the furniture in the villa. We did not buy the most expensive pieces of furniture because we could see those pieces being torn up by our students (namely the young men, who tend to have difficulty in properly using fragile furniture). The ceilings downstairs stood seventeen feet high. Hanging on the large walls in the living room were some expensive eighteenth-century tapestries, belonging to the Count. At first, he took down the tapestries, and the pictures we used to replace them looked like postage stamps in comparison. Thankfully, he decided instead to leave the tapestries there for us if we would pay the insurance for them. We were very happy and agreed to do so.

On October 21, 1984, we had a dedication for the villa at HUF. We had a choral group there sing a piece that Ken Davis had arranged for the occasion. The Count was thrilled by the event and very happy that his family's ancestral home would be used as an educational facility.

Some of the Board of Trustees wanted to see our new villa in Florence, so the following spring, on April 15, 1985, I flew over with some of the board members to visit the villa as well as Rome, Florence, Milan, and Venice. The board members enjoyed the trip so much so that the following year another group of the board members and their wives flew over with me to Rome, and from there we went to Florence again. After visiting Florence, we traveled to Sorrento, Pompeii, Vesuvius, Herculaneum, Capri, Pisa, Sienna, San Gimignano, Milan, and surrounding areas. On this trip, we saw much of the country that I had not seen before. It was a beautiful trip, especially when we were in the area of Capri and south along the Amalfi Coast. We took a road close to the edge of a cliff, where we would ride along and look down about a thousand feet to the sea. We stayed in a hotel located on the side of a cliff, looking down on the water.

We toured the areas and saw the places our students were visiting during their free travel times. At Sorrento we went to a factory that made inlaid wood products, like nesting tables and music boxes. We were all amazed at how the factory produced such beautiful items. On the Isle of Capri, however, we had our biggest surprise. A local woman was following us and stopping occasionally to listen to us speak. Finally, she came up to us and said, "You are from America. Where are you from?" We said, "Arkansas," and she exclaimed, "Oh, I have a friend in

Arkansas. His name is Erle Moore." We laughed, because Dr. Moore was head of our music department. When Erle was in the service in the Army during World War II, he was stationed in that area and used to go to this lady's home to play the piano and to sing. She was a six-teen-year-old girl at the time. Years later, Erle had taken his wife and daughter, Mona Lee, over to visit this lady's family. They had fallen out of touch, however, so she was thrilled to visit with our group, and she took us to her home and to a little souvenir shop that her family operated. We told Erle about our experience when we returned, and he was glad to hear from her.

After that extraordinary meeting on Capri, I decided I had almost reached the point where I would no longer be surprised by the people I met overseas who had a Harding connection. Almost. I still get a thrill whenever I meet yet another person in some remote corner of the world who has been touched by our school.

———————

That summer, I met several times with Bill Miller, a preacher for the Highbury Park Church in Nassau, Bahamas, who was interested in Harding's starting a Biblical studies program in his country. I presented his vision to the Harding Board, and they agreed to help the Highbury Park Church convert some of their church building to provide space. David Caskey, an American missionary who was working in the Bahamas, helped a great deal, and we flew various Harding professors to Nassau and back in order to staff the school.

On one of the trips to Nassau, I planned to take a teacher named L.V. Pfeifer and James Cone, Chairman of the Harding Board, along with about five hundred pounds of library books in the Harding plane. Unfortunately, a huge storm moved through Searcy the night before we were supposed to leave, and the runway was completely covered with snow. David Ridings, our pilot, decided that it would be safe enough to take off because he drove his truck up and down the runway to check for slick spots and couldn't find any. However, when we started down the runway, our Aero Commander reached the halfway point and suddenly began to slide. The left engine surged a little, and the plane veered off the runway toward the hangers. Fortunately, we hit a bump that turned us around and headed us back toward the runway before we hit any of the buildings, but we didn't quite get the plane back to the runway. About eight feet short of it, the plane stopped, but one of the engines sucked up gravel and was badly damaged. In fact, it cost about $50,000 to have it repaired. Needless to say, that trip didn't materialize.

Harding had a good program at Nassau for several years until we ran out of students who were living in the area. It was a shame that we weren't able to keep the school going, but I felt very good about the number of students who had graduated from it and were working with churches around the Caribbean.

———

The early 1980s were an important time in expanding Harding's reach. Besides HUF and the Bible school in Nassau, we also had the opportunity to develop the Walton Scholars Program with Sam Walton, whom I greatly admired. He originally lived about forty miles north of Searcy in Newport, where he had a small five- and ten-cent store in the 1960s. When he lost his lease and moved to northwest Arkansas, he developed another business that he called Wal-Mart. He soon began opening stores all over the country and took his business public.

I remember when Dr. Jimmy Carr came into my office one day and said, "Cliff, you ought to invest in some Wal-Mart stock. I think it's really going to do well."

I said, "Jimmy, I would just have to go to the bank and borrow the money, and I don't think I will do so." I figured I'd probably end up jinxing Walton's company if I invested in it anyway. Of course, now I realize that if I had borrowed $1,900 and bought a hundred shares of Wal-Mart stock and continued to reinvest it, the stock would be worth many millions of dollars today. That just shows how smart I am in investing.

When the first Wal-Mart store opened in Searcy, I attended the ceremony to mark the occasion. I arrived before the opening occurred and watched Sam as he climbed up on the counter and spoke to his associates. His message to his staff was so good that I wrote it down on some cards and kept them in my pocket for two or three years.

Sam opened a distribution center in Searcy in 1978 – the first Wal-Mart distribution center outside of Bentonville, in fact – and it provided quite a number of jobs for the town. I remember one occasion when he called me and said that he would like for me to be a judge for the music contest that he was sponsoring involving his Searcy associates. He had rented Harding's Administration Auditorium for the event.

"Sam," I told him truthfully, "I'm not a good judge of music."

"Neither am I," he laughed, "but I'm going to judge. Come on and judge with me."

I finally agreed to judge with him and really ended up enjoying it. Sam was a real encourager and showman. He was a very good businessman, but he also tried to help people do their work in an effective and enthusiastic way. I watched him with admiration when he climbed up on stage that night, saying, "Give me a W! Give me an A! Give me an L! Give me a squiggly!" as he had the audience spell out Wal-Mart.

I really appreciated how humble and down to earth Sam was, too. Once, I was invited to the home of Paul and June Carter; Paul was Sam's chief land officer at one point and, later, his chief financial officer. Sam and his wife, Helen, joined us for dinner, and I remember thinking that the only clue that he was an incredibly wealthy man was the new Lincoln he was driving. In fact, even after making his millions, every morning he would get up at an early hour to drive his old truck into town to drink coffee with his friends.

When I visited Sam and Helen in their home, I was amazed to see that it was built over a creek. I looked out the window on one side to see water flow under the house, and then walked to the other side of the house to see water coming out from under the house to flow down the stream. Sam had a good tennis court on his property, too, because his three chief enjoyments in life seemed to be playing tennis, hunting quail, and opening stores.

Sam Walton and Jack Stephens served as co-chairs for the American Studies Institute at Harding University for a number of years. After Sam developed cancer, he would come to the meetings carrying the medicine he needed to fight the disease. I appreciated how he was willing to attend the meetings even after he was so ill and how much he believed in the mission of Harding.

A result of Sam's association with Harding was an exciting program first proposed by Gabriel Galindo, a wealthy Panamanian diplomat and businessman, who was one of Sam's fishing buddies. Galindo suggested to Sam one day that he and Gabriel ought to work together to bring young people from Latin America to the United States so they could study freedom, democracy, and the free enterprise economy. Thousands of Latin American students were being recruited to Russia and Eastern European countries to study Marxism and Communism, and Galindo recognized what a danger that was to the stability and freedom of the region. Sam agreed.

In the spring of 1985, Sam asked the Board of Trustees if Harding would be interested in developing a program alongside John Brown University and University of the Ozarks to enable young people from Central America to study at their colleges. This would help those young people better understand the free world and would maybe inspire them to help develop a free, democratic society in their own countries. Sam said he would pay the entire cost – not only tuition, fees, room and board, but transportation and spending money as well. It was the best scholarship offer I had ever heard. The only real condition of the scholarship was that recipients must return to their home country to work for five years before they could move elsewhere. The goal, after all, was to encourage students to reinvest their skills and education in Latin America.

On March 25, 1985, I went to Bentonville to the Wal-Mart headquarters to help finalize plans for the Walton Scholarship Program. Sam agreed to send twelve to fifteen students to each of the three schools (Harding, John Brown University, and University of the Ozarks) during the first year and to increase the number of students as time went on. A few weeks later he, along with Jack Stephens and several other businessmen from Little Rock, publicly announced the program.

In May 1985, I went to Belize, Honduras, Costa Rica, and Panama to recruit the first Walton scholars for Harding. I was thankful I had studied Spanish for three years in high school in New Orleans because I was able to communicate a little bit in Spanish when needed. For ten years, I continued to go to the Central American countries to recruit students for the Walton program.

At first, Nicaragua was not permitted to join the program; President Daniel Ortega and the communist Sandinistas who ran the country made the political situation too instable. After two years, however, we were able to include Nicaragua, and I traveled there with a preacher from the country to serve as my interpreter. We met with one of the *commandantes* in charge of the educational program, a man named José Sándoval. He told me that Harding was the first school that had offered scholarships to his students, and he was very happy to approve the program. From then on, we easily recruited students from Nicaragua. The Walton program continued to grow and to do well, and more than two thousand students have been able to secure a good education at the three participating universities before returning home to help build their own countries.

Sam Walton was a very good friend of Harding for many years. He was a man of vision, and I was grateful that he came alongside Harding to help grow the school as well as Searcy itself.

My time wasn't solely focused on work, however. In March 1986, all eighteen members of my family went on a huge trip to Florida and the Bahamas. We flew to Orlando and took a Walt Disney ship across to Nassau and spent a couple of days in the area before returning.

In anticipation of the trip, we had one major obstacle we needed to overcome. My granddaughter Louisa was only about four years old and was dreadfully afraid of people who were dressed up in any kind of costume, such as the Harding Bison or Santa Claus. We knew this could be a challenge on a Disney ship, with so many characters walking around, so we decided to try an experiment to see if we could help her to overcome this fear. Debbie and Louisa came over to the house and watched me pull a Santa Claus costume over my clothes. Louisa was smiling as I talked to her, but the moment I put on the Santa coat, she began to whimper; when I put on the hat and beard, she started to sob. The experiment didn't work out very well, so we figured we would just have to take our chances and hope for the best. On the cruise, Louisa impressed us when she won a prize (a tee shirt), and to collect it she had to walk up to a stage with the costumed Disney characters. We all exchanged nervous glances, worried she would break into tears when she got close, but she stuck out her chin, marched down to the front, got her prize, and came back to us beaming.

Not only did we enjoy this vacation in Nassau, but we came back and went to Disney World and Epcot. We flew back to Little Rock together, and all eighteen of us went to The Shack for a final barbecue meal to punctuate a delightful vacation. That is a memory I will cherish forever; it is always a wonderful occasion when we are able to get our whole family together for a shared experience like that.

I was sixty-four, and I knew that things were going to be changing. The biggest change, of course, was my pending retirement. I had begun to slow down on speaking engagements and gradually even stepped out of the Citizenship Academy for high schoolers that I had enjoyed for so long.

By early 1986 I had decided I would retire from the presidency the following year. I wanted to give the board enough time to select a successor, so I notified them of my plans. They asked me to continue to serve another year, but I felt that since our other administrators were retiring at age sixty-five, I should do so as well. The Board and I set the retirement date for May 1987, but the agreement came with a catch – would I be willing to serve as the first chancellor of Harding University? Of course, I was honored to accept.

For several months, the board considered the applications for my successor. They asked me to give my opinions and evaluations, but I wanted to leave the decision in their hands – and I was happy when they chose David B. Burks to be the next president of Harding. David was well known, having been a student and later a professor at Harding for many years. He had served well as Dean of the School of Business and was loved by his students and colleagues alike.

In the winter of 1986 and the following spring, Harding began to prepare for the transition of leadership. At our faculty meeting on April 21, I spoke about my upcoming retirement. I expressed my deep appreciation for being able to serve for twenty-two years as president of an institution that I dearly loved, an institution that helped to shape my life. It helped to head me in the right direction while I was a student and gave me the privilege of teaching and serving many thousands of students through the years as both a professor and administrator. I encouraged the faculty to be loyal to Harding and its mission, and to support David Burks in his new role as president. I challenged the faculty to continue the great tradition of quality instruction and service to the students and to be firm in their faithfulness to the Lord and His word.

On May 7, 1987, the board provided an appreciation dinner and evening in my honor at the Heritage Building on campus, and it was a wonderful occasion of great memories. In fact, the placemat for each of the participants was a 14" by 20" sheet of paper with a photo of Louise and me in the middle with the words:

In tribute to President and Mrs. Clifton L. Ganus, Jr.

June 1965 through May 1987

Searcy, Arkansas

Around the placemat were other photos of important events and personal pictures that brought back old memories. Right above our picture was one of Louise being congratulated because an iris was named for her. To the right of that was one of Dr. Joe Pryor and me giving out diplomas to the graduates, as we did every year. Beneath that was a picture of me sitting on the sofa dressed in my Mao Tse Tung jacket and cap, representing the trip that I had made to China in 1978. There was also a picture of me holding up my softball glove. It was a relic; I don't know how many years old it was, but it was coming apart, so I bound it together with a white shoelace and kept on playing. The students laughed about that, as did the faculty. (People occasionally ask me if I still have that glove. I do.) Beneath that was a picture of Louise when she was awarded the Harding Distinguished Alumnus Award, which I had received just a few years prior. There was a photo of Dean Sears and me standing on the platform for the groundbreaking ceremony of Armstrong Hall, our first boys' dorm on the campus. To the left of that picture was one of Lott Tucker unveiling the Harding University sign in front of the student center. There was a picture of me teaching a class; another one of me standing in softball clothes, waiting a turn at bat; and one of Louise and me at a reception, dressed in our finery.

After the meal, we all went over to the Benson Auditorium for the evening program. I was surprised, but happy, when the Board announced that they were renaming the athletic center the Clifton L. Ganus Athletic Center. I had always loved athletics and enjoyed playing various sports, so that particular selection was very appropriate.

We had a very good crowd for the occasion, and I was honored that Sam Walton and many others were able to stay not only for the dinner but the program. It was a beautiful and meaningful presentation that celebrated my career and the years that Louise and I had invested in Harding, and I could not have been more grateful not only for the time and effort that went into the retirement celebration, but also just for the opportunity to serve Harding those many years.

Three days later, I retired as president and became chancellor. That same day, I was privileged to deliver the commencement address at the Harding graduation. David B. Burks began his presidency at Harding and for twenty-six years did a wonderful job directing the affairs of the school, developing it not only in size but in quality. I tried to stay out of his way and not to second-guess him; I did not always agree with his decisions, even as he would not have always agreed with me, but we had a very good relationship and tried to make it fruitful for Harding

With my retirement came even more travel. On August 2, 1988, Louise and I flew to Vancouver, British Colombia, and took an Alaskan Cruise with about sixty or seventy members of the Church of Christ from all over the United States. Dr. Benson and I were both invited as speakers, and we enjoyed being together and having our worship services and lectures.

We enjoyed Alaska so much that we went back the following summer, from July 31 to August 11, 1989. Louise and I flew to Anchorage, and I got a chance to fish with Tony Webb for salmon in the Kenai River and for halibut in the Cook Inlet. Louise didn't fish, but she enjoyed visiting with Connie, Tony's wife. When we were returning, we stopped at the Seattle airport. We knew we had a grandchild due at any time and were very eager to hear about the arrival. During our layover, I called to Charles's home in El Dorado and asked if the baby had come yet. Patty's mother, Nancy Sapio, answered the phone.

"Yes," she said. "The baby is here and is doing very well."

"Well, is it a boy or girl?" I asked.

"I don't think I am going to tell you," Nancy said. "I am just going to let Charles tell you...but he certainly has good lungs."

———————

As both our family and Harding continued to grow, I settled into my new role and continued to count my blessings; the Lord had seen fit to bless me with good health and a good life as I continued to help the university I loved in whatever way I could.

CHAPTER 21

GLOBAL LECTURESHIPS

One of the most meaningful pursuits of my life has been the lectureships of which I have been a part around the world; once a teacher, always a teacher, I suppose.

Besides the many presentations I delivered over the years on American civics and the importance of religious and economic freedom, I also had the great privilege of being invited to speak at a number of Christian conferences over the years. The most frequent one was the Caribbean Lectureships, which Louise and I first attended in 1983. I spoke for thirty-two of the next thirty-three years at these lectureships and became well acquainted with the brethren in the Caribbean. I learned to love and appreciate their tremendous work.

The first Caribbean Lectureship that I served as a speaker was in Antigua. When we finished on the island of Antigua, Louise and I went on down to Caracas, Venezuela, where Bob Brown was preaching. We spent a few days in Venezuela, traveling over the countryside with Bob as far as Mérida in the Andes Mountains. Bob had done an excellent work in Caracas, a very large city. There were many poor people who lived up on the mountainside in cardboard and wooden structures, but the church was strong there. Two of our people from Harding, Bill and Ava Conley, had been working with Bob in that area for many years. Dr. Arthur Shearin (a long-time music professor and eventual head of the music department at Harding for many years) also took his choir down to sing in that area on different occasions. Usually, though, we kept our travel confined to the Caribbean since, as we came to learn, there was incredible diversity and plenty to see in whatever nation was hosting that year.

Ken Dye, who was a preacher and missionary in Jamaica, had started the Caribbean Lectureships in the 1970s. Though always in a different location from year to year, the lectureships followed the same format every year and featured many of the same speakers. We would arrive on a Saturday and on Sunday would go to church at one or more of the congregations, sometimes splitting up if there were two congregations close to one another. After worship services was a potluck or catered lunch; then, that evening, we would have the first session – usually a devotional and church service. On Monday morning about 8:00 a.m., we would have a devotional and then begin the program, which continued until about 1:30 p.m. The afternoon was left open to allow us to tour the island, rest, or prepare for our next session. Then we would start again after supper and go for about two and a half or three more hours.

In addition to the speakers, we had field reports. People from the different islands would present on the happenings in their country. Several reports would be given throughout the four days of the lectureship.

Usually on Wednesday evening we would close with a session of a couple of speakers and the remaining field reports; then we all gathered around the room in a big circle – sometimes hundreds of people – and we held hands. Only twice in those many years I attended was a representative from Cuba able to attend. The other times, we left a gap in the circle to represent our brothers and sisters under Castro's communist rule on the island.

The number of people attending the lectureships varied a great deal, depending upon the size and the number of congregations on the particular hosting island. For instance, when Trinidad (more than thirty congregations) or Jamaica (more than forty congregations), hosted the lectureships, the locals of the island attended in good numbers. But when a small place like St. Kitts and Nevis hosted, the local members would attend, but not in numbers quite so large.

Freeport, on Grand Bahama Island, hosted the lectureships in June of 1984. The church was fairly strong in the Bahamas, with perhaps 120 or 130 members attending. In June of 1985, Barbados and Grenada hosted the lectureships. Grenada was an interesting location because of the spices grown there. In addition to attending the lectureships, we toured spice facilities and farms where those spices grew and were processed, and we brought home different kinds of spices for cooking.

Montego Bay in Jamaica hosted the lectureships in June of 1986. Located in the northwest corner of Jamaica, the host city had many congregations; Kingston, Jamaica's capital city on the south side of the island, had a training school for preachers. We had quite a crowd that year.

In 1987, Grenada again hosted the lectures, which happened shortly after the American invasion. A communist government had tried to take over the island and had built a large airport in Grenada; President Ronald Reagan decided to send American troops to push the communists back. Our soldiers had already left by the time of the lectureships, but we could see some of the results of the fighting.

The following years, we were hosted by the Cayman Islands, the Bahamas, St. Kitts and Nevis, and the Virgin Islands. In 1992 the honor went to Georgetown in Guyana, which is not actually an island, but a small country on the northern coast of South America. In 1993 I missed the Caribbean Lectureship, but it was for a good reason: For our fiftieth anniversary, I took Louise on a trip around the world and we spent the month of June working in Gorlovka in Ukraine. I started back again in 1994 in Puerto Rico, then the Bahamas, Grenada, and Jamaica. Trinidad, with its thirty congregations, hosted in 1998; nearby Tobago had even more congregations, and at least seven hundred people attended that year. The Dutch Island of St. Maarten hosted the 1999 lectureships, then St. Lucia, Aruba, the Bahamas, and St. Thomas.

In 2004, two Cuban members of the church finally received permission from their government to join us, completing the prayer circle at our closing session. They invited us to hold the lectureship in Havana in July 2005. We all looked forward to coming together again in Cuba.

Since I could not fly directly to Cuba from the United States, I flew to Nassau in the Bahamas and spent the night with Bill Miller, the preacher at the Highbury Park congregation. Unfortunately, we had bad weather and were not able to fly out of Nassau when we had planned, but it's hard to complain about an extra day in the Bahamas. Finally, we were able to make the short flight to Havana, but my bag got lost along the way, and for two days I had to do without most of my clothes and other possessions. I had to buy some clothes in Havana, but Cuba did not use the same numbering system on clothing, so they did not fit me very well. They did at least cover me up, however, and that's what I intended.

We had a good lectureship and enjoyed the Cuban hospitality and many speakers, as well as the classroom studies. Government officials welcomed us to the meeting, and Fidel Castro watched over us the whole lectureship; the church leaders had managed to secure an auditorium that would seat about four hundred people, and there was a twenty-foot-tall picture of Fidel Castro at the front of the auditorium. There was no way that you could avoid it while you were watching the speaker. The church of the Lord was growing well in Cuba, especially in the eastern part of the country. The Jamaica school of preaching had an overseas program in Cuba as well as other islands, and the result was that many more preachers were being trained and many were being baptized into Christ. Most of the congregations were very small house churches, because the Cuban government seemed to permit that type of spiritual activity much more so than unregistered, large assemblies. Unfortunately, the Cuban brethren have not been allowed to attend the Caribbean Lectureship again since hosting in 2005, but the government leaders did say at the end of that lectureship in Havana that they would be happy to have us return. Perhaps someday it will happen.

On July 2, 2016, my son Charles drove me to the airport to catch a flight to speak one more year at the lectureship held at Tobago. After the morning worship service, the lectureship group had lunch together in the lobby, prepared by the four Churches of Christ in Tobago. It featured the proverbial macaroni and cheese, beans, and chicken, which are three items almost inevitably found at a Caribbean meal. We officially started the lectureship that evening.

I was greatly surprised when I looked at the schedule. I was to speak on Tuesday morning, but I noticed the Sunday evening program said, "Award and Address: Clifton L. Ganus," and I wondered what that meant; had I forgotten about a presentation I was supposed to give? Fortunately, Michael Stewart, who preaches in Tobago, explained that in view of my many years of attendance and assistance of the lectureship, I would receive special recognition – no speech required. That evening, Ken Dye, who now works with the West End Church of Christ in Nashville, Tennessee, and who has been a good friend for many, many years, introduced me to the crowd.

The people of Tobago presented me with a handcrafted leather folder in which to keep my notes. They also gave me a beautifully carved board covered in Caribbean flowers and inscribed with the words "Prayer changes things." I was deeply moved by the gifts and recognition. Unfortunately, when I was coming off the stage, I slipped on the steps and fell backwards, hitting my head on the railing as I went. I'd like to say that only my ego was bruised, but my head was quite sore for several weeks afterwards.

In short, the Caribbean Lectureships are a major undertaking and tremendous encouragement to the believers in the region. Thanks to the decades of invitations I received to participate in the annual event, I've learned of many wonderful congregations in the area and met many, many fine Christians who love the Lord and love His kingdom. The sense of community those Christians in the Caribbean share is humbling and beautiful and a powerful reminder that the Gospel is being taught in every corner of the earth.

Rather than slowing down, my speaking actually seemed to pick up with retirement. On April 11, 1998, I flew to Anchorage, Alaska, and boarded a small commuter airline flying down to Soldotna to speak twice at the Alaska State Lectureship. About three hundred people had gathered in a school auditorium, and there were many RVs with people who had driven in from different parts of the state. It was in April, but it was snowing when I landed there. I stayed with Bob Townsley, who was the preacher at Soldotna, and I enjoyed visiting with brethren from all over the state.

That fall, I was asked to go to Germany to speak at the American Family Retreat, primarily for American military personnel and their families who were stationed in Europe. A few missionaries attended as well. Bill McDonough was there, along with Don Yelton from White's Ferry Road Church of Christ in West Monroe, Louisiana. It was extremely cold that year, and snow was everywhere, so we didn't spend much time outside, but rather in a very nice, comfortable army retreat center. There were approximately 150 people at the lectureship.

I spoke on two different occasions; one presentation was titled, "Give Us This Day Our Daily Bread."

In November of 1999, Louise and I flew to San Salvador, El Salvador, for me to speak at the Pan American Lectureship. Carl Mitchell, Jim Frazier, Howard Norton, and others came from the United States to be present for the lectureship. While I was there, I had an opportunity to visit the home of the assistant coach for one of the national basketball teams that my grandson John Richard Duke had played on earlier that year. He had been invited to come down and play for the team that won the national championship. John Richard stayed with the assistant coach, although he couldn't speak Spanish and the coach couldn't speak English. They each knew a few words in the others' language and got along very well.

I met the coach and his wife and children, who told me they really enjoyed having John Richard with them. The coach invited me to come back to the bedroom where John Richard had stayed. There was a small bed to which he pointed and said, "John Richard bed." Then, he put a stool down at the end of the bed and pointed to it and said, "John Richard feet." The bed wasn't long enough, since he was six feet, six inches tall, so his feet stuck over, and they put the little bench there to accommodate him.

In 2002, I spoke at three different lectureships all around the globe. In July, I flew to Antigua to speak at the Caribbean Lectureship, then later that month I flew to Europe to speak at the Pan-European Lectureship in Tallinn, Estonia. I had never been to Estonia, so I was happy to visit it, along with two other countries that I had never visited: Latvia and Lithuania. The lectureship in Tallinn was a good one with around 175 people present. About fifty were visitors from the United States, and the same number were missionaries from all over Europe. The remainder of the attendees were all church members in that area of the world.

Estonia, Latvia, and Lithuania had been a part of Russia for approximately fifty years, but they had been used as pawns in a game of chess between various countries – Russia, Prussia (Germany), Denmark, and

Sweden – for several centuries. During World War II Germany captured Estonia, Latvia, and Lithuania, then the Soviets took them over
after the war and occupied them as a part of the U.S.S.R. until 1991.

I had long admired the spirit of the people of those three small
countries. On August 23, 1989, more than two million of the citizens
of the triad had gathered on the highway from Tallinn, the capital
of Estonia, through Riga, the capital of Latvia, to Vilnius, the capital
of Lithuania, a distance of 420 miles, to join hands together and cry
out, "*Vabadus! Vabadus! Vabadus!*" which meant, "Freedom! Freedom!
Freedom!" Freedom took about two more years, but in the fall of 1991
these citizens were able to realize their dream. At the time of my visit
the people were free, independent, and proud of their heritage.

The lectureship was held in the lovely Radisson Hotel, which was
in the downtown part of Tallinn. It wasn't very far from the old city,
which dated back to the twelfth century. We had an opportunity to
visit and to eat in the old city on several different occasions.

The lectureship lasted from Sunday, July 28, until Thursday, August
1, at which time I decided to go down to Latvia with a number of the
members of the church who were going to lend support to the church
there. We drove a minibus to Riga, where we spent the night in a hotel
that was once a convent; even a barn and a horse stable had been made
into part of the hotel.

The old city was built on the Daugava River and contained many
stately and historic buildings, including some church buildings like
St. Peter's Basilica, where we climbed up to the top of the building
and looked out over all of Riga at the beautiful view. I loved walking
through the streets of the old city, visiting the little shops and the
restaurants. The structure of the city and streets was uneven and rather
hilly, so we wore our legs out walking.

After seeing all of Riga that I wished to visit, I decided to rent a car
and travel through the southwestern part of Latvia and into Lithuania
to visit the hometown of one of our basketball players, Reggie Butvydas.
Reggie was a 6'8" basketball player and a senior-to-be at Harding. He
lived in the town of Šilutė, a small city of about twenty thousand
people in the southwestern part of Lithuania. I got a map of Latvia,
Lithuania, and Estonia and marked out my five-hundred-mile trip.

221

I had some friends from France who had attended the lectureship at Tallinn who were in another car, and we drove together for a while. We wanted to cross over into Lithuania at a small border point near Skuodas. When we arrived at this border crossing, we found out that only people who lived in that area or Russian citizens would be able to cross at that border; everyone else had to cross over on the coast at a larger crossing point. We had to retrace our steps for several miles and go back up to Liepāja, a large town on the coast of the Baltic Sea. When we reached Liepāja, we stopped at a store, bought some provisions, and then headed south to Lithuania, crossing at the border near the Baltic Sea.

When I arrived at the border, I had trouble understanding the guard. The only thing I could make sense of was that he wasn't going to let me across the border without buying some kind of insurance, which I ultimately did just to get on with it. Finally, about thirty minutes after the other car I was traveling with was admitted, the guard permitted me to cross. The guard just repeated, "Car problem." I didn't know what he meant, and neither did my French friends who were with me in the other car, but I was grateful to finally cross the border.

Once we were in Lithuania, we stopped at a lovely spot to eat some lunch outdoors in a grove of trees. After we finished, we decided to head south on into Klaipeda, a large city with many thousands of people, which also had a Church of Christ meeting there. We arrived there on Saturday, and then I drove another forty miles south to the city of Šilutė. There I found Reggie, who was at a banquet for his sister's wedding, which had occurred that afternoon. I went over to the hall where they were having their dinner, but I didn't go inside, since I wasn't dressed appropriately. Reggie came out and visited a bit with me, and we agreed to meet the following day, which was Sunday afternoon.

I spent the night in Šilutė at a guest house, where an older man had a room available on the second floor. All of the hotels in town were full, so I was fortunate to find a room. I drove back early the next morning to Kaipeda to attend church service. The Church of Christ met on the second floor of a small building, and there were fifty or sixty people in attendance. After the worship service, I drove back to Šilutė to meet with Reggie.

That evening I decided to start driving back toward Riga and decided just to find a place to spend the night along the highway. It was late in the afternoon when I left, and darkness came pretty early, but I had a good map. If this sounds like the set up for a good adventure story, you're partly right; I had an adventure, but not a particularly good one. I drove for about a hundred and fifty miles into Siauliai, a city of about a hundred thousand people, on the main highway. As I drove into town, something strange suddenly happened to my car, and the horn started honking for no reason. I was looking for a hotel on a back street in a dark area, but the horn kept honking, periodically stopping and then starting up again. I parked the car even though I was still not sure where the hotel was. I didn't know what in the world was the matter, and I was embarrassed for making such a conspicuous arrival. I couldn't speak a word of the language, and the people who tried to help me couldn't speak English.

Finally, a man approached me, and he asked me for the keys, which had a remote-control device for locking the doors. I handed them over. The man looked at the key remote and said, "battery." Apparently, the battery had gone out and that what was causing the horn to honk. We walked a few blocks over to a big department store, but we couldn't find a battery that fit. The man called the police, who came even though it was after 10:00 at night. They put me in their car and drove to a couple of other places where they tried to find batteries, but we still couldn't find one. Finally, close to midnight, the horn stopped honking. When it did, the police towed the car about a block to the small hotel I hadn't been able to find.

The next morning, one of the hotel employees knew where I could get a battery, so he took off to get it. When he came back with the battery, I paid him, and we tried to start the car, but it wouldn't work. Apparently, after putting in a new battery, the device needed to be reprogrammed to get it to work. We called the car company at Riga and told them what had happened, and the company was thankfully able to walk us through the right procedure. I was finally able to get back on the road to Riga sometime after 9:00.

I drove about forty miles to the border between Lithuania and Latvia, and when I arrived at the border crossing I felt good because there was only one car ahead of me. "This is great!" I thought. "I'm going to be able to get out of here in a hurry."

The guard, who knew very little English, looked over the car, got my papers, read them, and then told me I had to wait. When I tried to get him to tell me why I was being held up, he just said, "Car. Problem. Car. Accident." I didn't know what in the world he meant, but it was the same thing the border guard had said when I tried to get into the country a few days earlier. Finally, he went into an office and used a computer to contact authorities in the city of Vilnius, on the south-eastern side of Lithuania. "Car. Problem. Car. Accident," he insisted.

"I didn't even go to Vilnius. I wasn't even within a hundred miles of Vilnius," I told him, in vain. Even if he couldn't understand my words, he could surely understand my gestures and confusion, but he was ada-mant. I finally got out my map to show him that I had already marked my route. He made me write everything down so he would have a summary of where and when I was on the trip. I complied, but he con-tinued his refusal to let me pass. After about an hour and a half of my insisting that I had not had an accident and his saying, "Car. Problem. Car. Accident," I took him out and showed him the car. There wasn't a scratch on it anywhere. Finally, he wrote something on a slip of paper in the Lithuanian language. He gave me that paper and then said, "Go." I quickly left and had no problem at the Latvian side of the border, and then I drove back to Riga and caught my plane back to the good old U.S.A.

That fall when school started, I took the paper to Reggie and asked him to translate it for me. He looked at it and laughed: "It says, 'You are to report to the police station at 9:00 Monday morning in Vilnius.'" I told him that I didn't think I would be going back over there, and I got a good chuckle out of it. I guess the border guard realized he had to do something with me, so he probably got permission from his authorities to tell me to report to the police station in Vilnius and let me go. My guess is that that since it was a rental car, some previous renter had been involved in an accident in Vilnius and did not report to court, and the company had repaired the damage to the car, but the charges still stood.

After that eventful summer, Louise and I left from Little Rock to fly to Uganda in December. We landed at Entebbe, spent the night there, and then went on to Jinja, where I stayed for a few days before going over to Mbale for the national meeting of the Churches of Christ. The church leaders all met at the church building, and many of the men and women slept in different parts of the building. But because Philip Shero and his family were out of town, Louise and I we were able to stay at their home in Mbale.

We enjoyed attending the lectures and worshipping with the brethren at Mbale. I spoke on the topic "Walking in Truth." Brethren came from all over the country, so I got to see a lot of missionaries as well as Ugandan Christians. They served several of their national dishes, prepared in a kitchen separate from the church building. There were three cooking areas with fires built from wood under big pots where people could cook large quantities of food like rice, beans, peas, and meat.

When I returned to Jinja, I observed the completion of the building that housed the Church of Christ, the Source Café, and other functions of the facility on Main Street. I also had the opportunity to teach at the Busoga Bible School while I was there for a couple of days. This was my second experience to teach there, and I had brought some materials to give to the brethren for them to take back to their villages to teach. My subject matter covered the Apostle Paul, his life, work, and his missionary journeys. We traveled to Rwanda, too, which was still recovering from the recent terrible genocide.

———————

I am grateful for the tremendous opportunities the Lord gave me to share with and gain ideas from other believers from diverse countries and cultures as we all seek to serve the Kingdom of God. I left every lectureship uplifted and encouraged about the many ways that God is using His various servants in every corner of the world to further the gospel, and humbled that I could be some small part of that beautiful work.

CHAPTER 22

AROUND THE WORLD AFTER 50 YEARS

O n May 27, 1993, Louise and I celebrated our fiftieth anniversary. Nothing seemed quite sufficient to me to celebrate everything our marriage and family represented, but since they meant the world to me, it seemed fitting to take Louise on a trip around the world. We left from Little Rock and flew to Los Angeles, boarded a plane to New Zealand, and made our first leg across the Pacific on a long but rewarding trip. We first stopped in Auckland on the north island of New Zealand, took a boat across the bay, rented a car, and enjoyed seeing part of the island. Then we went to the southern island and visited all the way south to Mount Cook, a national park, and across the island to Christchurch. New Zealand was a beautiful country – very green with lots of sheep and deer grazing on farms for exportation to Germany, where venison was dearly loved.

After New Zealand, we traveled to Brisbane, Australia, to the home of one of our students; we visited with his mother and sister and traveled through that area. We were planning to go up to the Great Barrier Reef, but I became ill and didn't get a chance to go. We did, however, get to go west to Toowoomba, the location of one of the Churches of Christ. We visited the building, which was being enlarged, and took the preacher and his wife out to lunch at a department store lunch counter, which felt like a step back in time, and we enjoyed Australian meat pies.

In Toowoomba, we saw people playing lawn bowling, where they would roll a special ball and try to get it as close to a target as they possibly could. They were all dressed in white – white clothes, white hats, white shoes – an interesting spectacle. Most of them were older people, and we enjoyed watching how good they were at lagging the ball up to the goal.

Of course, the Australians really love the outdoors and the sea, and we wanted to do the same. While there, we visited the Gold Coast, just about twenty-five miles south of Brisbane on the east coast. We also went west to one of the oldest and largest sheep farms in Australia, covering many thousands of acres. The farm was not raising many sheep at the time, but they did have some they used as examples to show people how they cared for and sheared the sheep.

We rented a car in Brisbane, and I temporarily forgot that, like the British, the Australians drive on the left side of the road. When I got in the car to drive, I thought, "What happened to the steering wheel? It's missing! And someone turned the rearview mirror." Then, it dawned on me that I was in the wrong seat. Thankfully, we went for almost five hundred miles and had no incidents, but I never could get completely comfortable driving on the left.

From Brisbane we traveled down to Sydney, one of the largest and oldest cities in Australia. It features a part of town which at one time served as the location for prisons for people who had been sent to Australia. Part of the old city still stands close by the great bridges, the department stores, and tall buildings, all by the waterfront.

We drove down to the capital city of Canberra. It's not directly on the coast, but about forty miles inland, and is much smaller than Sydney or Brisbane. The most interesting site to me was its relatively new parliament building, which sits partially underground. You can walk on the ground on top of the building.

From Australia, we flew to Singapore, where we stayed with David Hogan, his wife, and little daughter. I had visited Singapore before, and I found its mix of Chinese and English culture quite interesting. We were impressed by the country's cleanliness; there was no litter on the ground, and there was even a law against chewing gum. The government was restrictive in a sense, yet the country was very beautiful. We visited one of the museums representing World War II; Singapore held out a long time against the Japanese, but ultimately succumbed to them.

Singapore sits at the base of the Malaysian Peninsula, so we crossed over into Malaysia itself and visited a rubber and palm oil plantation. Those are two of the major products of the peninsula. We saw the rubber trees and could rub the white sap-like substance with our fingers, the heat from our bodies changing it from sticky liquid into rubber.

We next flew to Bangkok, Thailand, which I had visited in 1967. The traffic was terrible there; even at midnight, traffic was very congested. It was easy to get stuck and have to wait for a long time before we could move again. We decided instead to spend our time traveling around the countryside, visiting some of the many Buddhist and Hindu temples.

From Bangkok, Louise and I flew to New Delhi, India; neither of us had ever been to India before. Due to a flight delay, we arrived late at night, and we went to our hotel where we supposedly had a reservation. They had no room for us. I think since our plane was late getting in, they decided we weren't coming and sold the room to somebody else. The hotel suggested a rooming house just up the street to see if we could spend the night; they promised they would have a room for us the next day. Louise and I went outside and headed in the direction they told us, and we noticed bodies on the street. We almost stepped on them as we walked along. The night was so dark that we couldn't see clearly, but we knew there were dozens of people sleeping outside wherever we tried to step. We walked about a block and never could find the guest house they mentioned, so we went back to the hotel and told them that we would just have to spend the rest of the night sitting in the lobby until we could have a room.

It took until about 6:00 in the morning, but they finally did get some beds ready for us, and we walked up to the room. In the daylight I could look out of the window to see scores of people sleeping on pallets on the street. Since it was morning, the people were in the process of getting dressed, some of them bathing themselves, doing whatever they needed to do to be clean and ready to go to their work or other activities. I had imagined this scene on the previous night, as we were walking among them, but I had trouble grasping the full scope of it until I could see the whole thing. It was deeply sobering.

We visited with the preacher, whose name was Sunny David. Several members of his family also worked with the church in India. (His brother was a gifted musician who later visited Harding, as well as Lipscomb and Abilene, and really enjoyed being in America.)

There were many Muslims in India, as well as Hindus and Buddhists, which caused a great deal of conflict, especially in places like Delhi. We went through the Muslim section and saw some of the old city of Delhi, and they would tell us about some of the riots and problems that occurred. A lot of times it would start with the children, Muslims versus Hindus. Maybe some of the Hindus would throw a pig up on the steps of a mosque and desecrate it. Some of the Muslims, on the other hand, would kill a cow, sacred to the Hindus. The intentional antagonism was very sad.

Despite some of the religious clashes, India is a country full of beautiful memorials. We were able to see the tomb of Gandhi, whose body was cremated and the ashes spread in various places, including on the Ganges River, which is sacred to the people of India. We enjoyed seeing the many shrines to him to celebrate his pacifist approach to bringing freedom to India. On the day of our fiftieth wedding anniversary, May 27, 1993, Louise and I rented a car and a driver and went to Agra to see the Taj Mahal, which was built out of white marble between 1631 and 1653 by twenty thousand workers. It was a monument to love, commissioned by the Shah Jahan in honor of his wife, Mumtaz Mahal, who died at the age of thirty-eight, having giving birth to fourteen children. The Taj Mahal was a beautiful tomb with its intricate designs and engravings in the marble and its precious and semiprecious stones.

After leaving Agra, we went to Jaipur, "The Pink City," where the entire town is made of pink material. There is a palace of one of the Maharajas sitting high upon a hill, and tourists could actually ride up to the palace on an elephant. (We decided just to drive the car.) The building itself had an unusual layout with a common area in the middle, surrounded by all of the wives' individual quarters. The Maharaja only allowed his wives to come into the communal area in his presence in an effort to keep the peace between them.

From Delhi, we decided to fly to Kathmandu, Nepal, by Indian Airlines. I asked the clerk at the desk to reconfirm our reservation, and he told me that he had done so. Evidently, he didn't – because the plane left an hour early. We got out to the plane, but it had already closed its doors and moved out on the runway. There was no way that the plane would come back, so we had to wait until the next flight, which was not until the next morning. We caught the flight the following day, but Kathmandu is situated among the mountains, and the weather had turned bad in Nepal, so the plane couldn't land. The plane went back to Delhi, and we were told that we would be given a meal and a room at the hotel and would try to leave yet again at 8:00 the following morning. We had a real feast that night and went to bed, and then our phone rang around 5:00 in the morning. It was the airline calling us to say that the flight would be leaving early, and we needed to board the buses to the airport in just a few minutes. It was a rush, but we made it, and this time we flew to Nepal.

From Kathmandu we enjoyed going out into the countryside to see how the people lived in this little country. The area was filled with small farms, which people worked by hand. There were small rice paddies that were a little larger than my office at Harding. Most of the people were Hindu or Buddhist, but there was also a Church of Christ in Kathmandu, and the preacher came with his wife and two children to meet us at our hotel. We had dinner together and enjoyed our visit with them; I learned a great deal about religious practices in that part of the world. The preacher's father was a Hindu priest, and we discussed their worship rituals as we explored the city. We watched as worshippers kissed a big statue of a monkey which was, to them, one of their many gods. We also saw a temple dedicated to a young girl who was considered a goddess. She had been selected when she was very young, but she was probably twelve or thirteen now. The priests declared that she would never be allowed to marry, but when she reached the upper teens, they deposed her and put another young girl in her place. For a few cents you could see this young goddess in one of the temples. The preacher took us to the temple and paid the fee for us, and the mother of the young girl came out with her on the balcony. The "goddess" was eating a banana as she stood on the balcony a couple of minutes so that we could see her, and then she went back inside.

———————

When we left Nepal, we flew back to Delhi and then to London in order to catch a plane to Ukraine. We landed in Kiev, and there we took a train to Gorlovka, riding for seventeen hours in a dirty car on a very slow train that was made even slower by the fact that it kept stopping.

As we passed through the countryside, we noticed that the areas near the track were cultivated with little vegetable gardens, but there were no cattle roaming in the fields and no fences anywhere. People lived in villages and went out and worked on the collective or state farms. The government allowed the farmers a little plot of ground to work for themselves, the proceeds of which they could keep for themselves, but basically this area was a collective or communist type of agriculture.

Gorlovka was a city of about 400,000 people. A small Church of Christ had been established there with about fifty members, but the preacher had to leave to come back to the States for a while and wanted more experienced Christians to work there in his absence. He did not want to leave the new converts in Christ without guidance. Louise and I were there to spend the month of June with the congregation. At first we stayed at a hotel, a four-story building, which was not very commodious but met our needs. The sponsoring church in America had asked us to find an apartment and furnish it for the preachers who would come behind us to help the Gorlovka church. We eventually found an apartment just a couple of blocks away from the hotel on the corner of a main street and near where the church met. It was a good location for our purpose. We did our best to outfit the apartment, but we ate at the restaurant in the hotel not only while we were staying in the hotel but even after we were in the apartment, because of the difficulty of cooking. We were in Gorlovka for thirty days, and we had only potatoes, tomatoes, cabbage, and cucumbers. No gravy, no butter, and no dressing. I love all of those vegetables, but there weren't many calories in them. There were no cakes, pies, or ice cream, but we were served a candy bar for dessert. Since we were walking anywhere from three to six miles a day, I managed to lose thirteen pounds in that month, which was nice. It was much more difficult to keep it off when I returned home.

Furnishing the apartment was difficult. In fact, when we moved in it, there wasn't much there; just about everything had been taken out by the previous tenant. There was no telephone or water heater, and there was only one little couch that wasn't as wide as our couches here in America. But it was enough room for one person to sleep. It was a Saturday night when we arrived that the apartment, and, since I was going to preach the next day, my wife suggested that I spend the first half of the night on the couch, and she would sleep on an old, folded-up carpet that had been left there. Then, we would swap in the middle of the night. I started the night on the couch, and she finished the night on the couch. That Sunday at church we mentioned that we didn't have but that one couch on which to sleep, and someone said, "My dad has a little cot, a little, metal folding bed, and we just live a block from you. We would be happy for you to use it while you need it." So we agreed, and that Sunday afternoon I got the cot and carried it over to the apartment. It was a little fold-up metal bed with a light spring, and a little thin mattress. I couldn't sleep on it because I was too heavy, but Louise could. So, I slept on the couch and she slept on that little bed. That afternoon, I also went to the marketplace, which was open on Sundays but not on Mondays. When I was visiting the marketplace, I happened to see a single mattress for sale. The store would not deliver, so I had no way of taking it with me that Sunday afternoon. On Tuesday I walked about a mile and a half to the marketplace with Victor Parahkin, a young man who was learning how to preach. He took one end of the mattress, and I took the other end, and we carried it down Main Street to our apartment. It was so nice to have that mattress. We put it on the floor, but it was better than the couch, so Louise got to sleep on the mattress instead of the cot.

People had only recently been permitted to come into the country to preach, and the effects of Communist rule were still apparent. People had money, but there were no goods to buy. Whenever you found something, you had better get it fast because you may never find it again. I remember one time finding a jar of pickles, which I love, and so I bought it. I kept looking again for another jar but never found one. This was true of so many things. We had no sheets or pillowcases and no pillows. We never did find a pillow during the whole time we were there. Finally, just before we left Gorlovka, I was walking down a sidewalk and saw a pair of sheets and pillowcases on a table. Many times, people with goods that they wanted to sell would just put them on a table near the street and sell them, so they could make a little money. Toilet paper was something that you seldom could find. I found some just before we left. I saw a little boy out in front of a grocery store, sitting there with a cloth on the ground, and he had couple of rolls of toilet paper for sale. It was cheap. He probably made a penny or two in resale off the toilet paper, which was brown, rough, and coarse, but usable. We bought milk out on the street. A big tank full of milk would drive up, and people would line up behind it with their buckets, glass jars, or bottles; they would take it from a spigot at the end of the tank. I don't know if it was pasteurized, but I doubt it. Certainly, it was not sanitized, and people would just carry their milk home any way they could.

We could find fruits and vegetables fairly easily – at least, those that were in season. Apples were not the kinds that we have in America. Ukrainian apples were little scrawny things, and that's all they had. Canned goods were costly – a can of corn sold for more than a dollar. Anything that was processed or imported was very expensive. Only the local goods would be cheap. We finally got a telephone after a couple of weeks as well as hot water and enough dishes. We had to go twenty-five miles to Donetsk to find a kitchen knife because there were none anywhere in Gorlovka.

While we were there, Victor, the young man who helped me carry the mattress, did some preaching along with me. His teeth protruded a great deal, and he was very self-conscious of it, which made him shy. He didn't visit with the members of the church when they would come to service. He would just sit down after preaching and never talk to anyone, and so one day I said, "Victor, you know, it would be really great if you would be a little friendlier to the people who are coming. Meet them when they came to the door and say, 'Welcome! We are happy to have you.'"

He looked at me confused and said, "Why should I? They should come to church just like I do."

I agreed with him that they should, but I wanted to encourage him to be a little friendlier to the people in attendance. I think standing up in front of a crowd and preaching must have scared him enough for one day, so the thought of talking one-on-one with people was more than his bashfulness could handle.

While I was preaching at Gorlovka, we had some people who wanted to be baptized. There was no baptistery because the church was just renting a room in a school building, so we decided to have the baptism in our bathroom. Louise and I knew when the members were coming in the afternoon, so we were going to have water for them ready in the big tub. We turned the water on, and after about five minutes it quit. We were not able to get any more water, so when the people came we told them the situation and said we would just have to wait. Fortunately, after a little while, the water turned on again, and we filled up the tub. A mother, a father, and their two teenagers were baptized that day. We had already had several young teenagers or those in their early twenties baptized while I was there, but this lady was bigger than I was. She was really heavy, and I was worried about baptizing her. We baptized the young ones first – the boy and girl were no problem. Then, the daddy was baptized, and he was no problem because he was small enough; but when it was the lady's turn, she filled up the whole tub, and when I pushed her under, even though I did it gently, the water splashed out over me and over the floor. But she was under the water, and we all celebrated that happy day together.

The church was made up mostly of women, some children, and a few young men. Many of them were students. A technical school and a language school were near our meeting place. One Saturday afternoon I was in a little grocery store getting some bread. I pointed to a loaf of bread and said, "I would like a loaf of the bread." The lady didn't understand English, but she saw me point to the bread, and she brought it to me. When I started to leave, two young men – a tall, blond man and a shorter, dark-haired man – came up to me. The short one, whose name was Val (the other was named Andy) said, "We speak English."

I gave them my name and told them that I was visiting there in Gorlovka. After a little bit Val said, "I believe in Jesus."

"Great! I believe in Jesus, too," I replied. "In fact, I am preaching here tomorrow afternoon at the language school." They were both students at the language school and both studying English. I invited them to come to the service the next day.

Val added, "I have written to a preacher in America to get me a Bible."

There are an awful lot of preachers in American, but just to make conversation, I asked, "Who was the preacher?"

"Eddie Cloer."

I had to laugh. "Eddie Cloer teaches with us at Harding University and lives just two doors down from my daughter in Searcy." We talked for a while, and the next day they came to the service and listened as I preached. I gave them each a Bible and they had me inscribe the Bibles for them.

When we finished working in Gorlovka, we took the long train ride back to Kiev and then flew to London and to the United States. It was wonderful trip around the world for our fiftieth wedding anniversary, but it was also very good to be back home again in our own beds with our own food, friends, and loved ones.

I have always been grateful for the experiences God has given to Louise and me in our many travels. Our time in Ukraine that summer had much more significance to us than just a tourist visit, and I decided I wanted to return the following year to see how the country and the people were growing.

It had not been easy to find goods and supplies in 1993. When I went back just one year later, things had changed – but now there was a new issue. There were many more goods, but the real problem in 1994 was that the people in Gorlovka had no money. Their salaries were low, and the pensions for the older people were very little. Even those that were employed often didn't get their salaries for as long as five months after they should have been paid. There were many coal mines in the area of Gorlovka, so mining was the main type of available work, but there was an oversupply of coal, and they had a hard time selling it. Therefore, the companies didn't have enough money to pay the miners.

During that year I corresponded with both Andy and Val. Val was single. Andy was married and had a little boy, perhaps six or eight months old. On my next visit to Ukraine, I met Val first and saw he had really studied his Bible. It was all marked up, and he knew many scriptures. In fact, I would quote a part of a scripture, and he could finish it for me. He said, "I want to be baptized." We talked for a little while, and I felt excited about his decision. We called Victor, the young man who was still preaching there, and I had Victor baptize Val because I felt it would be better for the local man to do the baptizing.

Andy didn't visit me at first; in fact, it was several days before I got to see him. When he finally did come, we talked and visited for a good while. About 10:00 at night when he was getting ready to leave, he suddenly said, "Why did you come back to Gorlovka?"

I replied, "Well, I have come back to baptize you and Val, and I am halfway through." He looked at me kind of funny. He wasn't baptized then, but just a short time later that same summer someone from Memphis, Tennessee, was visiting and working with the church, and Andy was baptized as well. Both of those young men became preachers of the gospel. Val attended the preacher training program at Gorlovka and was the top student in the class of about twenty. Later, he was asked to move to Russia to preach at a small congregation, which he did. Andy went on down to Torrez, and he became the preacher for the church in Torrez. Both of these young men came to America eventually. Andy studied for a degree in economics in Memphis, and Val (who was now married with several children) worked with his wife in New York City and attended the church there.

It was amazing to me that something as simple as connecting by chance with two young men while I was attempting to buy a loaf of bread ended up being a moment that led to the spread of the gospel in Eastern Europe. God never wastes an opportunity, and I am very grateful to have been one small instrument through which He accomplished His will in that part of the world.

———————

On March 8, 1995, Louise and I flew to Istanbul, Turkey. We landed late in the evening and picked up our rented car to drive to our hotel. I had the address, but we were not able to find the building. We turned onto one-way streets and kept driving over and over again past the place where the hotel was supposed to be. Finally, we looked up and saw a tall building several blocks over to the left that had the initials of the hotel on top. We figured out how to get over there and, sure enough, it was our hotel. To get in, however, we had to go through security checkpoints, like at the airport.

We visited several mosques and took a boat ride up the Bosporus River, and we enjoyed seeing the homes near its banks. Most of the homes in Istanbul were masonry, but on the river there were some beautiful wooden houses, which were a rarity, because wood is so scarce in that part of the world.

When we left Istanbul, we drove down the coast into southern Turkey, visiting Biblical places we really wanted to see, like Troas, where Paul left to begin his journey into Europe. Troas had been called Truva earlier, and Troy before that. A replica of the famous Trojan horse stands in Troas now. From there, we went to see the locations of the seven churches of Asia in varying stages of excavation. Pergamum was one of the first we visited, and after we had been there a day or two, we hired a young man to go with us to some of the other locations. He had his own tourist agency, and he also had an uncle who owned a restaurant. We went to the restaurant, and I had soup made of the brains and cheek jowls of a sheep. I took one bite of it and didn't really care for it, so I let Louise eat it. I decided to have a gyro instead, which was mutton cooked and sliced thin and prepared like a wrap sandwich here in the United States. It was very good – better than the brain soup, anyway.

Izmir is now the name of the city that was called Smyrna in the days of the New Testament. The remains of old Smyrna are almost gone, with only the *agora*, or marketplace, remaining of the ancient city. Izmir is now a great port city and is situated on hills at the edge of the Aegean Sea.

We enjoyed Turkey, and from there we traveled to Albania. Ellen Ruth Walker, a friend from Searcy, was a missionary in Tirana and still lives there. Albania is a very poor country, and for a long time it was under Enver Hoxha, a communist dictator, who was the most rabid anti-Christian of any of the eastern European communists. In fact, the constitution of his country even carried the death penalty for those who practiced Christianity. He tried to make the people believe that the United States was going to invade Albania; as a result, he installed thousands of "pill boxes," small concrete structures along the seashore, so the people would have a place to fire at the invaders. These pill boxes all faced in the same direction, to the west, and Hoxha used them as a tool for keeping control over the Albanians and making them think that the Americans were their great enemy. There are now churches throughout Albania, so I guess Christianity proved stronger than communism in the end.

―――――――

When we returned home from that trip, I found myself reflecting on all of the incredible places we had visited and the people we had met – not just on that adventure, but throughout our lives. I could not have done it without my beautiful bride at my side, nor would I have wanted to do so. Apart from my salvation, Louise was the greatest gift God gave me in this life, and I am grateful for everything she made possible through her patience, steadfastness, support, and love.

CHAPTER 23

EASTERN EUROPE

My interest in the welfare and politics of eastern Europe was as strong as ever as the Iron Curtain began to fall and many former communist countries began to shake off their oppressive governments.

In the summer of 1990 Louise and I flew to Vienna, Austria, where we joined Mike and Molly Dawidow as well as Rubel Shelly and his son, Tim. The six of us then made a trip in the Dawidows' van to several different countries. First, we drove from Vienna to Bratislava and Prague, both in Czechoslovakia, and then returned to Vienna. After that, we drove south and east to other eastern European countries, beginning in Budapest, Hungary and continuing on to Romania, which had recently been freed from the dictator Ceaușescu – by execution. Just over the border we had stopped for some gasoline and were taking pictures. A man came up to me and said, "We have freedom here in Romania. Before the fall of Ceaușescu, we could not even talk to you, but now we have freedom. Those people down in Bucharest are not going to take it away from us." That word, "freedom," was the most common word we heard in Romania.

We experienced a fairly large earthquake while we were in Bucharest, and about eighty aftershocks throughout the day and the night afterwards. One of the worst was at about 3:20 in the morning. I happened to be awake, and suddenly the bed began to shake. I shook my wife and said, "Louise, Louise – it's another earthquake." In fact, I did that twice, and she didn't even budge, she was sleeping so deeply. Finally, I thought, "Oh, forget it. We are on the fifteenth floor of a building. It either goes down or it doesn't." I walked out to the window and looked out. The city was still standing and so was our hotel, so I went back to sleep.

In Romania, we visited some orphanages to assess what the children needed and how our church could help. The government didn't have enough money to take care of these children, and most of the time their parents were alive but too poor to feed them. One of the places we visited housed very young children, up to two years old, and they were each in a bed. Often, the bed and their clothes reeked of urine. The children stood in the bed, rocking back and forth with blank looks on their faces.

Later, we went to another orphanage on the outskirts of the city where Mike had previously taken toys, food, and medicine. When we entered the orphanage grounds officials told us, "Don't touch the children. They have ringworm and lice in their hair, so please don't touch them." When we walked inside the gate, we saw the children, about seventy-two of them, seated on benches alongside the sidewalk. They were very quiet, but when we got close to them, they jumped up, ran over to us, and put their arms around our legs, they were so desperate for love. Louise broke out into welts because of the shock of the experience. We talked about those children all the rest of that trip and made plans to help get them a washing machine, food, clothing, and a bunch of shoes. It was heartbreaking to want to do more but to feel overwhelmed by the degree of need.

We continued as a group through Bulgaria and Yugoslavia (which dissolved just two years later), then Louise and I traveled on our own to East Berlin to see how much had been accomplished in the thirty-three years since our first visit in 1957. East Berlin had gone through a great deal of rebuilding. It was not comparable to the growth and development of West Berlin, but it was much improved.

The congregations in Romania had been wanting to give a little more credence to their work and to get a little more publicity, so I flew back over in November of 1991 to lecture at some of the universities about the American way of life – freedom, democracy, private enterprise economy, and America's history. I was to be part of a five-day program at some of the universities where I would have a couple of hours each day to speak to the students who understood English.

I first traveled to Sibiu, where I lectured from 10:00 to 12:00 each morning for five days to about forty-five university students. I enjoyed speaking with the young people. They were all older teenagers, and they knew English well enough that they could understand me, so I did not have to have an interpreter.

My first night in Sibiu, I was staying in a private home in a basement room with a television set, and I turned it on to find Dallas with J.R. Ewing. I had never seen an episode of Dallas, so I didn't know much about the program except what I had heard about it in the United States; but I learned that Ceaușescu, the now-defunct dictator, had stopped showing the program because he had to pay royalties to get it. After his death, Romania started showing it again three times a week in the evening, and it was all the rage. The next day, knowing the students all watched Dallas, I began my lecture by stating, "My name is Clifton Ganus, Jr. I was born in Hillsboro, Texas, which is very close to Dallas, Texas." Immediately, a shout came up from the room from several of the students: "Dallas! J.R. Ewing! J.R. Ewing!" They had been watching the show and loved it. So I was already a celebrity.

After leaving Sibiu, I went to Cluj-Napoca, where I lectured at a university that prepared medical doctors and nurses. I enjoyed staying in an apartment owned by a local family, and I tried to talk to them about Jesus and the Bible – I spent a good bit of time at it, in fact – but without a good response. Many of the people did not believe in God because they had been brainwashed for decades by the communists, and it was sad to see the results. Still, I enjoyed my time in Cluj – especially the food. There was a hotel restaurant where I could have a full meal for the equivalent of about $2.50.

After that, I went to Bucharest, where I spoke at the University of Bucharest. We had more trouble getting me in there than at these other places, but at least I was scheduled to lecture. The Sunday preceding the day I was to speak, I went to a church that met in an old theater building. There were probably sixty or seventy people there, including Russ and Rosemary Burcham, who, along with some others, were doing short-term mission work in collaboration with Dale and Imogene McAnulty. I preached that morning, and during my sermon I became very dizzy. On the brink of passing out, I asked for a chair. The members brought me one and I finished my lesson. It turned out that I had contracted the flu, and that was not even the biggest challenge of the week. I was staying at the apartment of some church members who were in the north of Bucharest while the husband worked on a dam for the government, and I managed to get myself back to the house. But that night it snowed and snowed for twenty-four hours until it was over thirty inches deep. I didn't even get out of the apartment at all on Monday, and unfortunately, I had to cancel at the university because of my illness. I got well later that week and then flew back home. As I was flying back on December 15, 1991, Dr. Benson died at the age of ninety-three.

I arrived in time for his funeral, and it was a beautiful celebration of his incredible work and legacy, but also sad in that marked the end of an era in many ways. Still, I was glad he lived long enough to see communism begin to crumble in Europe, since that was a cause dear to both of our hearts.

On May 20, 1996, I flew back to Ukraine to work with the churches in Gorlovka and Torez. I went by bus to Torez, about sixty miles from Gorlovka, where my friend Andy – one of the young men I had met during my visit in 1993 – was now preaching for a small church of thirty or forty members. I stayed in an apartment owned by the church on the fifth floor of a school building and had an opportunity to visit with one of the ladies who was working with the Bible camps in the summertime.

While I was there, I went to Andy's home to eat with him after the service. He was living by himself at the time because, tragically, his wife had left him and taken their little son, because Andy was a Christian and she wasn't. Andy was staying at his grandmother's little half-acre farm, where he had a garden at the rear of a small, run-down house. Andy fixed us a meal of spaghetti with fried eggs on top. We also had very good pickled tomatoes that he had made the previous fall. He had a few chickens, which meant he had his own eggs, and a few vegetables. My heart hurt for him, since I knew he was going through an extremely rough time, but I did find it interesting to see how an average person lived in Torez.

The following year, I traveled to Ukraine again, this time to work on a campaign in Donetsk and to speak for the churches in Gorlovka and Torez. I stayed with an elderly widow in Gorlovka; she was a retired schoolteacher living on a pension of $27 a month. She spoke only a few words of English, and I didn't know many words of Russian, but we managed to get along and she was very kind. I tried to take all my meals away from her home so she did not feel obligated to feed me, but every evening when I came back, she would make me eat something. Even though I would tell her I was up to my neck in food and didn't need anything, she still cooked and basically growled at me until I cleaned my plate.

I preached at the church in Gorlovka and then went to Torez by bus. I was supposed to preach, but when I arrived I found out that since I had been invited by the church to preach in Donetsk but not officially invited to preach at Gorlovka or Torez in the same manner, I was being watched to make sure I did not overstep. Previously when I had been over there, I could preach anywhere at any time with no question, but now they were reinterpreting the law differently, so I could not preach unless I was explicitly invited to preach at each individual place. I was supposed to check in with the religious arm of the government when I arrived, but because my bus didn't get there until Saturday afternoon they were closed, so I couldn't take care of it. On Monday, David Ingram went to the office to check for me, and the officials asked, "Where is he?"

"Oh, he's gone over to Gorlovka," he replied.

"Why did he go to Gorlovka?" they demanded. "He should have checked in here before that." So, Ingram called me and told me that I was in trouble, and the guy had told him that I had better not preach in Gorlovka or Torez. At that point, I had already preached in Gorlovka, so there was nothing I could do about it, but I decided that I would not preach in Torez even though I was planning on it.

I did not want to do anything that would get anybody else in trouble, so I only led communion in Torez rather than preaching. Still, it was a joy to be with the brethren and to have lunch with them. In fact, we went out to a park and had a picnic, and while we were there a lady wanted to be baptized. There was only a dirty little lake, but she had her sins washed away in that murky water.

After visiting Torez I went back to Donetsk, where I was scheduled to preach and speak twice in a lectureship the church was hosting while a campaign group from Texas was visiting. I stayed with David and Janette Ingram and enjoyed meeting the other brethren in Donetsk. The church was meeting in a hall that had pictures of World War II on the walls in honor of the people who had died in what they called the "Great War for National Liberation." The church had a good group meeting there, probably sixty or seventy, and the singing was very good. There were a number of young people, and it was good to visit with them, too, to get a glimpse of the next generation of church leaders.

———

In the summer of 1998, Cliff III was planning to take his Chorus to sing in eastern and northern Europe – Poland, Ukraine, Russia, and Finland – and asked if Louise and I would be interested in going.

The Chorus sang at the technical university in Gdańsk and presented an evening concert at the Sopot Church of Christ building. The building was not yet complete but was well under way, and everyone was interested to see how the acoustics would be. It turned out that the acoustics were very good for the concert, and everyone was really pleased. The Chorus also performed at the Catholic Church building in Gdańsk, which was the home congregation of former Polish President Lech Wałęsa – a significant figure in world politics who came to speak at Harding as part of the American Studies program just two years later.

The following day, on Monday, I went with Mike Dawidow and Cliff to meet the mayor of Sopot, and I was able to present a letter to him signed by Harding President David Burks, the mayor of Searcy, one of our Congressman, and Senator Tim Hutchinson from Arkansas. The purpose of the letter was to help the relationship of the Sopot government and the Church of Christ in that city. There had been some suspicion on the part of the government about the new building and what it would mean to the city. The reception was very good, and the local church members were encouraged by the presentation of the letter.

After leaving Sopot, the Chorus sang in the southern part of Poland at Kraków in a very old Catholic church building. From there, we went to Kiev, and after a tour of the city the Chorus sang a joint concert with the choir of the St. Alexander's Church in Kiev. There was an excellent crowd of about 550 people, and they gave a very fine reception to the Chorus. In fact, every audience we sang for was amazed at how well the Harding Chorus sang.

From Kiev, we went to Moscow and arrived about 3:30 in the morning at the hotel. Our bus driver, who was with us the entire trip, did a wonderful job in getting us safely to our destination despite the long hours of driving late into the night. On Sunday, May 31, we met with the church in Moscow and sang for the members there in a brief presentation.

When the service was over, I asked if anyone had heard of Yarnell's Ice Cream because I knew that even though it was produced in Searcy it was being sold in Moscow and St. Petersburg. About ten hands went up. They were very familiar with Yarnell's, which was so much better than the Russian ice cream and considered a gourmet dessert. They told me where to go to find Yarnell's, and I bought a pint of Death by Chocolate. It cost me about $3.25, whereas we would get it in Searcy for $.99, but it was very good and tasted like home.

From Moscow, we went to Dubna, which was a secret town during World War II. People were forbidden to enter the town unless they lived there because they were producing rockets, while most people thought they were just producing baby buggies. Secretly, there was a large nuclear accelerator in Dubna, one of the biggest in the world. For years, the Russian people themselves didn't know what was taking place in this small town deep into the woods north of Moscow. One of our Harding students was from Dubna, and we had a very warm welcome as the people came out when we arrived by bus. They met us with their traditional bit of bread and salt, which was a symbol of welcome. There were approximately three hundred people each at the first and second concerts at the House of Culture, and about 180 at the Bolshoi Volga performance. While we were in Dubna, we also met some of the largest, most aggressive mosquitoes that we saw on the whole trip.

We departed Dubna about 8:00 a.m. on Saturday and drove all day to St. Petersburg. We arrived at our residence in that city to find we were staying at a subpar hotel with absolutely no hot water. The running water was frigid, and we were all reluctant to take a shower. I finally took a cold shower because I really needed it, and I survived, but it was brutal. We were happy to stay only three days there.

We managed to have a church service together at the hotel on Sunday morning and then visited the Hermitage Museum. At 4:00 p.m., the Chorus presented a concert at the Beloselskiy-Belozerskiy Palace, with approximately two hundred in attendance, and the performance was very well received. The Chorus also sang at an arts magnet school, where they were joined by three of the school's singing groups. We were able to visit the Peter and Paul Fortress at St. Petersburg and the Peterhof Palace, that had been constructed by Peter the Great and had beautiful gardens.

The Chorus gave an evening concert in Lomonosov, near the Peterhof Palace. We met several of the church members there, including one of the young men that we had helped to baptize in the city of Gorlovka in Ukraine. He and his wife had moved to St. Petersburg, where he was preaching. His wife was pregnant, and later we found out that they had a little boy.

Early the next morning we left for Tampere, Finland. Arnold Pylkas, the former swimming coach at Harding, and his wife had been working in the city for several years and had started a church there. When we got to Tampere, we met the Pylkases and also a young lady named Hanna who became a very important person in our lives. She was Finnish, and her father owned four McDonald's stores in Tampere, one of them downtown. We ate there, and it was a good treat to have some typical American food. Hanna was our guide while there as well as our interpreter; later, Hanna came to Harding, stayed a few weeks and took a course. She was baptized in the fountain on Harding's campus.

We were well received at Tampere and had an opportunity to go out to Viikinsaari Island, where the Chorus had a concert that had been arranged by the city's Cultural Affairs Director. The Chorus also sang in the children's ward of a local hospital. It was a very rewarding experience.

On Saturday, the Chorus had time to do some shopping in Tampere before their concert that evening at the Tampere Cathedral. On Sunday evening, the Chorus performed a concert at the Hervanta Lutheran church building and had an excellent crowd before catching a flight to Helsinki and then back to the United States.

Louise and I still hadn't had enough of eastern Europe, though, so in June 2003 we made yet another trip, visiting several countries that were part of the former Yugoslavia. In Zagreb, Croatia, Mladen Jovanivich was the preacher and served as our gracious host. We stayed for two nights in Zagreb at the church building, which had been a private home at one point. It was three stories tall, and the sleeping quarters were on the third floor, up winding steps where it was difficult to maneuver a suitcase. In the building downstairs, they had a Bible study, a preacher training program, and church services. We took the train from Zagreb through Slovenia and on to Trieste in northern Italy, before visiting with the workers at Avanti Italia, a ministry in Scandicci, just outside of Florence, where native English speakers teach English using the Bible. I loved witnessing the progress of so many of these new nations as well as supporting and encouraging the Christians who had served the Lord so faithfully through so many years of governmental persecution and difficulty.

In 2012 Cliff decided to take his Chorus to sing in several Eastern European countries; he asked me if I would be interested in going with him, and I immediately said yes. I was excited to go back to see the people that I had taught several years before.

Once again, I was deeply impressed by our Harding students, both for their talents and their hearts for sharing the word of God with the world.

We traveled to Germany, Ukraine, Romania, Hungary, Slovakia, Austria, and the Czech Republic. I loved visiting with the church in Gorlovka, since it had been almost ten years since Louise and I had worked with the church there. In 1993 the church was meeting in a school auditorium; recently, however, they had been able to acquire a nice two-story building, which was used not only for church services but also as a school. I took the preacher and one of the ladies who worked in the building to lunch before we went to the program that afternoon. We used public transportation, which was a trolley car, and enjoyed our lunch together. Our program was at a beautiful old movie theater called the Shakhtar Palace. When I arrived, I had wonderful surprise: the lady who arranged for the program and was our translator and guide had been a five-year-old girl in 1993 in our Sunday school class. She remembered our being there many years before, and her father, who had been very much opposed to the church during our earlier time there, had become a Christian and was now a faithful preacher of the gospel. It was certainly good to visit with her again.

The next Sunday we sang in Odessa, where we visited and worshipped with our brethren. The church there had split some years before, and the preacher, whose name was Misha, had hoped that the Chorus's visit would help bring them back together again. Two of the groups did meet together, and I pray they have a better relationship now because of the singing of our young people and the joy of the occasion.

The next day, there was a very long drive to Romania, plus several hours at the Moldova border, and we arrived in Bucharest about 11:30 in the evening. Much of the next day was spent visiting and sightseeing in Bucharest, and that evening the Chorus participated in a joint concert at the Orthodox School with two of the local choruses. One was a professional cathedral choir, and the other was a male choir from a theological academy. Both of them were very good, but (of course) I felt that our Chorus was even better. It was a very congenial evening.

There were several performances in Hungary and then we pushed on to Bratislava, Slovakia, where we found that our hotel was more than just a hotel – it was a boat on the Danube River.

When the Chorus arrived the next day at the Jesuit church building where they were to perform, more than three hundred people were present. The priest in charge wanted the Chorus to sing only music that would be appropriate for the occasion, so they sang all of the sacred songs that they knew in different languages, which took just about an hour, and then they sang, "The Lord Bless You and Keep You." The audience was enthralled with the singing and followed them outside and wanted them to sing some more. Outside they lined up along the church building and sang secular songs for another twenty minutes or more. It was a great evening, and everyone enjoyed it – both the Chorus and the audience.

As the trip wrapped up with stops in Vienna and Prague, I marveled at how much had changed during my lifetime and what opportunities were available for our students now that I never would have dreamt we could do while I was still president of Harding. I am so grateful that I had the chance not only to see eastern Europe shake off many constraints of its history, but that young people now can travel there with messages of hope, healing, and the good news with a freedom that once seemed impossible.

CHAPTER 24

HUG

L ouise and I had the distinct pleasure of visiting several of Harding's overseas campuses a number of times, including the campus in Greece (HUG). In November 2000, Jeff Hopper, the dean of Harding's International Programs, asked if I would be interested in teaching the upcoming semester at HUG. At first, I said, "Oh no, I don't think that I could." But Jeff said they needed someone to go, and he thought it would be great if I would be able to make the trip. Don Shackelford and his wife were going, and Don would direct the program as well as teach, but they needed another teacher. I would think about it. Almost immediately after I got home that evening, I received a call from Don Shackelford, saying he would love for me to go. After thinking over the decision and choosing what courses I might like to teach, I agreed.

One class would deal with the apostle Paul, his life, writings, and journeys. Another class would cover Greek culture and history. And, lastly, I would teach American History up to 1887. Once I made the decision to go, I immediately purchased books to prepare for all three of the courses. I did an awful lot of studying and preparation through the rest of November and December while getting ready for the trip in January. I had not taught the course on Paul and his journeys for the last fifty years. I had taught American History ten years previously, but I had never taught the course about Greece, its history, and culture. Getting ready to teach those three courses took quite a bit of preparation.

At the start of the term, we flew over to Greece, landing at the airport in Glyfada, a southern suburb of Athens. Then Louise and I traveled about forty minutes to the little town of Porto Rafti, which was on the Aegean Sea, approximately twenty-five miles southeast of downtown Athens. Normally, it had about ten thousand people, but in the summertime it swelled exponentially because it was a sea-side resort. Porto Rafti means "the port of tailors," and a small island stands a couple of miles off of Porto Rafti's coast that hosts a large statue of a tailor, built in tribute for the workers of Porto Rafti's origins and namesake.

Harding had recently purchased the Artemis, a seven-year-old resort hotel in Porto Rafti, to house the students and provide educational facilities. Located on the main street of Porto Rafti, Harding's new resort hotel was a beautiful building with accommodating apartments, designed perfectly for our students. Stepping out of the front door of the Artemis, I could see a tall mountain, accessible for climbing – for the students at least. (I tried climbing this mountain once, and after I made the trek a third of the way, the briars on the trails discouraged me from going higher.) We had a vineyard across the street from our building, where during our time from January to early May we watched the vines as they turned green and as they grew grapes to about the size of peas before we headed back home. I was sorry we weren't able to see them through to harvest in the fall, but it was certainly very interesting to watch them grow.

Right next door to the villa was a public school with an outdoor basketball court where our students could play. The school also had a fitness club, and Harding enrolled all of our students and staff in the club so that we could use the machines, treadmills, and weights almost any time, even on Sunday afternoons. It was nice to go next door and try to stay in some kind of shape. Of course, we did a lot of walking while we were there, which helped with that, too.

Harding's building not only housed our students, but it had four businesses in the front part of the building on the ground floor. One was a very nice bakery with beautiful pastries. There were also a woman's boutique and a barber shop for men and women. Goody's, a restaurant somewhat like a Wendy's, stood on the other side of the building's entrance. Headquartered in Thessalonica, Goody's restaurants had locations all over Greece. They served hamburgers and other sandwiches, spaghetti, salads, and ice cream. It was one of the two restaurants that catered some of our meals for the students and staff.

Each apartment had its own kitchen, and we prepared or purchased our own breakfasts, evening meals, and Sunday meals. Six days a week we all ate a late lunch together at 2:00 p.m. This lunch was catered on Tuesday, Thursday, and Saturday by Goody's and on Monday, Wednesday, and Friday by a restaurant across the street that had a large grill where they cooked beef, pork, chicken, or lamb.

The building has three stories. The four businesses occupied most of the first floor, but the middle entrance leads to the reception desk, the visitors' waiting area, and, to one side, a large room that was once an office but now serves as classroom for about forty people, with desks, projector equipment, and a blackboard. Farther in are large, well-furnished living, game, and dining rooms, the latter seating almost one hundred people – all with beautiful marble floors. Greece has sixteen different kinds of marble, but it does not have much wood, so wood is usually quite expensive. But in this building, we had some beautiful wooden wall panels. When Harding bought the facility, they purchased everything: sheets, towels, dishes, pots and pans, furniture, TVs, telephones – the works. The owner, who was past retirement age, was tired of operating a resort hotel, so he handed over the key and walked out. I loved discovering that the hotel had secret rooms. We could open panels in the walls and find rooms full of dishes, furniture, and equipment.

The area behind the hotel is walled, for security and privacy, with a large swimming pool fourteen feet deep at one end. There is also a large round stage where programs can be presented. We occasionally had chapel out there, surrounded by beautiful flowers and shrubs. There were dressing rooms for the swimming pool and an additional house for the caretaker.

Steve and Debbie Stamatis lived and worked at the building. Vicky Tsakou, a friendly young evangelical woman, worked behind the desk. Parascos, also an evangelical, was the caretaker who looked after the building. Joanna was the cleaning lady who also did the laundry for the students and staff. We also had a man who worked the desk at night. Leaving the property unattended in that area was dangerous, so we had someone attending the desk at all times. Since the building had once been a hotel, people were always stopping by to try to rent a room, not knowing it had been changed to a Harding University campus. The staff put up big signs, but visitors still walked in or made calls to reserve a room.

Joyce Shackelford was our unofficial cook, and from time to time she made tacos or other delicious food for the students. Occasionally at night there would be leftovers, and the students would come in the dining area to eat, but we usually ate our evening meal in our rooms. There were several bakeries close by, so we could buy sandwiches or almost anything we desired. Greek gyros were favorites of the students and staff. Mrs. Shackelford baked a cake every time someone had a birthday. Louise and I had birthdays while we were there, and we had birthday cakes big enough to feed everyone. Occasionally, she made a cake that she called the "unbirthday" cake. It wasn't anybody's birthday, but she just wanted to make a cake. We were always happy when she did so.

Our classes, which met every day, were one and a half hours long, which allowed us to get in all of the required work. We had classes six days a week while we were on the campus, but when we were traveling, which was a lot, we did not have any classes. Every once in a while we would have a day off, but not very often, so we were kept pretty busy studying, teaching, or traveling. There were twenty-eight students – sixteen girls and twelve boys – in the group. That made a pretty good mix; and out of this group, incidentally, came two marriages.

On Sundays, the students were free to go into Athens to shop in the *plaka* or to visit in museums, and at 6:00 in the evening we would meet for the church service downtown at the church building near Omonoia Square. The Greek group met in the morning at 11:00, in the late afternoon they had a Bible study, then came our evening English service. The church building was well used. Dino Roussos was the regular preacher, but I preached some, and so did Don Shackelford and others who visited occasionally. It was an English-speaking service, but there were many different languages represented. One evening for the Lord's Supper we had nine different people leading prayers in nine different languages.

After the service was over, quite often the congregation would have refreshments. Occasionally, there would be a small meal, sometimes just drinks with cookies or cake, but it was a time for fellowship. Our song leader from Bulgaria didn't speak English, but he was a music director. He would study the English words of the songs he was going to lead on the following Sunday, and he always did a good job in leading singing for the church.

Our group went to church by bus, but occasionally the faculty would go by van and stop to have dinner somewhere along the way at an American, Italian, or Greek restaurant. Then we would meet the students at church, but the bus would always be there to pick us up and take us all home at night. Usually, the ride home would take forty or fifty minutes, but sometimes over an hour, depending upon the traffic. The students especially enjoyed shopping in the area just a few blocks away from the church building. We all enjoyed visiting famous places in Athens like the Acropolis and the Parthenon, but other sites in the city as well, such as the location where the modern-day Olympics were restored in 1896.

We occasionally had visiting speakers for our students. Our lawyer was involved in business and government and knew a lot of people, so it was interesting to have him come and speak to us on different topics. We were fortunate enough to be able to visit a private hospital in Athens and to listen to one of the private sector doctors. This doctor told our group about the differences between the public and private sectors of medicine in Greece. Forty percent of the Greek population used the private sector of medicine and hospitals for health care. We also visited a well-known private school, which had about nine hundred students, and our American students talked with the Greek students and teachers. We all learned quite a bit about the educational system in Greece.

One of the most interesting events that we attended was at the invitation of the Indonesian ambassador to Greece. Our lawyer was a friend of the ambassador and attended an evangelical church with him, so the ambassador invited us to come to his home. He wanted us to meet with his staff, learn about Indonesia, and enjoy Indonesian food prepared by the wives of his staff members. The ambassador lived in a rented home, which was beautiful and very spacious with a large living and dining area. The space accommodated not only our twenty-eight students and staff, but a few others who had been invited as well, including the ambassador from Honduras, who was there along with his wife and daughter.

The evening began with two or three of the ambassador's staff members telling us about different aspects of life in Indonesia, such as business, government, social life, and religion. After this we had an unusual meal served in buffet style. We started with seaweed soup, and then we walked around a large table with all kinds of food, such as tiny frogs, less than three inches long, and we were told to eat the entire animal, not just the legs like we do in America. We also had calamari, or squid, which resembled onion rings (at least that's what I thought the dish was at first), but calamari tasted more like rubber, battered and fried, to me. The buffet also featured mutton, chicken, and vegetables, a variety of Indonesian food, and a little bit of Greek food as well. The food was all good, and when we had finished the dinner we all gathered back in the big room for an evening of entertainment. Some of our guys did a little mimicking/singing/lip-synching, and everyone enjoyed it. After that, the ambassador's daughter sang, and three teenage girls who were children of the staff performed in their native costumes. Then came a Greek dance with many of the visitors – Greeks, Indonesians, and some of the Americans – joining in. This dancing reminded me of the movie *Zorba the Greek*, when Anthony Quinn played the lead role and danced by himself to express his feelings.

We needed to get up early the following morning to depart for Thessalonica, so around 11:30 I told the host that we were going to leave pretty soon. But he said, "We have dessert!" So we went back into the dining area, where our hosts served two different kinds of delicious flan with lots of fruit. Then we went back into the big room – and our host still didn't want us to go! Finally, at midnight, we told him we truly must leave. I think he would have kept us with him until 2:00 or 3:00 in the morning had I not politely insisted. As we left, we all signed the guest registry. The ambassador was so impressed with our students that he invited us to come back for a farewell party before leaving Greece, but we just couldn't work it into our schedule.

The group really enjoyed the trips we made throughout Greece and other countries. We were fortunate to have hired a very good bus and a good Greek bus driver named George, who spoke just a little bit of English – at least enough to get by with us. He took us to church and back most of the time and also made the trips with us throughout Greece. I sat near the front of the bus all the time and watched him as he fingered a string of beads that appeared to be similar to Catholic rosary beads. But these, called "worry beads," were for a different purpose; men would fumble with them, one bead after another. I watched George many times as he used his left hand to drive and his right hand to fumble the beads; then, every once in a while, he would flip them and go through the beads again. He had two sets of them. I had read about worry beads and knew they came originally from Turkey, but the Greeks picked up the practice and it became a Greek tradition. We saw sets of worry beads all over, and we could buy them at many different stores as souvenirs. I brought back some of them and gave sets to some people who I felt needed them.

We made a comparatively short trip to Corinth, an important commercial city in the time of the Apostle Paul. Close to it sat the Corinthian Canal, which was quite a feat of construction. Four miles of earth needed to be cut through across the peninsula, but those four miles of canal would save about three hundred miles of sailing as people traveled from the Aegean Sea or Athens around the Peloponnesus west to Italy or up the coast of Albania. The canal was very slow in developing; it was started by Nero in the first century A.D. and was not actually finished until 1892, by the same man who developed the Suez Canal. The canal was 227 feet deep, and as we stood on the bridge crossing the canal we were fortunate to see a vessel beneath us being towed through by a tugboat.

Corinth itself was an important place with many ruins and a museum that housed hundreds of ancient artifacts. Many statues and portions of buildings that remained intact in Corinth were related to Biblical stories. The judgment seat, or bema, before which Paul testified, was still there, and we went to the middle of the ancient city to see it.

We also visited Mycenae, the location of King Agamemnon's palace, a very ancient castle, dating to about eleven hundred years before Christ. Near the palace were some famous tombs, built in the shape of a beehive, and the acoustics inside were such that we could put our ears along the wall and hear someone whisper a long distance away because of how the sound reflected between the curves of the wall.

From Mycenae we went to Epidaurus, the location of one of the best-preserved ancient theaters in the world. The theater seated about eight thousand people, and a speaker could stand on the stage, talk without accessory amplification, and be heard anywhere in the seats. There was a museum there and a forest of beautiful trees all around, which was unusual because there were not many trees in Greece.[30] The theater still served as a venue for musical and dramatic programs.

One of my favorite trips of the semester was a six-day excursion to Macedonia in the northern part of Greece. We first traveled to Delphi, the city famous for its oracle. Our journey to Delphi by bus was not so difficult, but ancient Greeks had to travel on donkeys, wagons, and chariots, so making the trip to the top of the mountain was a challenge. Delphi was a lovely spot with a large area devoted to games of various kinds. There was a stadium on the very top of the mountain, located above a theater that would seat a couple of thousand people. Below the theater was the Temple of Apollo, which was also fairly well preserved. Several treasuries were there, as well, where offerings and donations from various cities were stored. Delphi was the place where all Greek citizens – rich or poor, important or unimportant – came to get answers regarding their life choices. Citizens would ask questions to the priest or priestess, who would go back into a secret place to receive an answer from the female oracle. The questions ranged from "Am I going to get married?" to "Am I going to succeed in business?" to "Am I going to die soon?" to everything in between. Even Alexander the Great came to listen to the oracle for an answer to the question, "Am I going to be successful against the Persians or the Syrians?" Today, many tourists come to see not only the location of the temple and the theater but also the museum which houses many beautiful artifacts, especially The Delphic Charioteer, a famous well-preserved bronze statue of a chariot driver.

From Delphi, we went on up to Meteora, near the city of Kalambaka, famous because of its rugged mountains and monumental stone pillars. At the beginning of the fourteenth century many monks went to live in that area and carved caves in the mountains as places to live. Later, they built monasteries on the tops of the pillars, so that the only means of access was by rope ladder or rope and pulley. Because they stood perched on top of these sheer stone mountains, getting up to them

---

[30] Greece is predominantly rugged, mountainous, and rocky, and many trees had been used for building ships or had been burned in forest fires.

was difficult, and they provided a retreat where the monks could pull up their ropes behind them and maintain privacy and security. There were probably twenty-five monasteries at one time. Only six were still in use, and we were able to go in a couple of them via modern elevators or bridges.

After Meteora, we went north in Macedonia as far as Kabala, which at the time of Paul was called Neapolis and was the first stop he made on European soil. Kabala was a busy little seaport, and from there we went to Philippi, which was an important Roman military city in Paul's day.

There were many different things to see in that region that connected to New Testament history. We all knew the story of what happened at Philippi when Paul converted Lydia and her household to Christianity and was then beaten and put in prison. After going to prison, Paul baptized the jailer and his family. We visited places mentioned in the Bible and followed the journeys of Paul. We passed through Amphipolis and Apollonia as we traveled to Thessalonica, where there was much of historical interest, including excavations disclosing how different eras had produced different levels of the city. We also visited Pella, the home of Alexander the Great. He grew up in that area, as did his father, Philip.

After visiting Thessalonica and Pella, we came to Berea and saw the monument that was made to the Berean people who in the book of Acts were declared to be more noble because they searched the Scriptures daily to see if Paul was speaking the truth. This account from Acts was inscribed on the monument and depicted in mosaic with pictures of Paul and others in the city.

We stopped at the foothills of Mount Olympus at the city of Dion to see the grave of Alexander's father. The grave site, only recently discovered, displayed many artifacts from Philip's life. We passed by the statue at Thermopylae where a famous battle took place a few hundred years before Christ lived. The Persians defeated the Greeks because a Greek traitor showed the Persians how to get behind the lines. In this battle, some three hundred Spartans gave their lives trying to slow the progress of the enemy. There were others who died there as well, but these Spartans got most of the tribute. We took pictures at the location of the Battle of Thermopylae and then returned to Athens.

Our next trip was a cruise among the Greek Isles. We boarded our ship, *The Odysseus*, at the port city of Piraeus and were given our stateroom assignments. Sailing out of Athens, we passed the Temple of Poseidon at Sounion, which was the last thing ancient sailors saw when they left Athens and the first thing they saw when they returned to Greece. On the cruise, we went first to Mykonos, a small picturesque island surrounded by the beautifully blue Aegean Sea. Mykonos and its surrounding islands provided bright visual contrast to the blue of the Aegean. Almost all of the masonry on the islands was white with blue trim (blue shutters or a blue roof or a blue door), like the colors of Greece's flag. The islands also had many beautiful and expensive boats docked at their wharves, so I could tell that many rich people visited the islands.

After Mykonos, we sailed to Patmos, a small and pretty island where the Apostle John was exiled. We went by bus to the top of the mountain which overlooked the little bay and the city to see the cave where John supposedly lived. There a little piece of rock jutting out inside the cave was claimed to have been John's pillow. A monastery was built at the top of the mountain, and we were able to walk throughout the whole area. Then we walked down the hill part of the way to the bus and went back to the ship.

From Patmos, we went on to the mainland and landed at Kusadasi, the port city for Ephesus, a famous city where excavations documented settlements dating back thousands of years before Christ. We stopped there only for a short period of time, but we were able to disembark and do some shopping.

The next island we visited was Rhodes, ten or twelve miles off the coast of Turkey. Because of its proximity to Turkey, we noticed Turkish influence there. We were able to visit one of the old palaces, important before the days of Christ. We also visited a pottery shop and watched the workers make the island's beautiful distinctive pottery – black with gold trim.

From Rhodes, we sailed to Crete, the largest of the Greek islands. Paul left Titus in Crete to get things in order and to appoint elders in every city. From there, we sailed to our last island, Santorini, the home and birthplace of Dino Roussos, the preacher for the congregation we attended in Athens. In fact, his mother still lived there. Santorini was distinctively shaped by a volcanic explosion that occurred about sixteen hundred years before Christ and was so devastating that it blew out one side of the island, leaving only a semicircular arc of land. We sailed in just below the city, which stood about eight hundred or nine hundred feet high (eighty or ninety stories up).

Visitors could reach the city from the sea in one of three ways. You could walk, you could ride a donkey up the trail (so you had to be very careful where you stepped if you walked), or you could take a funicular, a tramway, which was what Louise and I did. It cost the same amount of money to ride the donkey or to go up by tram. I think it took three minutes to go up the tram, and it took quite a bit longer to go up by donkey, but our people chose to go both ways. Santorini offered an unusual view from the height of the city, looking out over the sea and ships. Several hundred people lived in that city at the top of the broken volcano, and most of the city catered to tourists: shops, tourist attractions, and restaurants. The ships did not come in to the dock, so passengers had to be ferried by small local boats for three or four hundred yards.

From Santorini we sailed back to Piraeus and Athens. Overall, we had a wonderful cruise, because even though it only lasted four days we saw several beautiful islands. The food was good, and we enjoyed being on the ship. We did have rough weather one day, and it really shook us from one side of the ship to the other. We couldn't walk straight at all, but it wasn't too bad for very long, and I don't think many of us got too sick.

For our next trip, we flew by Olympic Airlines to the island of Samos. Some of the islands along the Turkish coast belong to Greece and some belong to Turkey. Samos, just twelve miles off the coast of Turkey, belongs to Greece, and we landed there, ate dinner, and then took a small ship over to Turkey. The ship, probably 110-120 feet long, could carry about fifty people, and it served as a ferry, though it was built more like a ship, and it took us back to the port city of Kusadasi. This short voyage gave us an opportunity to see Turkey from a distance and to experience crossing, as so many people did, from the islands to the mainland.

From there, we went to Ephesus, which was probably twenty-seven percent excavated at the time. Then we went to the old city of

Pergamum, perched high on a hilltop with the new city of Pergamum down below it. The old city was built upon the top of a hill for protection, and it had a beautiful view looking out over the whole valley.

After Pergamum, we went to Sardis. Sardis, Pergamum, and Ephesus were the three best preserved of the seven cities of Asia mentioned in the book of Revelation. The city had an ancient synagogue whose walls and beautiful mosaic floor were next to the gymnasium, which was for education and training as well as physical exercise. The area in which the king and the notables sat to watch the games or competitions was well preserved. Sardis also had the foundations and some of the original columns of an old temple, as well as a small Christian church, built near the temple in perhaps the second or third century.

We also went to Hierapolis, close to Laodicea, another one of the churches mentioned in the Bible as the home of Epaphras, one of Paul's close associates. Hierapolis had beautiful, calcium rich hot springs that flowed down over the side of a hill, leaving flows of calcium deposits that looked like snow from a distance. I walked in the shallow water of the pools. Hierapolis also had a very nice theater as well as many tombs in a wonderful old cemetery located near the city. We spent the night in a lovely hotel where there were different sets of swimming pools. Some of the pools had very hot water, some were warm, and some were cold. We could take our choice of where to swim, and we could switch from one pool to the other.

We came back to Kusadasi, spent the night in the hotel, and prepared to leave the next day, only to find that we could not sail to Samos to fly back to Greece because the weather was so rough at the port. No ship was getting out, and the authorities were not sure we could get out the next day either. We started trying to figure out some way to get back to Porto Rafti. Interestingly, the weather was actually beautiful; it was just very windy. We decided to take our bus back up to Izmir (the old city of Smyrna), where we could catch a Turkish Airlines flight to Istanbul, where we could then get a flight on Olympic Airways back to Athens. We didn't get home until about midnight. It was quite an experience, but at least we were able to finish our trip from Turkey back to Athens.

The last of our trips for the semester with our students was a trip to Egypt. We had been scheduled to go to Israel, but because of suicide bombings that spring traveling in Israel was not advisable. Therefore, we switched the trip to Egypt. A few years earlier some militants had killed members of a group from America and other countries as they visited Luxor. This, of course, was on our minds, but we decided it was safe enough at that time, so we flew from Athens to Cairo, which wasn't a very long trip.

When we landed in Cairo, we boarded the bus we had rented and met our driver and our guide. Everywhere we traveled in Egypt, we not only had our own guide (in our case, Dino Roussos), but we also had to hire a local guide. We stayed in a hotel near the pyramids of Giza. In fact, when I stepped out of the hotel in the morning, I looked up and there stood the largest of the pyramids, not more than half a mile away. We were in an area that had been developed since I was there the last time in 1965. All of it was new to me, but when we got out to the pyramids, that view was still the same, just as it seemed to be thirty-six years earlier.

The hotel where we stayed had very good food, and we enjoyed being there for several days. Don Shackelford warned the young people to be careful what they did or said because we were in a country that followed the laws of the Koran closely – more so than Turkey, which was much more secular. "Please don't say anything that could get us in trouble," he urged. Well, one of the young ladies in the hotel that night decided that she wanted a pizza, so she called and ordered one, and the man on the phone asked what she would like on it.

She said, "Canadian bacon," and he immediately began to berate her. "Don't you know this is a Muslim country, and we do not eat pork? Don't ever ask for pork in Egypt!" Her roommate was laughing so loud, she had to put a pillow over her face. We learned pretty quickly what to do and what to say and what not to.

We saw all three of the pyramids as well as the Sphinx. Some of our students went inside one of the pyramids, but we could not climb them because a law had been passed against it. Of course, in 1965 Cliff and I had climbed one, but too many people had lost their lives climbing the pyramids since that time, so the government forbade anyone else to do it. In fact, there were guards all around the pyramids to keep people from getting too close to them, except around the entrance. The day was hot, so Don and I each bought one of the little Arabian headdresses to keep the sun off of our head and necks, which helped a little bit.

We visited the museum and were amazed at the number of guards there, as well as at the pyramids. At the museum, the guards all dressed in white uniforms and were called the Tourism Police. Every bus had someone resembling an FBI agent to greet them, dressed nicely with a coat and tie. Beneath the coat, each guard had his radio and an automatic weapon that he kept ready at all times. One was with us everywhere we went, and when we boarded the bus, he was there with us. When we would shop, he was there with us. We were well guarded.

At the museum we visited many different exhibits, obelisks, statues, and tombs, including the area for King Tutankhamen. He supposedly was a very young king when he died, although the guide who was with us said that King Tut had actually lived longer than most people believed. It's amazing that he had more than four thousand artifacts in his tomb, some of them very large, like the stacked golden coffins. The tomb also held furniture, clothing, and jewelry. When King Tut's exhibit had come to the United States a few years earlier, Louise stood in the rain for three hours in New Orleans to see fifty-seven pieces that came from the tomb. But here in Cairo, we saw the whole collection. The museum was tremendous, and after seeing so many beautiful artifacts we all felt overloaded and overwhelmed.

From Cairo we flew to Aswan, about 550 miles south on the Nile River. The great Aswan dam was built back in the 1970s. Egypt asked the United States to help construct the dam, but the United States refused to do so at the time, so the Russians helped to build it, allowing a very long lake to form on the Nile River to the south of the dam. That lake was only about six miles wide, but it was over three hundred miles long, controlling a huge amount of water. At Abu Simbel, where the new lake would have flooded monumental ancient temples and statues, the government moved those antiquities at a cost of millions of dollars in a project that was internationally supported and observed.

At Aswan, we watched a papyrus demonstration where we saw artisans slice the papyrus reed and then put it in water to sit for a week in order to remove the sugar. Then the workers pressed the reeds under rollers, drying them. Next, they interlaced strips in crossing perpendicular lines by threes until completing the sheet. They then rolled and pressed the sheets for a week before they were ready to use. Workers also demonstrated writing and painting on papyrus sheets. I bought several sheets for souvenirs. Aswan had a lovely botanical garden on one of the islands in the Nile River, which was started by Lord Kitchener of England when he came through Egypt. He was heading down to Khartoum in the Sudan to rescue General Gordon, a British general who was trapped there by the Sudanese rebels. In the meantime, he heard that General Gordon had already been killed, so he decided to stay in the area of Aswan and ended up developing the botanical gardens. The gardens held tall trees, all kinds of shrubs, and flowers, which were all irrigated from the Nile River.

From Aswan we took a boat down the Nile River and stopped at temples that had been built some three thousand years ago. Sand had almost covered them, except for just a little part of the tops sticking out, and no one paid much attention to them until the 1800s, when people decided to excavate these areas. The excavators found beautiful temples, statues, and paintings on the temple walls and ceilings – all still preserved after all this time because they had been completely buried by sand.

We took a three-day trip down the Nile River, heading north, and I enjoyed seeing the points of irrigation all along the way. Some Japanese engineers did a good job in helping the people with irrigation a number of years earlier, and I would often see both big and small pumps along the way as people diverted water out of the river onto their land. Otherwise, nothing would grow in Egypt. We could see greenery all along the banks of the river as far as the people could irri- gate. Beyond that area was nothing but dry sand, with not even a sprig of grass growing.

When we came to Karnak at Luxor, we arrived at the end of our boat trip. There were two great temples there, joined together by a long avenue probably a mile long, with rows of sphinxes on each side. Luxor was also home to the Valley of the Kings and the Valley of the Queens, the location of the burial of pharaohs. There were approximately six- ty-two tombs of the kings and a similar number for the queens. We were able to go inside a couple of the tombs. It was very hot there, but it was enjoyable to go back to Luxor, which I had visited thirty-six years before.

From there we flew to Cairo, boarded our bus, and headed back to the same hotel where we had stayed previously. The most enjoyable part of that day's trip was in the middle of the afternoon. We had not had lunch and were very hungry, so we instructors arranged secretly to have Kentucky Fried Chicken bring each of us a boxed lunch and a cold Pepsi. We stopped on one of the main streets, where delivery workers brought the food out to us. When they put the food on the bus the students immediately passed it around and started eating. I laughed at the kids hollering excitedly about having Kentucky Fried Chicken; it tasted like home. We went back to our hotel, and that evening we went out to the Sphinx and the Great Pyramids to see a performance under lights and to hear about their history. While we were there, Louise looked up at the Great Pyramid close by, the one Cliff and I had climbed in 1965, and she said, "When I get you back to the hotel, I am going to spank you."

"Why?" I asked.

"For taking my son up to the top of that pyramid!" she said. She could just imagine us looking like little specks on the side of the pyramid, and she realized how dangerous it was. "Why did you choose to do that?"

"It was there," I shrugged, "so we climbed it."

The next day we flew back to Athens and spent the rest of that day and the next preparing to go back to the United States. Most of the students were going to travel a few days somewhere in Europe before flying home. Quite a number of them left on a private bus, riding to Patras to catch a ship for Italy, because there was a national strike in Greece at the time. Louise and I stayed at Porto Rafti until the next day, when we were going to fly to Florence, Italy, and then on to Uganda. Everyone was leaving, and we were left alone. The next day we went out to the airport only to hear, "Sorry, but there is no flight today. The airlines have decided to go on strike." So we had to go back to our villa and stay until the next day at the same time. For twenty-four hours, when everybody else had gone, Louise and I were the only two there. Staying at the villa by ourselves was quite lonely, but the next day we took the plane and flew to Milan where Sherrill, our granddaughter, met us. We went by train together down to Florence. We stayed there a couple of days and then caught a flight out of Rome to go to Uganda. Jay Walls got up about 2:00 in the morning with us, and we drove to Rome, caught the plane to Brussels, and from Brussels flew to Entebbe. We stayed a few days in Uganda with our granddaughter Johnna and her husband, Bret Raymond, and visited with the team working there. Then, we flew home to the United States; it was good to get back home again!

We went back to Greece several times, including in 2004, when my son Cliff and his wife, Debbie, were the visiting faculty. On those trips, we were able to visit even more locations around the region, like Olympia, birthplace of the Olympic games, and Istanbul and Gallipoli in Turkey. But, really, my favorite part of every trip was watching the students discover new cultures and seeing how they represented Harding beautifully around the world.

A few years later, Louise and I visited my son Charles and his wife while they were living in St. Albans in England. Charles had been sent to head up Murco, a subsidiary of Murphy Oil, which had about five hundred service stations and a refinery in Wales. Their apartment north of London was small, with two little bedrooms, a small kitchen, and a fair-sized family room, but it was close enough to his office that he could walk to work most days. And they used it well, especially for visitors who passed through London from time to time – mainly Harding University students who had been studying in Italy or Greece. In the two years they lived there, they kept over a hundred people – one night keeping twenty-two Harding students at once. They blew up air mattresses and let the students sleep on the floor. Patty cooked for them and prepared sandwiches and snacks for them to take on their excursions. It made me happy to know that Harding students had welcoming places like Charles and Patty's place that felt like home as they were traveling around the world – the world they are going to change.

CHAPTER 25

A TRIP TO UGANDA

O ne of the most important efforts of which I have ever been a part is with the work of the Lord in Uganda. I never dreamed that I would begin an extensive chapter of mission work that has been so rewarding, though also difficult and frustrating. In fact, I have been engaged with work throughout Africa, but the efforts in Uganda have been especially dear to my heart, and I have visited the country twenty-seven times.

In January of 1994, five young couples – the Moores, the Abneys, the Smiths, the Taylors, and the Bartons – were applying for permission to serve as missionaries in Jinja. They had been training for years in the United States and were looking forward to the work, but they had encountered a problem. Every congregation and every preacher in Uganda had to register with and be overseen by the country's Non-Governmental Organization Committee. Two Ugandans controlled the registration for the Uganda Churches of Christ, but it appeared that these two were interested in supervising the missionaries especially because of the money those missionaries spent. Our young missionaries understandably did not feel they could work under the supervision of either of those men. In fact, in my visiting with the government office that oversaw the non-governmental organizations and churches, I learned that the government was not at fault for our not having more American missionaries in the country, but those two church leaders were.

Two American missionaries, David Jenkins and Greg Carr, had already found themselves at odds with the Uganda Churches of Christ (UCC) group and had registered under the name of New Testament Church Ministries. Jenkins was a graduate of Harding, and Carr had graduated from Abilene. But the UCC people were calling them imposters because they did not have a scriptural name.

As a result, on January 15, 1994, three other church leaders and I flew to Uganda to see what could be done to alleviate the situation and make it possible for our five families to be allowed to work. The others with me were Mark Berryman, who had been to Uganda many times and knew the people; Cliff Fridge, an elder at a congregation in southeast Houston; and an elder from the Pleasant Valley Church of Christ in Little Rock.

Some locals met us when we landed at Entebbe, and we all traveled the twenty-five miles to Kampala, the capital, where we met the Carr and Jenkins families. We wanted to evaluate the churches in the region before we addressed the major issue at hand, so after worshipping with a rural congregation we went to Jinja, about fifty miles east of Kampala, driving through heavily populated areas with small shops and factories of various kinds, through big sugar cane fields, and through tea plantations.

In the mid-1990s, Jinja had a population of about one hundred thousand, and it served as the government headquarters of that area as well as the seat of power for the Basoga people. This was where our young missionaries wanted to work. There was no congregation meeting in the town, but there was a very small one meeting in a rural area outside of Jinja, under a large tree at the compound of David Oketch and his family. The houses were circular and made of mud and were divided with living quarters on one side and an area with mats for sleeping on the other side. They cooked in a separate mud hut or outside.

After visiting in Jinja, we drove to Mbale. There was no congregation in town at that time, but there were a couple of congregations in the vicinity. One of them was a few miles east, at the home of Nathanael Odokotun. Nathanael was a hospitable elderly man who had a school at his compound as well as a little church building, and he was a leader of the church in that area. As soon as we arrived, he invited us to stay with him. We spent the night on the dirt floor of the church building. Our dinner was late that evening because Nathanael had someone catch a chicken, and they prepared it for us from scratch, along with beans and rice.

After visiting Mbale and learning about the work of the Lord in that area, we traveled back to Kampala because we wanted to talk with one of the Ugandan UCC leaders in hopes of sorting out the conflict. We called and told him that we would be glad to come by and visit with him for a few minutes. When we got to his home, not only was he there with his wife, but he had also assembled the other UCC leader, a German couple who had been supporting his work, and four young men who had been in a preacher training school down in Botswana. We were all introduced to each other, sat down, and started talking. Our conversation turned into an unpleasant two-hour debate. I was glad we had the opportunity to meet the people there and to know some of their feelings, but the conversation was uncomfortable. The young men had written down questions to ask us on little cards, and most of the questions were very pointed. Their questions suggested that we were loose in the faith and not as strict in the Word as we should be.

While we were talking over the various issues, Mark Berryman finally announced, "Brethren, we have got to quit this lying. It's just not good; it's not right."

One of the two leaders replied, "What do you mean 'lying'? There's no one lying."

Mark turned to the UCC leader we had contacted, and asked, "How is your heart? Are you feeling better now? Are you having any problems?"

The leader bowed his head. He didn't say anything, but Mark replied, "This is what I am talking about." The man had been sending letters to America, telling people that he had a serious heart condition, and that he was bedridden and needed help. Mark added, "This is what I mean, and it just needs to stop – this requesting money from America under false pretenses."

One of the young men, who was very harsh and hard in his questioning, was being supported by Cliff Fridge's church. Cliff asked this young man to come outside so they could speak alone, and they were gone for about fifteen minutes. When they came back in, the young man didn't say anything more. It was not an enjoyable evening by any stretch, but it was an important one.

We were able to work with David Jenkins and Greg Carr to change the name of their registration from New Testament Church Ministries to New Testament Churches of Christ, so the accusations that their name wasn't biblical would be moot. When this was done, we felt that our mission team that was so eager to get to work could come under the registration of the NTCC, and they did. In the spring of 1994, they were able to get into the country and set up shop to begin to work in the Jinja area among the Basoga people. I flew back for a follow-up visit in December 1994, and I was pleased to see that the mission team was already making an impact.

In fact, Louise and I made visits to Uganda quite regularly for a number of years. On December 19, 1995, we left for Uganda and Ethiopia in East Africa, and Ghana and Togo in West Africa.

Communists had taken over Ethiopia in 1971 and immediately began to shut down churches and to imprison or exile preachers. Our brethren had a difficult time, and one was killed in Addis Ababa near the compound of the church. The communists were ousted in 1991, but many people continued to distrust the government for years after-wards. Louise and I were warned about spies who might try to entrap us, including taxicab drivers, and others told us that we had to be careful about where we took pictures. There was a beautiful and unusually designed bank building downtown, and I wanted to get a picture of it, but our Ethiopian friends told me not to do it because there was a government building next to the bank, and I could get in trouble for taking the picture if someone suspected I had ulterior motives.

It was sobering to see how the systemic distrust lingered, but it was quite inspiring to get to know a believer named Behailu Abebe and learn more about the work he had done to build the church and keep it going under communist rule. He was the son of the governor of one of the provinces about seventy miles from Addis Ababa. His father, a well-to-do lawyer, was a learned man who spoke seven languages. He sent Behailu to live with his sister and her husband in Addis Ababa when the boy was fourteen years old. There, Behailu met one of the American missionaries who had Jule Miller's filmstrips. He borrowed the projector and the strips to show to young children, and in so doing he learned a lot about the Lord and the Bible and was baptized. When he was baptized, his family disowned him for leaving the Coptic faith. In fact, they declared him dead and would not have anything to do with him. When he would call home, his mother would say, "Why have you called me?"

He would say, "Mother, I called because I love you."

His mother would reply, "But you are dead."

His sister gave him an ultimatum, "Either you get rid of the film-strips, or you leave my house." He left the house.

Behailu was passionate about sharing the gospel, and among those he helped to convert was a young lady whom he later married. They have a family and live next to the Church of Christ building in a compound in Addis Ababa.

The compound, consisting of about three acres, had come about because the daughter of Haile Selassie had a deaf son and was interested in the possibility of a school for the deaf. When missionaries first moved into Ethiopia, they were not permitted simply to open a church and start preaching. Instead, a missionary had to provide some kind of service for the country. Gary Blake, one of our Harding graduates, and Linnie Darden,[31] an African-American missionary who, though hearing, had studied at Gallaudat University (which primarily educates hearing-impaired students), decided in 1962 that a school for the deaf in Ethiopia was the best way to go. They tried to get parents who had deaf children to let them attend the school; unfortunately, they were up against some longstanding cultural beliefs. Many people in Ethiopia believed a deaf person could not be taught; their philosophy was, "They're deaf and dumb, and, therefore, no one should waste time or money on them. One should work with someone who can be taught."

Finally, our brethren went out on the streets and found three little urchins who were deaf, and the missionaries followed them home and asked their parents if they could bring them to the school. The parents said, "No. These children are begging and bringing home money for us, and we need it."

The missionaries made a counter-offer: "What if we give you the amount of money that they are bringing home plus food and clothing. Would you let us teach them?" The parents finally agreed to do so. This

---

[31] Linnie Darden's grandson, Jason Darden, now teaches at Harding.

was the beginning of the school for the deaf that eventually grew to have three separate campuses and more than eight hundred students. Building up the school was a long, slow process, but it worked.

In the southern part of Ethiopia, when the communists first took over, the leader of the party was closing down the Churches of Christ. Behailu traveled down to help his brothers and sister there, and they prayed all night long after his arrival. The next day at 8:00 in the morning, Behailu went in to see the communist leader and told him that if they closed down the Churches of Christ, then the church would close down the school for the deaf.

"You can't do that. Why would you do that?" the communist demanded.

Behailu said, "Well, because the school is supported by the Churches of Christ in America, and if you shut down the Churches of Christ here, they will stop their funds. We will be forced to shut down the school for the deaf children."

The leader repeated, "You can't do that." He called in some of his men and asked, "Who gave the order to shut down the Churches of Christ?"

There was an awkward silence because no one wanted to say, "Sir, you did." They finally just responded, "Well, we thought it was best to do so."

"We will not close down the Churches of Christ," the leader ordered, and that was that.

As a result, during this period, our brethren were able to continue to preach the gospel and carry on the work of the Lord despite the fact that the communists were in control. The situation didn't keep church members and leaders from being harassed or even imprisoned at the time, but it meant that the Churches of Christ were not wiped out as they might otherwise have been. Behailu was imprisoned for a while when he refused to join the Communist Party, then was exiled to Kenya. He worked in Nairobi for a few years before returning to Ethiopia.

From 1984 to 1986 Ethiopia had a terrible drought, and an estimated one to two million people died. I'm glad to say that many Churches of Christ worked independently as well as banding together to help in every way possible to alleviate the conditions. In one area alone, around 180,000 people were saved because of the help from our brotherhood.

The church today is very strong in Ethiopia, even without a single American missionary in the country. At the time we were there, a Brother Clark from California was coming over two or three times a year, but no one lived in the country full-time except the national preachers. Ethiopia had more than sixty thousand members of the church and about six hundred congregations. Many of them were very large congregations of several hundred, and one had as many as fourteen hundred members. I preached at one of these congregations that had five hundred members in the southern part of the country. There wasn't even a road to the building; our Land Rover made a path as we went along. I don't remember even seeing a bicycle there, and yet there were five hundred members attending the services of the church. These brethren had built their own building. They put tall poles in the ground, wove in branches, and then caked mud and patted it on about eight inches thick with windows placed in and a tin roof on top. The tin and windows were the only things they had to buy; all the rest of the materials were brought from their home communities. The floor was just straw-strewn dirt, but there were seats and benches; every seat was filled, and there were about fifty more people sitting on the ground in the straw. It was a very inspiring worship service.

Because of the country's ties to England, many people spoke English as well as one of the seventy-five or so local dialects throughout the country. The congregation asked me to preach that Sunday morning, and I spoke in English. It was translated into the native language, and then someone translated it from the native language to the dialect of that particular tribe, so I would have to stand and wait while two other translations occurred. Anticipating this, I wrote quite a short sermon. The Lord's Supper, on the other hand, took about forty-five minutes, not because of too many people speaking, but because while the members were passing the bread, they tried to fill the cups to go around for the entire audience.

From Ethiopia, Louise and I traveled west to Ghana. In the airport, I saw a couple with their children and heard them speak American English but paid no more attention to them. When we boarded the plane, I happened to sit behind the man and one of the children. After a little while, I leaned forward and greeted him. When he looked at me, he said, "I think I know you."

I said, "Oh?"

"Yes," he replied. "You are Clifton Ganus from Harding University."

"Yes, I am!" I exclaimed. "How did you know?"

"I am Mark Ward, and my daddy is Doyle Ward."

"Oh, do you mean Pete?" I asked, using Doyle's nickname.

Mark laughed. "Yes!"

Pete and his wife were in Searcy for several years, and we played a lot of basketball and softball together. I mentioned that to Mark, and he smiled. "Yes, I know. I was five years old, and I was out there watching you many times as you were playing."

Mark was now an engineer with an American oil company and was stationed in Nigeria, where his family was heading. I asked him about the possibility of my getting off the plane during our layover in Lagos, and he said, "Oh, no, I wouldn't do that if I were you." I remembered our visit to Lagos at the airport in 1972, and our problem with the taxicab driver, so we didn't disembark after all.

Ghana's capital city, Accra, is located on the coast of the Gulf of Guinea off of the Atlantic Ocean. Accra, a large city, had many Churches of Christ as well as a preacher training program. The members of this church had constructed a building that was almost finished, and we had a chance to visit with a wealthy native Ghanaian businessman who was a member of the church. He had a couple of different offices (the main one was located in Accra), and his company was involved in fishing supplies of various kinds. It was encouraging to see the remarkable things our brethren were doing both with churches and in their local economies.

The next leg of our trip was a journey up to Yendi in the northern part of the country, which was Muslim territory. On the way, we passed the very large city of Kumasi, which has several Churches of Christ, including one of about eight hundred members. I preached there on Sunday, and the singing was remarkable. We also had a chance to see the nearby hospital where three Christian nurses worked and traveled to the countryside to teach people how to care for their children, educating about cleanliness and preventing disease.

When we left Kumasi, we drove to Yendi, and just before we arrived there we passed the town of Tamale – what I thought was an unusual name for a city, since I always associate it with Mexican cuisine. The region was overseen by tribal chieftains; one chief was over about eighty thousand people and another ruled over four hundred thousand people, which included the eighty thousand of the other chief's people. We were able to visit the smaller tribal chieftain and to enter into his house. He was sitting on pillows like a potentate, and people bowed when they came in to see him.

The two tribes predominant in the area were the Dagumbas and Concabas, and they didn't really care for each other. In fact, a couple of years before we were there those two tribes had been at war. One group had cut off the heads of about eighty people and stuck them on poles in the village as a warning to others. Several thousand people were killed in this war before the government sent troops in and stopped the conflict. Even though this was primarily a Muslim area, there was a sizable Christian population in Yendi, and during the war some of the Concabas had slipped into the village and warned the Christians that there was about to be a major conflict and they should leave. That warning saved many lives.

None of the property belonging the Church of Christ in Yendi was damaged or destroyed during the conflict; however, next door was Catholic property, and that building was completely destroyed. The Churches of Christ had been involved in drilling water wells all over that area, and people really felt good about them as a result. Finding clean water was quite a problem; usually, women and children would walk five miles or more carrying containers on their heads to get water and then walk back home. Even then, the water might be impure. There were at least thirty different kinds of diseases people contracted because of unclean water. Having a good, convenient well that reached as much as 120 feet deep in the ground with covers of rock over it really turned many people to Christianity. They saw what Christians were doing for them, and they became interested, started studying the Bible, and became children of God.

The enmity between the Dagumbas and Concabas was still very strong. In fact, I was asked while I was at Yendi to speak on the subject of leadership to the two tribes. The Dagumbas met at the Yendi compound of the church, and I talked to about forty or forty-five of these men from the various villages of their tribes. Then they took me about six miles over to another church building, where I spoke to about forty or forty-five leaders of the Concabas. When I was finished speaking to the Concabas, who are more warlike than the Dagumbas, I sat there with Dan McVey, a Freed-Hardeman grad who had been living there for thirteen years, and listened to them talk in their own language. I didn't know what they were saying, but they were very animated. One of the young men stood up and was talking, and Dan McVey described to me what he was saying, which was that during the war with the Dagumbas he had not participated: "I just could not kill Christians, and therefore, I did not participate because I knew some of the people would be Christians."

Dan then said, "This young man also did not participate." And he had the youth stand up.

Some of the church members frowned at what that man said, so when we went outside the building, I said, "Dan, did some of these church leaders participate in the war?"

"Oh, yes," he replied. "Many of them with gusto." Even Christians were fighting against Christians in this area because their animosity was very strong. At least while we were there, peace prevailed, but it was impossible to get the leaders together to talk about their differences

I visited one of the villages where there was a well and a pump. Women and children were pumping water into their buckets and carrying it back to their huts. While I was there, about ten or twelve children, dressed in loin cloths, underwear, or stark naked, came up to me, and I taught them how to do high fives. We would do it over and over again, and they would laugh and have more fun. When I finished, I looked down at my hand, and it was brown because of the dirt on the children. I was rather tickled by the evidence of our game together. They had a great time, and I enjoyed playing with them.

Wells were still a major source of goodwill in the region around Yendi for the local Christians. Church members drilled wells for the villages and generally were successful in doing so. They charged a small amount for the drilling to make the villagers feel they had an interest in the well and appreciated it even more. While we were there, they were about to drill another well on the church compound where the preachers would meet. There was no well close by the building, so they decided to drill near it. Before they began the drilling, they asked me to lead a prayer that it might be a successful well, which I did. They drilled down, and at sixty feet they hit a good flow of water. It was a good well at just half of the depth of the other two wells on the compound. The members requested that I stay and pray for all the wells they were drilling. Of course, I couldn't do that, but it was nice to have a good well there for the preachers who would be coming in for training in that area. The house for the church leaders in Yendi was in a compound that also had a brand-new clinic, which was very pretty and commodious. The members there decided to name it in honor of Glenn Boyd because of his help in that area. We got to see the building before its dedication and even before Glenn saw it.

When we left Accra, Dan McVey drove us to the border of Togo. There were several Harding couples at that time serving in Tabligbo, which was really just a large village with a few shops and stores. There used to be a cement factory close by, but it had closed down, and they were hoping that something else would replace it. Sandi Wright was there for a few years, along with Frank Bunner and his wife, and Jeff and Brenda Holland and their son, Josiah. They worked out in the countryside in the various villages and established congregations in that area. We went with them to one of the villages where we saw the home of one of the witch doctors. All around his house he had different talismans, which he used in his practice of voodoo. Inside his house, he had feathers, bones, trinkets, and various things hanging on the wall. Voodooism was strong in the culture of the Togo, and from there it was exported to Haiti in the Caribbean.

When I returned home from Africa, I spoke to Dr. Burks about an idea that I had been forming. I was extremely impressed with Behailu Abebe and the tremendous work that he had done in Ethiopia, and I wanted to do something that would help him further his efforts. Behailu had finished high school but never had a chance to go to college and had no degree, but many of the other people who worked with him did have college training. It seemed to me that giving Behailu an honorary doctorate from Harding University would be helpful to his ministry, especially in view of the wonderful work and leadership he had provided through all his years in Ethiopia and in Kenya as well. After I presented the idea to Dr. Burks, he agreed.

I went back to Ethiopia on March 12, 1996, to make the presentation, which was quite the ceremony. I took my own robe, hood, and mortar along with a set for Behailu. Normally, for honorary doctorate ceremonies, we give only the honorary hood to the individual, but I gave Behailu the full regalia. The church compound at Addis Ababa held the ceremony with about two hundred people present: visitors from education and government, members of the church, and friends of Behailu. We had a big dinner in the building after the presentation, which consisted of goat, lamb, chicken, and several vegetables. I sat up at the head table in the church building, but I could watch people preparing Ethiopian coffee on the floor. The beans were green, so they roasted them in a little furnace, and when they had finished roasting them, they put them in a little grinder. Then, they brewed the coffee and passed it around for people to drink. I enjoyed seeing the process – from the green coffee bean picked fresh from the tree to the finished product – all made while we were having dinner. It was wonderful to see that part of their culture woven so seamlessly into the celebration.

Behailu and his family, of course, were all thrilled by the honor, and I am sure his degree helped him through the years as he continued on in his great work in Ethiopia. His vision for the church and tireless dedication has accomplished a great deal for the people of eastern Africa and the kingdom of God.

I continued my interest in supporting the work of the Churches of Christ in Africa, with a special emphasis on Uganda, and visited them frequently. In May 2004, my grandson Landon Ganus accompanied me on a trip. Grace Nyanga and Moses Oparah met us in Entebbe and drove us to Jinja, where we stayed for the next several days at a bed and breakfast called Arise, Africa. I always took a lot of American chocolate candy with me to Africa, which two employees at Arise really liked; they called me The Chocolate Man. We had a prepared breakfast every day with eggs, pineapple, bread, butter, jelly, and orange juice. The rest of our meals we ate mostly at The Source Café, and a couple of times we ate with Erica Pearson, a Harding alumna who was the only American missionary there at the time.

Catching a ride on a boda boda in Jinja

I preached one Sunday at the church in Jinja, with 165 people in attendance, and one was baptized, a Muslim girl. After the service the congregation presented a bicycle to a young man named Charles, who was an evangelist, so that he could go out to the villages to preach. Then church members all had dinner together, which was simply rice with just a little bit of meat in it, and there were also cold drinks for all of the audience.

That evening I spoke to a group of people who had AIDS or were HIV positive. There were thirty-one in the group, including the three counselors. For a starting point, I used 1 John 1:7: "If we walk in the light as He is in the light, we have fellowship one with another." I did this because the only thing that bound them together then in fellowship was the fact that they were HIV positive, but as Christians they would also have Jesus and a much greater fellowship with a much greater reward. AIDS could only promise death, but Jesus promised life. After it was over, I shook hands with every one of them, and many of them said, "Thank you very much for coming to speak to us. We appreciate what the church is doing for us because most people just look upon us as being outcasts and won't have anything to do with us."

I also gave a lecture for the Busoga Bible School on the topic of leadership. These were students who had already finished the first round of courses and were in the advanced study. The Bible School was doing a fine job in training young men to be preachers and leaders of the congregations in the villages.

I also went out to visit the village of Nawangoma, where Harding Christian Academy, a secondary school, had a new building under construction with two rooms already built and others underway. The plan was for the Busoga people to send their children to receive an education and learn the word of God, to become Christians and leaders in God's kingdom. My family and I were helping with the school and looked forward to its being very effective in the future.

I was extremely impressed by our visit to Budoola, which was in a very rural area about fifty miles from Jinja, where people walked miles to come together to worship each Sunday. We traveled in a van over highway, gravel road, dirt road, and, finally, through a field until we came to the church building and James Okumu's house about 150 yards away from the church. James started the congregation in 1996 with five members, and it had grown to have sixty-seven baptized believers as well as children. They had a traditional mud building with a tin roof, but they were trying to build a stone building as well. They already had the walls up, made from rocks the members themselves had plucked out of fields and carried to the building site. We were helping in their project as they put the roof on and the doors and windows.

James had a little stone house that he built himself, along with a few mud huts around it, which were used by a total of twenty-one people. Thirteen of them were children: six of his own daughters (he had lost two sons) and seven from two of his brothers who died with AIDS. He owned twenty acres in which he planted sweet potatoes, cassava, corn, vanilla trees, and other things, as well as thirty-one goats, a dog, a cat, and lots of chickens running around loose. The compound he had built himself was snug and clean. James was an outstanding preacher and teacher, one of the best in Africa. I had known him for a decade and had been fairly close to him, and we helped him in several different ways, such as getting him a brick machine so that he could make bricks to sell. We also helped educate his children. Just recently, he baptized a preacher of the AIG, the African Independent Group, which was an evangelical group with several nearby congregations. He baptized the preacher and twenty-three of the members of his congregation after he had taught them about baptism, the Lord's Supper, and other fundamental Biblical truths. Those members of the AIG were now committed to trying to be like the New Testament church.

The most difficult area of the work I helped undertake was the Christian school, which we began working on in February of 2003 and opened the following year. Many years ago, there was an attempt to begin a primary Christian school, but it lasted only a short period of time and became a government school near the village of Nawangoma. Some of the brethren in the late 1990s attempted to start a secondary Christian school, but after constructing the walls of two classrooms they ran out of money and could not get any support. The effort failed. A year or so passed by, and others wanted to try to build a school and asked me to help them to fund it. I was told that in six years the school would be self-sufficient. After considering the request, I told them that I would give them some assistance to get the school started. It was located on the hill near Nawangoma, and the city fathers gave us permission to build on the area. The Church of Christ in Nawangoma had been given permission to build a small church facility there as well. They did not have money to finish the building and asked if I would help them to complete it. I said I would do so if they would permit the Christian school to use the facility during the week for classrooms, and they agreed.

The campus has a beautiful location. Since it's on the top of the hill, you can look down in every direction. Over time, we were able to provide funds to erect an office complex, a large classroom building, a girls' dormitory, boys' dormitory, library, headmaster's house, faculty room, and a kitchen and dining facility. We also built a basketball and volleyball court and a small building as a concession stand. Through the years, we have been able to develop a good educational program and to provide spiritual instruction as well. Based upon the program at Harding Academy in Searcy, every student at Harding Academy in Nawangoma has a Bible class, and there is a chapel assembly for all students five days a week.

Issuing diplomas at Harding Academy of Nawangoma

As a result of the school, great numbers of students through the years have been baptized into Christ, and many of the young men have learned to preach and to participate in the services of the church. Two of our alumni married and began another small Christian primary school about forty-five minutes away. Others have helped to establish congregations in the villages. Much good has been done as a result of that school.

At the school's beginning, there wasn't much opposition to its being in the area, but when it became more successful there were locals who wanted to get in on the act. They began to raise challenges and to make claims that they should have a role in the school's operation. It is hard to be involved in a project from eight thousand miles away, which is why I have visited the country so often. Most of those trips have been with the purpose of assisting at the school and protecting its assets from people who might try to jeopardize them. I also am in constant communication with the administrators of the school and have stacks of email documents several feet high to attest to that communication. Still, it is difficult, and sometimes I feel inadequate to give advice to a culture set in such a different world than mine. Many times equipment was purchased or promises made without permission, and I found myself responsible for payment of bills.

We have encountered problems over the years that were extremely difficult to negotiate, the difficulties being compounded by geographical distance and cultural differences. However, the situation has improved in the last few years, as Maanda Wilson became chairman of the board. He is also the director of Harding Christian Academy, and he does an excellent job in those roles. A young lady serves as our headmaster, and we have a good staff of teachers. The school has achieved status as an examination center, which is a feather in its cap, and our A-level students will be able to take their government exams each year on the campus instead of having to go to some other school for that purpose. The atmosphere has improved tremendously, and the spirit and attitude on the campus is very good.

Once each month, about twenty-five or thirty of our students and four or five of our teachers are taken by bus to participate in what is called "Super Sunday," a time when members of the church from different congregations gather at one of the church buildings to worship together. On that Sunday, some of our students participate in the church service, and one or two of our teachers will also speak. They worship together, eat together, sing together, and have a rousing fellowship. They love it, and it's good for the students as well as the congregations. Oftentimes, baptisms occur on these occasions. When we had a "Super Sunday" on the Harding Christian Academy campus in Nawangoma, seventeen of the students were baptized as well as two of our staff and a government official who had been listening to our radio program on Sunday evening for over a year and had come to the conclusion that the Church of Christ was teaching the truth. He wanted to be a part of it.

Since there is little money in the homes of so many of our students, the fees are kept very low, and we have to provide approximately $80,000 each year for the operation of the school. That seems like a lot of money, but if the Lord is correct when He states that a soul is worth more than all of the money in the world, then I think we're getting a bargain when we baptize scores of students every year, many of them going on to help to evangelize the community in which they live.

I know that it has been so frustrating at times, but two or three years ago, I just said to the Lord, "Father, I can't do it myself. You're just going to have to take over and do it, and I'll try to help you as I can." I think He truly is with us, and, despite the frustrations, the costs, and the difficulties that we have faced, the results and possibility of doing much more good keeps us going. Christian education has meant so much in the Lord's work in America, and it has in other countries as well. May God help us to continue to do what we can to help others help themselves and be a blessing in the community in which they live, wherever it may be in the world.

CHAPTER 26

THE AMERICAS

O ne of my favorite parts about retirement has been the opportunity to travel even more than I did before, and to see parts of the world I had not yet visited. Even more than the sights, however, when I travel I love seeing people whom I know and love or whose work for the church I've admired. (On a slightly less noble level, I will admit that I also love traveling for the sake of trying new cuisines.)

In March of 1994 I took Louise with me to Guatemala to recruit students for the Walton Program. When we finished the work part of our trip, we headed north in a small plane to the largest Mayan ruins in the world, at Tikal. Tikal encompassed a large area, but much of it had been taken over by the jungle. The government cleared back a number of the trees so that tourists could see the ruins – two pyramids and housing areas built by the Mayan people – and visitors could still climb one of the pyramids. I scaled about ninety steps up to the top of the first pyramid; they were small steps for my big feet. The platform at the top served as a place of worship and sacrifice for the Mayan people, so I waved at where Louise was standing on the ground with a camera, and she took a picture of me. Then I realized there was no way to get down except down those small steps with nothing to hold for support, and if I took a misstep, I would fall all the way down the pyramid. I thought, "You nut. What are you doing up here? You are seventy-one years old. You shouldn't be up this high." I crawled down the pyramid by turning around and backing down.

—————

I always enjoyed going to Central America, especially the trip we made the following year with Helen Walton to attend a reunion in El

Salvador for the Walton Scholars' Program. The group had about forty-two students representing a number of countries and all three of the Arkansas universities in the Walton Program. Those of us who came from the United States all stayed in the same hotel. The owner of the hotel was happy to see Mrs. Helen Walton; I think he wanted her to start a store in that area. Helen was just as common and comfortable as an old shoe and fit in very well with everyone. She had no pretentions at all. She sat in the middle of the floor with kids all around her, just like a hen with her chicks. Everyone enjoyed having her there.

I relished these trips to Central America because they gave me the chance to see the fruits of the work of The Baxter Institute, a Christian school and preacher training program in Tegucigalpa, Honduras. A good friend of mine, Harris Goodwin, started the school and had been its president for many years; he was helpful to us in selecting students from Honduras for the Walton Program. The Baxter Institute trained young men and women from all over Central America who wanted to serve the Lord's kingdom both on their very fine campus in Tegucigalpa and also via their correspondence program. I occasionally lectured on world missions at the Baxter Institute and always left encouraged and inspired by the remarkable work of the leaders who graduated from the programs.

———————

Louise and I took a cruise from New Orleans through the western Caribbean in 1997 and even had a chance to visit with my nephew, Trey Billingsley, and his wife, Jamie, on Grand Cayman, where they live. In Jamaica, the preacher of one of the congregations in Montego Bay was nice enough to come out and meet us. He took us downtown so that we could do a little shopping outside the tourist areas while we were there.

———————

For Christmas a few years ago, my son Charles and his wife, Patty, gave Louise and me a surprise. For many years I had often drawn a picture of what our present to an individual would be and let him or her guess what it was. This time, Charles surprised us by drawing a ship. I guessed it might be a cruise, and I was correct! Less than a month later, the four of us drove down to New Orleans for a weeklong cruise through Central America.

Before we embarked on Sunday, we went to church at the Carrollton Avenue Church of Christ – the same congregation our family helped established in 1935 when I was thirteen – and then we headed to the river to board the ship. It was a beautiful vessel, a little over three football fields long, weighing 92,250 tons, and staffed with more than a thousand crew members for the three thousand passengers. We checked into our cabin, which was a beautiful stateroom with lovely furniture and a little balcony. But, because I always like to be where the food is, we went straight to the Venetian dining room and had our Sunday lunch of popcorn shrimp, fried chicken, mashed potatoes, and caramel flan.

At 4:00 we left the dock and began the hundred-mile journey to the mouth of the river. Technically, there are four mouths of the river, but only one is navigable by large ships. It was a lot of fun to see the city go by and then to see other areas a little beyond the city, like where Andrew Jackson defeated the British in the Battle of New Orleans in the War of 1812. Charles especially enjoyed watching the refinery owned by his former company as we passed by. We also saw American Bay, where I used to fish with my Uncle Van, as well as a number of small villages along the river. Finally, we came to Venice, the last place on land before we hit the Gulf. It took six and a half hours to go down the river until we hit open water.

We enjoyed eating through the buffet line on the top deck for dinner. The big show that evening included a magician, acrobats, singers, and dancers – kind of a preview of what we could expect for the entire week. Every night there was a different show, and most of them were very good.

Before the program began, the master of ceremonies said, "We have many children onboard our ship, and many old people – some of whom have been married a long time. Let me see the hands of those who have been married fifty years of more." Several hands went up, then he asked about fifty-five years. There were fewer hands. Then he asked sixty and sixty-five. Finally, someone yelled out that they had been married sixty-eight years, and the emcee started to declare them the winners, but my hand was still up and someone yelled out: "There is another man and his wife over here."

The emcee looked over at me and said, "Who are you, where are you from, and how long have you been married?"

I yelled back, "We are Cliff and Louise Ganus from Harding University in Searcy, Arkansas, and we have been married seventy-three years."

The audience erupted into a standing ovation. The emcee replied, "That is wonderful. What is your secret for such a long married life?"

I replied: "Don't die and don't divorce. It's easy."

———

One of the most meaningful trips I have taken was in 2013, when I had the opportunity to visit Haiti for the first time. Speaking at the Caribbean lectureship each year gave me an opportunity to visit many of the islands, but I had never been to Haiti. Finally, I had an opportunity to join Harry Hames, who works for Healing Hands in Nashville, Tennessee, and travels many times each year to Haiti. I was happy to go and set foot in my 117th country. Haiti is a small nation of 10,714 square miles and ten and a half million inhabitants. By comparison, Arkansas is five times as big in land area as Haiti with less than a third of its people. Haiti is the poorest country in the western hemisphere and one of the poorest in the entire world. There have been many earthquakes in Haiti, the most recent on January 12, 2010, when more than three million people were affected by a terrible quake and months of aftershocks. It is estimated that between 100,000 and 160,000 were killed. Some 250,000 residences were destroyed along with about thirty thousand commercial buildings. Tremendous help was needed, and many nations poured money, materials, and men into the devastated country.

On October 4, 2013, I landed at Port-au-Prince, the capital city, and was met by Harry with a truck. Evidence of the earthquake was everywhere, despite the fact that it had been more than three and a half years since it occurred. There were piles of rubble, especially in the medians of the thoroughfares. There were also many vacant lots and damaged buildings not yet repaired. The city was full of temporary shelters and tents, and there was evidence of construction everywhere.

We made only two excursions out of the capital city. One was of forty or fifty miles to the west to visit Regis Duval, a preacher in the Petit-Goâve area. He also was a schoolteacher for a small elementary Christian school that had been damaged by the earthquake and repaired to some extent. While there, we were able to visit his apartment. Sometimes missionaries who are supported from the United States live very well, but not in this case. Brother Duval is supported by brethren at Harding Place in Searcy and is in contact frequently with Dr. Winfred Wright, who speaks French fluently. We were amazed at the small austere housing area that he and his wife occupied. It was a tiny space divided into two rooms and a closet area. His children, a boy and a girl, could not even live with the family but stayed with relatives nearby. It was truly a very humble abode. He teaches during the week and then preaches on Sunday at the local Church of Christ.

The other excursion was about a hundred miles to the northwest, to the city of Gonaives. A sixteen-year-old boy named Peter went with us because he knew the language and the area well. As we were leaving the city, we witnessed the beating of a thief. Often, when a thief is captured, instead of taking him to jail the police beat him, sometimes with lethal force.

As we drove north of the capital we saw many small homes that had been built to help take care of those who had been displaced by the earthquake. We had planned this trip to visit with Pacius, a preacher who worked with the church in that area and had visited Searcy, and we had arranged for him to meet us when we arrived at Gonaives. Entering the city, we stopped for Peter to call Pacius on the phone at a bus station where there were a great number of buses coming in from the hills surrounding the city. As we drove just a little way to wait for Peter, two men and a girl on a motorbike hit us gently from behind. Immediately, we knew that we were in trouble. Harry and I were sitting in the truck, waiting for Peter to return when a crowd of people gathered. Naturally, the driver of the motorbike blamed Harry for the accident. With dollar signs flashing before his eyes, he demanded $250 for damages. Of course, there wasn't much damage. All we could see was a dent in the fender covering the front wheel of the bike. It probably would have taken no more than ten or twenty dollars to repair it, but the demand was insistent, and the crowd became angry. We didn't speak their language and wondered what would happen. We rolled up the windows and locked the doors, waiting for Pacius to come. Peter joined us and told us that he had succeeded in reaching him and that he would be there in a few minutes. Fortunately, Pacius arrived shortly and began talking with the locals. It was a very heated exchange, but he finally won the battle. He learned that one of the riders felt that he was injured and needed to see a doctor. Pacius had a relative who was a medical doctor, and he agreed to take the three of them over to talk with him. They agreed, and nothing further came of it.

We waited at Pacius's home while he took the riders to the doctor. When he returned we had a wonderful lunch with him and his wife and talked about the work in that area. It was in that location that Dr. David Smith, a Harding alumnus who lives in Little Rock, had worked for some time, had built some facilities for the Lord's work, and had established a program for feeding poor people in the community. While we were there, we were able to see one of the feeding times. About eighty young children came in from all over that area, each one bringing a pot in which food could be placed. There were two very large kettles of food that had been prepared by members of the church for distribution, and each child received a potful. Some of them began to eat immediately; others took the food back home to help feed siblings or parents. For many of them, it would be the only meal they would receive that day.

We then visited one of the buildings of the Church of Christ in a poor section of the city. It was a primitive building made mostly of sheet iron, with a dirt floor and backless benches. There was a water well and a pump – and also a large pig that had wandered onto the church property. The neighborhood was just about as poor as the church building.

The second structure that we visited was much different. It was on the other side of the city, about a mile or so away. It was well built of concrete and steel and would hold a few hundred people. On the second floor was an area for classrooms, not only for church use but also for a school. It was not yet complete, but it promised to be a very fine structure for the church in that area. There is much good work that is being accomplished in that vicinity by Pacius and others who work with him, much of it with the support of Dr. Smith.

Most of our time on the trip was spent in the capital city. On Sunday morning, we drove to the largest Church of Christ, where there were more than four hundred people. The building had been damaged by the earthquake but was being restored. The lower portion, where the church assembled, had already been completed. The second and third floors had not been entirely finished, but classes were being held there. It was a friendly congregation, and I was asked to preach for them, which I was happy to do. That evening I spoke at a country congregation that had only fifty or sixty members. Their nice building did not show any evidence of having been damaged by the earthquake. They also had a school nearby and had begun the construction of a dormitory for their preacher training program.

We had the privilege of visiting some of the orphanages operated by the church. The first one was surrounded by a large fence. Inside the gate was an open facility where small meetings could be held; on the left were classrooms, and on the right rooms for housing. In the back of the lot was a large pen for chickens and goats. Classrooms were well equipped, thanks to donations from Christians in Japan. The entire facility would be considered substandard in the United States, but in Haiti it was pretty good. You should have seen the faces of the children when we opened packages of clothes and shoes we had brought for them.

In the residential area of Port Au Prince, we drove to a church building that was attractive and well decorated. We were able to visit with a caretaker, his wife, and two children, who lived on the complex. There also were five or six tiny buildings that were used as classrooms. On the backside of the church building was a small grove of trees, including coconut trees. The caretaker got down a coconut for us and cut it open so that we could drink the milk and eat the coconut. We enjoyed visiting with the children.

One evening we were able to visit with American missionaries David and Charlene May, who were working in Port-au-Prince, and were pleased to discover that Charlene was the sister of Louine Woodroof, a friend of ours in Searcy. They had prepared a good meal for us, and we enjoyed visiting not only with them, but with seven or eight ladies from the United States who were there to assist them on a short-term basis by teaching sewing and other skills to the nationals there.

One of the most interesting places we visited was the home of Roberta Edwards. It was a large two-room house, where she kept eighteen orphans, ages two to eighteen. It was in a compound that was surrounded by an eight-foot wall, which was common in that area of Port-au-Prince. In fact, much of the residential city is walled in. As you ride down the street, you don't see much of the houses, just tall walls and security.

Roberta was an American who had married a Haitian. He left her, but she continued to live in Haiti and care for orphan children. She was a faithful member of the church and was doing a tremendous service when we were there. In her compound, she had a large house, a garage big enough for the truck she used to transport all her children to and from church services, and an area with three small ponds where she raised fish. One was for the fry (baby fish), another was for the medium fish, and another for the larger fish, so they went from one pond to the other as they grew. Roberta's family not only ate fish but also sold some. They had a large garden, as well, to produce food for their own use. In addition, there was a large covered area where every day she fed about a hundred people from the community who were poor and needy. In addition to caring for the children, she homeschooled them and had a large room with a library and desks for their studying. Peter, who went with us to Gonaives, had been one of her boys.

For lunch on Sunday, we all met under the roof out in the compound. It was a great experience to eat with the children and Roberta and a couple of ladies who were helping her. We had roast beef, mashed potatoes and gravy, beans, and good, warm rolls; then at the close of the meal, she brought out a gallon of Blue Bell ice cream. I must have looked shocked to see Blue Bell ice cream in Haiti. She laughed and said, "I guess you may wonder how we're able to have this ice cream here. Well, I have a sponsor who gives me $25 every month just to buy a gallon of Blue Bell ice cream." A gallon of it costs about $23 in Port-Au-Prince. Each one of us received a little scoop of ice cream. "We get three meals out of one gallon each month," she explained. I almost felt guilty in eating some of it, but not too guilty. I wolfed it down.

In addition to her work with her children, Roberta had ten ladies of different ages whom she was teaching to sew. She had some machines that had come from the States, and she helped the ladies to make aprons, bags, and different items that they could sell. She then paid the ladies, and by this they not only learned a trade but were able to provide for themselves. I was very impressed by the dedication of Roberta Edwards. She was doing a tremendous work and was helping so many people in many different ways. Sadly, just a few months after we visited her, she was murdered. She was driving her car at night and another car followed her a while and then blocked her. The driver shot through the windshield and killed her. She had two children with her at the time: a twelve-year-old and a four-year-old. The older child jumped out and ran, but no one knows what happened to the four-year-old, nor were the police able to determine exactly why Roberta was murdered. Shortly before, she had had a man picked up by the police for stealing, and some people think it was retaliation.

I will never cease to marvel at the lives and determination of so many quiet saints whom I have had the honor of meeting in my travels. The challenges and the very real evils that they encounter on a daily basis often seem unimaginable to many of us living in the United States; but their work persists, and the gospel is not quenched, despite poverty, violence, and corruption. I pray for these men and women fervently.

CHAPTER 27

SOUTHEAST MEETS FAR EAST

I n 2003, only about six weeks after I got back from fishing in Alaska, I left for China at the invitation of Milo Hadwin, who was working with the Pacific Rim Education Theatre. He wanted me to represent Harding at the one hundredth anniversary of the Central China Normal University, which had about eighteen thousand students and was located in the city of Wuhan. I agreed to go, and he helped me make arrangements. I was also asked to speak at the global forum of university presidents on education in America. I left Searcy at 4:30 p.m. on Sunday, October 5, and flew from Little Rock to Dallas and Los Angeles, followed by a nonstop flight of about fourteen hours to Guangzhou, which was the old Canton. I arrived Tuesday morning at 4:40 and waited eight hours at the airport for a flight to Wuhan, arriving at 3:30 in the afternoon. Some of the university staff met me and took me to my hotel, where I learned that there was to be a dinner that evening, and I had to hurry to get dressed for it. There were about 230 people present at the dinner, including the president of Central China Normal University, Dr. Ma Min. He had studied at Yale University, as well as in China. I was also pleased to see David and Vicki Bearden from California, who supported work with the church in China.

We had a very nice formal dinner with a lot of different kinds of dishes, some of which I didn't even recognize. The next morning at 10:00 we attended the celebration at the new gym on the campus, which could seat more than eight thousand people. The school boasted colorful banners, flags, signs, and inflatable plastic arches, which had been brought in especially for the occasion. There was also a fifty-piece band. On the floor of the gym there were several hundred students who were also in the military, dressed in their uniforms and sitting at attention the whole time, faces straight ahead toward the main speaker's platform. They were very quiet except on cue, when it was time to applaud. They all applauded in unison, and then put their hands back on their knees and left them there, sitting like statues until it was time to applaud again. It was interesting, but also a little bit eerie to watch. There were people filling up the entire gymnasium on the floors and as well as in the stands. I sat with the dignitaries at tables that had ice water and cups of hot tea. We were treated well during the long ceremony.

When it was over, we went back to the hotel for a nice buffet lunch with a few surprising items, including swan feet. I knew that Tyson Foods sent many tons of chicken feet to China each year, where it is a popular dish, but I had never even imagined that swan feet might be similarly regarded. There were a few other items I couldn't identify, which I mostly avoided.

That afternoon, the global forum of the presidents met with about 220 people. This was in an auditorium on the campus, and I was one of seven speakers. I represented the United States along with a man from Silicon Valley in California, and there were other men and women speaking from as far and wide as South Korea, New Zealand, and France. After the presentations, which were translated simultaneously, we toured the campus, visiting the major buildings. That evening, we had a gala festival outdoors. There were probably two hundred performers over the course of the evening, with drama, comedy, music, and dancing. Of course, I couldn't understand the jokes, but everyone else seemed to think they were all very funny. The festivities lasted until late in the evening and ended with fireworks exploding over our heads.

The next morning I went down to breakfast and met with Edward Meyers, one of the American Christians who taught at CCNU, and with Thomas Peng, who had also formerly taught at Wuhan University. Thomas worked for Truth for Today in Wuhan, and I had visited his office while I was there. We all had breakfast and talked about the possibility of some relationship between Harding and the university in Wuhan, hoping that perhaps someday something could be worked out. Milo Hadwin was trying to work in that area, as was David Bearden. After breakfast, we went to the History and Culture Building to meet with Dr. Wang, Dr. Yao, and some of their faculty and staff, including a young lady who had spent a semester at Harding University. It was good to visit with her; in fact, there were two teachers on the faculty of CCNU who had been to Harding.

David Bearden and I spoke to one of the classes. There were fifty-two students in the class, and forty-two of them were young ladies. After the speaking there was a question and answer period. One of the students asked, "Why do young people in America go to college?" I gave many reasons why I felt that they did. After having taught at the same institution for more than half a century, I felt like I had a pretty good grasp on understanding American college students.

After we left the group at the university, we went with Dr. Wang, Dr. Yao, and a couple other staff members, to a traditional Chinese restaurant near the campus for lunch, and Dr. Yao ordered for all of us. It was a very interesting meal, and as we entered this restaurant, several of the hostesses met us at the door, three or four on each side of the entrance, bowing and welcoming the customers as if we were long-awaited guests. Later in the afternoon, two of the young Chinese students, Sally and Rebecca, took me on a walking tour; we also took a taxi out to the Yellow Crane Tower, the construction of which started in the second century A.D. There was a big park on the top of Frog Hill with a tower. We were able to walk through the park, see the tower, and catch a beautiful view of the city.

We went back to the hotel, and at 5:00 Ed Mosby and his wife picked us up in a taxi. We drove to his apartment where there were twenty-two American Christians waiting for us. These were people who were teaching English at the different schools and universities and were, on the side, teaching the Bible in home churches. They could not have any large groups of people meeting together without drawing the attention of the government, but they could have ten to twelve people studying in each group and varied the meeting times and sometimes the location so that they didn't draw too much attention. They couldn't do any public teaching or proselytizing, but they could speak freely to anyone who asked them a question about the Bible or about Jesus. They all were happy with their work and were being paid enough by the universities to live well and to take care of all their expenses while they were in China. It was surely good to see a number of Harding people in the crowd. I guess you might say that this was the first Harding University alumni meeting in Wuhan, China.

That night we had Memphis-style barbecue, served with potato salad, slaw, chips, cookies, and drinks – just like in America. After several days of delicious but also sometimes surprising meals, it was nice to eat something that I recognized and that tasted like home. I told the people there about what was happening at Harding, and they told me about their work in Wuhan. It was an interesting evening.

The next morning I had one more meeting at the university before Edward took me back to the airport to fly to Guangzhou, Los Angeles, Dallas, and Little Rock. I had to wait for seven hours at Guangzhou for my plane to Los Angeles, and for eight hours at LAX for a 1:45 a.m. flight to Dallas. Then it was a quick hop to Little Rock, arriving at 9:07 Saturday morning.

That trip took about thirty-five hours each way, but, since I left on Sunday afternoon and got back on Saturday morning, I was gone actually less than six days. I hardly had time to get over my jet lag before I turned around and came back. After that trip I corresponded with the president of CCNU and also with one of the young guides on campus who wrote me to practice her English through email. It was exciting to have helped build the relationships between our two universities, and the next summer, when my son Cliff took the Harding University Chorus to China, Thailand, and Singapore, they performed a concert at the university in Wuhan.

On Tuesday, May 18, 2010, I joined Larry Long, Milo and Karen Hadwin, and West Ling, a former student from China who worked for Harding, as we embarked to China to visit various universities to recruit potential Harding students.

We were supposed to land in Hong Kong first, but there was a terrible thunderstorm over the city, and we had to land in Taipei, Taiwan, instead. From there we continued to Guangzhou, where university personnel met us and took us to a beautiful hotel in the international convention center. We finally got to bed about 1:30 a.m.

The following day we went to the campus of the Guangdong University of Foreign Studies in Guangzhou and met with administrators to work out an agreement that would permit them to send students to Harding. We had an opportunity to visit with about forty students who were prepared to come to our school over the next few years. Some were able to speak English well enough; others needed a little more training. We went to the new campus of the university and met with some of the administrators and professors in the undergraduate program. Later that evening we met with United States consulate officials, and they helped us make arrangements to get visas for the Chinese students joining us the following year. We were also fortunate to be able to visit with some Chinese students who had been on our campus in years past.

Two days later we took the world's fastest train, which traveled more than two hundred miles an hour, from Guangzhou to Hengyang. The trip of 330 miles took us less than two hours, including four stops, during which we admired the scenery.

We arrived in Hengyang, where staff from the University of South China picked us up and drove us to the Shen Long Hotel. (Larry Long claimed the hotel was owned by one of his relatives.) Mark Wang, who had been a student at Harding before being hired by Harding to recruit students in China, met us at the hotel. He drove us to the campus of the University of South China, where we met with the president and other administrators. They hung large banners to welcome us and gave us a tour of the campus as well as a very nice dinner.

On the following day, we ate breakfast in a beautiful revolving restaurant on the top floor of the hotel with a wonderful panoramic view of the city. Later we went to the apartment of Edwin and Mary Myers, good friends of ours who were doing mission work as well as teaching in that city. It was Sunday morning, and we had a worship service with them in which we were joined by Steve Shaner and a group of Harding students traveling with him. Our students on short-term mission programs had been doing a wonderful job in helping to teach the Chinese students interested in learning more about Jesus, and there were many Bible studies taking place at the time. The Chinese Christians were not permitted to worship with the Americans, so they met in another area of the city.

The Harding administrators then loaded in a little car that Mark had borrowed and drove to Changsha. On our drive, Mark pointed out all of the new construction taking place in China; new buildings were springing up everywhere. We went to the Southern Pearl International Hotel and had a meal at a very large restaurant that was modeled after the buildings in the Forbidden City in Beijing.

On the following day we went to the Hunan International Economics University, the second largest private university in China. There, we met with the vice president, and Larry Long signed an agreement between that university and Harding that we hoped would result in getting students from there to come to Harding. Larry and I also had the opportunity to speak to a group of a thousand students about our work at Harding. We showed a video about our campus and were interested in the reaction of the students. They seemed to like the views of the campus, but two things made the greatest impression: we heard a lot of "oohs" and "ahs" when they saw our dormitory rooms and how nicely they were furnished; and we heard the "oohs" and "ahs" again when they heard the affordable cost to attend our university.

We went to the home of Mr. Zhao, a man we knew who had visited Harding in the past with pieces from his wonderful collection of ancient Chinese woodcarvings along with paintings by his extremely gifted thirteen-year-old son. Then we went back to the hotel, and Terry and Alan, two Chinese former students at Harding, took us to a new Dairy Queen where we were able to enjoy something from home – Blizzards.

On the following day we met with the president of Changsha University, who was planning to come to Harding to visit with us in the fall. We had a wonderful experience there and were able to show the Harding video to between two hundred and three hundred students. Their reaction was similar to that of other locations, which was encouraging.

Later, we went to West Lake restaurant, the largest restaurant in Asia – it could seat five thousand guests – for dinner and then to the airport to fly to Beijing. In Beijing, while Karen and Milo Hadwin went to visit their son David, who was teaching school there, Mark Wang took Dr. Long and me to see the Forbidden City and the Great Wall of China. I enjoyed visiting them again because I always managed to see something I had missed on previous trips. After a visit to the Silk Market to get souvenirs to bring back to America, we went to dinner with a former student who was living in China.

On the following morning, our team went with West Ling to the airport to begin the long trip back to America. It was a good trip, and a very productive one, since we were able to secure many students who planned to join us at Harding in the following years.

CHAPTER 28

CLOSER TO HOME

A s much as I love traveling around the world, I also enjoy traveling and connecting with people within the United States, and some of my favorite experiences have been along the Mississippi River. The river has been a part of my life for as long as I can remember, from the time I was a boy in Louisiana through some of my favorite memories with my sons, grandsons, and family friends on some harebrained adventures we cooked up. Specifically, we boated from Searcy to New Orleans – almost seven hundred miles with all the twists and turns – just to see if we could.

In June 1972, my brother James, my son Charles, my nephew Robert, and I decided to take a trip down the White River and the Mississippi River. James drove a trailer up from New Orleans with his boat, an Aristocraft, which was a nice new eighteen-footer with a metal top. We put the boat in the water at Nimmo on the Little Red River, about a half hour southeast of Searcy, and went down the Little Red to the White River (about eight miles); then we cruised down the White River to the Mississippi, and on down the Mississippi to New Orleans.

The first night, we stayed on the White River and slept on a sandbar. We took plenty of food with us and mosquito netting for sleeping at night. During the day, I wore a swimsuit and cooked dinner over a big, roaring fire with no mosquitoes whatsoever, but when darkness came, the mosquitoes came in droves – along with miller moths. We didn't get any sleep that night because the mosquitoes feasted on us and the moths were constantly smacking into things. Evidently, the mosquito netting had holes. I tried to cover up with a sheet and leave my face out to breathe, but the mosquitoes bit me on the face. Then, I covered up everything but my nose or my lips, and they would bite me there. None of us slept well. To make matters worse, I set out a trotline to catch some fish but accidently backed the boat motor over it, cut the line, and lost it.

The next morning, we left to travel down to Greenville, Mississippi. Our first stop on the river was at Rosedale, Mississippi. It was only a couple of miles from the levee and we needed gas, so we took our extra gasoline cans, walked over the levee, hitchhiked into town in a pickup truck, got our gas, and came on back to the river. Then we arrived in Greenville, where we met up with Charles Weeks, a Harding graduate who had worked with us in New Orleans and also taught for our Christian school there. Greenville had a Frostop Root Beer shop and Pasquales Italian Restaurant, and Charles brought Lot-O-Burgers and cold sodas out to the boat for us. We really enjoyed them.

Just as we were getting ready to leave Greenville to spend the night on the banks of the river again, my brother said, "Cliff, since we didn't sleep at all last night, do you think it would be all right to stay in a motel tonight?"

I wouldn't have asked that question, but I was so glad *he* did. I said, "Yes, I think we can," so we spent the night in a motel there but still felt we were being true to the spirit of adventure we had set for that trip.

And adventure comes in many forms. The third day we got stuck in the middle of the river. The Mississippi, a river half a mile wide and up to two hundred feet deep, can also be so shallow that even a small boat can get stuck on a sandbar; in fact, we got stuck twice on that trip. After the mosquitoes, though, nothing seemed that bad.

By the third night, we had made it all the way down to Baton Rouge and spent the night in a hunting lodge. We just left the boat tied up to a big barge and hitchhiked in a truck to the lodge for the night. It had screened windows, so we were very fortunate that there were no mosquitoes.

None of us had called home from the time we left on Sunday morning, and this was a Tuesday evening, so I decided to call Louise. There was no phone at the lodge, so the boys and I walked up to the hospital to find a telephone.

"Where are you?" Louise asked when she answered.

I looked around me. "Well, I'm in the hospital at Baton Rouge."

"In the hospital?" she gasped. "What happened?"

"I had to come in the hospital to get a telephone to call home," I explained, and she breathed a little easier after that.

The next day, we started on down the river. South of Baton Rouge we began to meet a lot of ocean-going vessels. We looked like a cork on the sea floating around these giant vessels – oil tankers, container vessels, and various other ships.

We finished the trip to New Orleans without incident and enjoyed staying there a couple of days. Louise drove down to meet us and brought a family friend with her to help pack everything up. As usual, my main concern was with food; we ate well on the trip but still had plenty of food left over. Given that I had accidentally cut the trotline that first day, it was a relief that we didn't starve. It was a wonderful trip that just made us want to do it again.

It took almost thirty years, but I did.

In the summer of 2001, my grandsons John Richard and David Duke talked with their cousins from Alabama about the possibility of taking a trip down the river to New Orleans. I thought about it, and one night when I couldn't sleep from about 1:00 to 4:00 in the morning I planned a trip with all of the stops. I then told John Richard that if he would like, I would be glad to take the boys in my boat during the Thanksgiving holidays when they were free from school. He was happy about the idea and contacted his brother, David, who was doing mission work and teaching school in Kenya at the time.

David was interested in going, and the two cousins, John and Scott Picken, who were sixteen and fourteen, said they would love to go, too. John and Scott came over from Montgomery to Searcy on Friday evening, November 16; our plan was to set off early the next morning. David and I had already secured everything we would need. The boat was stocked (maybe a little bit too much) with all of our gear, sleeping bags, a tent, cooking equipment, and plenty of food: canned soup, clam chowder, Treet, Vienna sausages, pork and beans, green beans, and different kinds of cereal. We were well prepared for the four and a half days that we figured it would take us to make the trip.

We left about 8:30 a.m. from Searcy and drove to Georgetown, twenty-one miles away on the White River. At this time the river was very low with sandbars everywhere. We all loaded, took pictures, said goodbye to our families, and headed out. Everything went well for about three miles, and then, suddenly, we heard a terrible sound coming from the area of the prop. The motor began to vibrate a great deal. We stopped immediately, raised the outdrive, and looked at the prop; one of the three blades had completely broken off near the hub. Of course, we couldn't use that prop at all. Fortunately, I had a spare prop that was slightly damaged, but was still usable. David took off the old prop, put on the other one, and we headed on down the river.

We did, however, call my son-in-law and asked him to check around to see where we could get another prop. There were none at Des Arc, which was the nearest town, but he found one at DeValls Bluff, some sixty miles below Georgetown. A man came out to meet us with a brand-new prop, which we promptly put on and continued on our way.

Our first stop, aside from our unscheduled visit to DeValls Bluff, was at Clarendon, a small town on the eastern bank of the White River. Arriving there about 1:00 p.m., we found a large houseboat on the river with a porch that had a table and chairs. It looked like a public place, but it turned out that it was owned by an organization called The River Rats. We just pulled up alongside it, took out our food, and made Treet and cheese sandwiches with chips and cold drinks. We had a good time. We needed to get gas, so the boys took the cans, walked about a quarter mile, and bought thirteen gallons from the station. While we were there, two of the River Rats came down and visited with us. We told them what we were doing, and they were very interested in our trip. Like so many others we talked with on the river, they were envious of our adventure.

We decided to spend the first night on the White River, where it would be calmer and more private than on the Mississippi. We went all the way to mile fifteen on our map, which meant fifteen miles from the mouth of the White, where it joined the Mississippi. We chose to spend the night on the west bank of the river on a point that stuck out into the water.

This first night happened to be when the Leonid meteor shower took place just before dawn. I awakened about ten minutes before 5:00

a.m. and began to watch the shower. I could see the streaking lights as meteor dust would come into the atmosphere and burn up. Some of the flashes were very brilliant, and they occurred as often as eight a minute, according to David's timing. It was a beautiful sight.

In the morning, we left around 7:30 and traveled the last fifteen miles down the White River and past the lock and dam that leads from the White River to the Arkansas River at the Arkansas Post Canal. Barges and ships go up through this lock to Little Rock and on toward Tulsa. A short time later, we reached the Mississippi River at mile point 599, which meant we were that far from the mouth of the Mississippi. From this point to New Orleans was only a little over five hundred miles. When we entered the Mississippi, we experienced quite a churning as the two rivers met because the eddy formed there was very strong. We gunned the engine and headed out into the Mississippi, which was perhaps only a third of a mile wide at this point, but still an imposing sight as we left the comfort of the White River.

The White River had been very smooth compared to the Mississippi, which we entered about 8:00 on Sunday morning, November 18. At times this river was over a mile wide. Because of its width, we thought it should be plenty deep for our little boat, but even in the middle of the river we could see sandbars. We hit one just a few miles north of Greenville, Mississippi, and before we knew it our boat stuck on the sand. The boys all got out of the boat in water that was just about a foot deep, and they worked hard to get the boat off the sandbar, which took about fifteen minutes. But we finally got loose and continued toward Greenville, where we were planning to stop and go to church. Greenville sits near, but not quite on, the river; it is actually situated on a small bay leading off from the Mississippi. We had difficulty seeing the entrance of the bay because of the way it was shaped, so we actually passed by it. When we reached the bridge crossing the river we knew that we had gone too far and backtracked a mile or so upstream, found the entrance to the bay, turned into it, and followed it about five miles until we got to the yacht club.

Incidentally, this was the only location on the Mississippi River below the White River where we could actually get gas right on the river, pumped directly into our boat, so we gassed up fully and filled up all the cans there, taking about thirty-seven gallons of gas. I remember very clearly that we had to pay $1.59 a gallon, the highest price on the trip. The rest of the time we would carry the plastic gas cans, hitch-hike in a pickup truck, and fill them up with gas at the nearest station. Then we would take the cans back to the boat and pour the gas into the boat tank.

In Greenville we docked next to two casino gambling ships. Charles Weeks met us, as he had in 1972, and took us to church and then to his restaurant, the Frostop. We got Lot-O-Burgers and fried catfish, both of which were very good, and we finished it all off with good, cold frozen mugs of Frostop root beer. After lunch Charles took us back to the boat, and we headed down the river toward Vicksburg. We decided to stop just a few miles before we got to the city and spent the night on the east bank of the river. We made camp and had a very good evening except for the big tugboats that continued to push barges even in the dark. We could hear them throughout the night as they were chugging up and down the Mississippi and sounding their horns. We seemed more bothered by the noise than were the three deer who came to our campsite to drink from the river, though.

We got up Monday morning and went about ten miles to Vicksburg, turned up the Yazoo River, and found a landing where we could leave our boat. We called a taxicab, and all of us, with our plastic gas cans, went over to see the Civil War battlefield and museum. On the way back, we got the cab driver to stop at a Wendy's and ordered sand-wiches and fries, and then we picked up seventeen gallons of gasoline and went back to the boat. We left Vicksburg about 11:00 a.m., ate an early lunch on the boat – good ol' Wendy's sandwiches – and went on to Natchez.

Natchez was an interesting city perched on the bluffs on the east side of the river. Below the bluffs there used to be gambling and houses of prostitution. But above and to the left there were many beautiful homes – mansions with colonial-style columns. On the west side of the river near the bridge we were fortunate to meet a man who was working with a barge company and a lime company, spreading lime on farms in that area. He was friendly and took us into town to get some more gasoline. We were probably half a mile or so away from the gas station, and he made three trips with us until we were able to put thirty gallons of gas in the boat's tank and fill our gas containers. We always tried to have full cans of gas with us whenever we left a gas station to be sure we could get to the next available sources. They were few and far between on the river.

When we got about twenty-six miles below Natchez, we came to a wide place in the river where we had agreed to meet with Harrell Freeman. He was on the Board of Trustees at Harding University, lived in New Orleans, and loved to fly. He owned a small acrobatic airplane, so he flew up from New Orleans to meet us and drop some food. While he was flying in, we saw him and talked with him on a little walk-ie-talkie which he had given to me earlier so that we would have it available. He flew overhead and circled us about five hundred feet high and dropped a package. It was taped in a life jacket so that it wouldn't come apart on impact and would float on the water. We fished the package out of the river. Harrell circled around and dropped another package, and then he circled again and dropped a third one. We got all three of the packages, waved goodbye to him, sailed back to the west bank of the river where we pitched camp, and had a wonderful supper of boiled shrimp, cocktail sauce, and big chunks of pineapple. Some of the kids made shish kabobs out of shrimp and pineapple, heating it over a fire on a stick. We had a great dinner, eating all the shrimp and fixings we could hold. The next morning we had ten shrimp left over. Since there were five of us we divided them, and each of us got two to go along with our breakfast. It was thoughtful and generous for Harrell Freeman and his son, Will, to fly up from New Orleans just to bring us shrimp and the trimmings and then fly back home again.[32] It was a meal that was definitely appreciated and enjoyed!

On Tuesday morning we left our campsite and motored toward Baton Rouge. On the way we stopped at St. Francisville, a little town on the east side of the river at mile point 265. The town was about a mile and a half away from the river, but a ferry crossing was there, so we stopped near the ferry, and I was able to get a car to take me in to town.

---

[32] When we arrived in New Orleans on Wednesday night, we went to church at Hickory Knoll where Harrell and his family attended and had a chance to visit with them and to thank them for bringing the shrimp to us and to return their containers. Not many people who travel by river have friends who would drop their supper to them in the Mississippi River!

The driver was in line to get on the ferry, but since the ferry was being filled with diesel – a process that took several hours to complete – he figured it was worth it to drive me into town and then attempt to cross at one of the bridges at a different location. I was able to get thirteen gallons of gas, and a fisherman who was pulling his boat in a pickup volunteered to take me back down to the river. We put the gas in the tank and headed on south toward Baton Rouge.

At Baton Rouge we were not able to find a fueling station on the river, so we decided to leave the boat and go over the levee and into town to find a gas station. That didn't work – we couldn't find a station that was close – so we decided to try to make it down to the next point where we hoped we could get some gas. Our hunt for gas did allow us a great view of the state capital building at Baton Rouge. In fact, we could see all of downtown pretty well, even though we didn't get off the boat.

At one place as we were looking for fuel, we chatted briefly with a man who said, "You do have a VHF radio in your boat, don't you?"

"No, I don't," I told him. "I have a little cell phone but that's all."

He fussed at me for not having a radio and told me how dangerous it was to be on the Mississippi, especially without a radio: "You don't know how many times I have been out rescuing people, saving boats that were sinking and boats that had ropes caught in their propellers and other kinds of problems."

What I wanted to reply was: "Well, in the first place, we are sober. In the second place, we have a good boat, and in the third place, we are trying to be careful." But I held my tongue and simply thanked him as we pushed on.

Between Baton Rouge and New Orleans we were dwarfed by many ocean-going vessels, big oil tankers, and cargo ships of various kinds. Thanks to a collection of huge barges that were blocking our way as they were being towed near Donaldsonville, though, we finally got our next round of gasoline. It was a long way in to town to the service station, so the man who was in charge of the barge business and had a large tank of gasoline that he used for his own trucks told one of his workers to give us gas, which he did. They gave us twenty-four gallons and wouldn't take anything for it, but I tipped the man who helped us with it. He had to hand pump it from the tank into our cans, but we were really blessed in being able to get the gasoline we needed. We left there about 3:30 on Tuesday afternoon, trying to go as far as we could down the river.

When we found smooth water, we could make forty miles an hour, but much of the time we were behind big barges – as many as thirty to forty in a bunch. One tugboat could churn up the river and chop the water, and for about two miles behind the boat we had rough going, but then it would smooth out again until we hit our next group of barges or ocean-going vessels.

We stopped about 5:00 on Tuesday evening on the west bank of the river behind some barges, and the kids set up camp on the levee on some concrete slabs (I slept on the boat). We started a fire and cooked our supper. We were going to go in to find a restaurant so we could have some "real food," as the boys called it, but we couldn't find any place open. So there, at mile 138, we spent the night behind some barges. Early the next morning, when we started to go, we got stuck again on a sandbar. It was hard to believe there was a sandbar at a place where the river was supposed to be so deep, but because the barges had been parked there it's likely that the sand had built up behind them. It just took a few minutes to get off and to get out in the flow of the water again. Then we headed on to New Orleans, our destination.

On Wednesday, about 9:30 in the morning, we arrived in downtown New Orleans. We passed the Huey Long Bridge, and I told the kids about my experience hiking twenty miles out there as a Boy Scout and sleeping on the levee. I even told them about how I climbed out on the superstructure while it was under construction, which I realize now was a very foolish and dangerous thing.

The next two bridges we passed were close to Canal Street. There we stopped in the middle of the river for a little while to look at the buildings downtown. Then we went a little farther along, stopped at the French Quarter, and took pictures of Jackson Square, the St. Louis Cathedral, the museum, the Cabildo, and the Pontalba Buildings, which were the first apartment buildings in the United States.

When we came to the Industrial Canal, just a couple of miles from Canal Street, we started to go through the lock. Since the lake where we were headed was about seven feet lower than the river, it was necessary to pass through the lock system. However, there was a large ship in it when we arrived, and we had to wait about forty-five minutes until that ship went through going north. Then coming south were six tugboats all in the lock at one time. When they came out, we were the first boat in, and we drove all the way up to the front of the lock. The water level was changed to the proper level, and we entered the Industrial Canal.

Once in the Industrial Canal we had to wait while they raised three bridges for us. The bridges were so low that even our little boat couldn't get through. One of them took about fifteen minutes to move because the attendant said he didn't see us, although I honked several times and circled around out where he would have had clear visibility. I think he was probably taking a nap.

It was about five miles to the lakefront and then another six miles or so to the yacht club. It was windy, choppy, and rough, but we were talking to our family on cell phones, so they knew where we were. Finally, we could see them waiting for us. They took pictures of us in the boat, and then we went to the yacht club where we pulled the boat out of the water. Louise and I spent the night with my sister-in-law, Doris Ganus, and the rest had motel rooms.

The next day we had Thanksgiving dinner together at Shoney's, a restaurant where my nephew, Tim Ganus, was the general manager. All thirteen of us enjoyed turkey and dressing with all the trimmings and pumpkin pie. After the dinner, everyone started to head home. Louise and I left New Orleans and towed our boat back to Searcy, arriving about 9:45 p.m. and brimming with wonderful memories from the past week with those boys.

———————

Early in 2010 I began to hear the call of the wild again, or at least the call of the Mighty Mississippi. Nine years had passed since I took my last trip in my little boat down to New Orleans, so it was time to go again. I asked Cliff III if he would like to go because he had never been with me on my Mississippi River trips. We also invited Jim Woodroof, who had preached for many years at the College Church and was a good friend of ours, and his son Tim. The four of us began to make preparations to leave in March.

The trip required six gasoline containers, an ice chest, all the necessary food, sleeping bags, a tent, and other equipment that would be necessary for the expedition. Jim Woodroof would also have a birthday while we were on the trip, so his wife, Louine, added a beautiful birthday cake for us to enjoy.

Cliff was very good at preparing for a trip like this and even planned for comforts we had not enjoyed on our previous trip, like a homemade toilet. Cliff took a commode seat, added four legs and strengthened them, and we had a functional toilet. We also took a little souvenir shovel that I had acquired when we constructed a building on the campus. This shovel was good for covering up what we needed to.

Early on Monday, March 8, we loaded up the boat in my backyard and then pulled it out to Georgetown, twenty-one miles from Searcy, to launch our expedition. We waved goodbye to our friends and loved ones who had come to see us off and started our journey. We had no difficulties in going down the White River. Our first point of interest was Dondie's, a seafood restaurant on the banks of the river in Des Arc, constructed to appear as a steamboat but up on the shore. We had boated down to Des Arc to eat at Dondie's many times.

The weather was pretty good while we were on the White River, but it became rainy and foggy on the Mississippi, slowing us up a bit. We stopped the second night near Transylvania, Louisiana, just north of Greenville, Mississippi, on the west bank of the river. It had rained a lot in that area and where we docked was very muddy. Two Harding alumni, James and Jeff Thornton, who had played football for the school, came to meet us. When I tried to get off the boat, I got stuck in the mud and both of my shoes came off. The two farm boys had on boots and were well prepared for the weather. They got on each side of me, and I put my arms around them as they lifted me up and carried me to firmer ground. While they were doing so, my pants decided they missed my shoes that were stuck down there in the mud, and they fell off all the way down to my ankles. I'm glad there were no cameras handy at the moment. Once I got my pants and shoes back, we enjoyed visiting with the young men, and they took us to a hunting and fishing camp owned by a friend of theirs near the levee of the Mississippi River. We had a wonderful supper prepared on a grill and a good night's sleep in real beds.

We dealt with some dense fog and a couple of broken propellers, but the biggest scare we had on that trip was from another vessel. South of Baton Rouge we were joined by ocean-going ships and oil tankers that were traveling to and from the Gulf of Mexico. We did not pass very close to them but could still feel the effects of their waves on our little boat. When we stopped on the side of the river to pour gasoline from our containers into the tank on the boat, we spotted a large ocean-going vessel coming down the river. We wanted to move on before it got there, but we couldn't leave fast enough and got stuck behind it, which was frustrating, since it was only going about twenty miles an hour and we were used to cruising at thirty-five. I decided to pass it on the left; but, unfortunately, I got just a bit too close to the ship when I did. The bow wave kept pulling me closer to the ship and stepping down from the crest was dangerous. After a few scary moments, I finally broke free, and we passed the ship, but it was a little touchy for a while. The captain of the ship, of course, never even saw us.

Camping on the Mississippi with the Woodroofs

I always enjoyed coming to the city of New Orleans by way of the river; my hometown was a welcome sight. We passed through the Industrial Canal and went to the marina in Lake Pontchartrain, where we met Clay Beason, who had pulled the trailer down from Searcy. Our first stop after loading the boat on the trailer was at Deanie's. We could hardly wait to get a good, hot meal that we knew we would really enjoy. Dondie's is my favorite spot at the start of the trip, and Deanie's is my favorite spot at the end of it. Everyone enjoyed the seafood, a good night's rest at a motel, and then our drive back to Searcy. It was a wonderful experience, and I hoped this wouldn't be my last trip. It wasn't.

Dinner at Deanie's with Woodroofs and friends after river trip

"Just one more trip. Just one more trip." That was my thought early in 2012. It had been two years since Cliff, the Woodroofs, and I made the trip down the Mississippi, and even though I'd traveled to the other side of the globe and back in the meantime, I was ready to have another adventure on the river I'd grown up loving. We did all of the necessary preparations and asked Lathan Garnett if he would be interested in going. Lathan was on Harding's first football team in 1959, when we restarted intercollegiate football. He talked to his son Phil, who lived in Dallas, and they both agreed that they wanted to make the trip. Phil was a master at putting together videos and brought his camera and a rod that would stretch out four to eight feet to document our adventure. We were fortunate on this trip that Phil could record the sights and sounds of our journey as we never had been able to before.

On March 5, at 9:00 in the morning, we arrived at Georgetown. Clay Beason again brought us over with the trailer. We also had several friends and family members who came with us to see us off. We passed Dondie's at Des Arc again and stopped at Clarendon for our first acquisition of gasoline, as usual.

After having lunch and fueling the boat, we headed south on the White River. We had no problems on this trip until we came close to the mouth of the White River where it flowed into the Mississippi. For some reason, we could not get the engine to start. We paddled and floated downstream for a while until someone came by in a small boat and graciously pulled us the remaining few hundred yards to the government facilities, located on the south side of the White River. It was a large, concrete, restricted area, but the officials there were very nice to let us stay as long as we needed. We eventually had to call a mechanic who lived several miles away in a small town, but while he was still on his way Phil finally somehow got the engine started. We put on a new battery and everything seemed to be running well. When the mechanic arrived after dark, I gave him a hundred-dollar bill for his trouble, and he went home happy. We decided to spend the night on the concrete, and the next morning started our way to the Mississippi River.

We were glad to see that muddy river again the next morning, but it wasn't long until we got stuck on a sandbar, and everyone had to disrobe and jump out to work the boat free. I was always fascinated with how I could be on a small boat in a great river, and yet the water would be only one foot deep in certain areas. I guess I never did learn to stay in the channel as I should have.

We arrived at Vicksburg, where some of my friends from the church not only took us to get gasoline but also brought us barbecue and all the trimmings. We had a wonderful meal thanks to their generosity. Moreover, this time the local newspaper people heard of what we were doing and sent a reporter and photographer to interview us. They took pictures and wrote a wonderful story about our experiences.

We saw several things on that trip I had never seen before. First, there were thousands of birds passing us overhead; it was breathtaking. Secondly, south of Baton Rouge, we spotted sixty-three barges together

– seven wide and nine deep – with a tugboat that looked as if it were about forty or fifty yards long. It looked like a small hotel, and the waves it made were formidable.

There was only one mishap on the final leg of the trip. When we got about thirty or forty miles from New Orleans, we hit a submerged log and tore up a prop. Cliff put on a life jacket and jumped into the water to replace the prop. We were afraid that he might drop the prop or the wrench, and we would then be in a heap of trouble, but he expertly got the job done, and we headed on our way. We didn't realize how bad things were, though; the log had damaged the outdrive seal, and gear oil was leaking. Fortunately, we were close to New Orleans. Otherwise, we might not have made it.

We saw the usual giant cranes and ships as we got closer to the city. We passed through the Industrial Canal and had to wait a good while for the bridge to be raised so that we could get through, even in a small boat like ours. Clay Beason had pulled the trailer down from Searcy to meet us, as he had two years earlier, and we loaded up the boat and headed for our usual stop – Deanie's – before a good night's sleep in a motel and the drive back to Searcy in the morning. We were all happy we had successfully completed the trip and enjoyed one another's company on a river cruise.

One day in the late fall of 2013, Debbie Howard, the director of Harding's History House, was looking at a picture of Louise and me standing in our little eighteen-foot Bayliner, which she had framed for the History House. Lathan Garnett happened to be there and mentioned that I had made four trips down the Mississippi River, three of them in that very boat. Debbie decided that it would make for an interesting evening to have people share their adventures from our trips. However, she quickly discovered that the History House would not be big enough to host the event, so they decided to move it to Cone Chapel. She began making arrangements with Liz Howell, one of Harding's vice presidents, and they soon discovered that that Cone Chapel would not be big enough, either. We finally decided on having the event in the Founders Room.

Debbie talked with Sebastian, the head chef with Aramark on Harding's campus, and they worked up a themed menu for the event, which included jambalaya, shrimp étouffée, and what he called "Spam Milanese," which was simply breaded Spam, which we had eaten on our trips down the river. They also served varied desserts, such as egg custard from the old Ganus restaurant menu, and grilled pineapple with chocolate sauce. The number of people who planned to come soon rose to over three hundred.

On February 25, 2014, we had a wonderful evening in the Founders Room on Harding's campus. The evening was almost as much fun as traveling down the river in our little boat. Phil Garnett, Lathan's son, was the emcee. We watched the video he had made of our trip down the Mississippi River in 2012, and Jim Woodroof, John Richard Duke, Lathan Garnett, Cliff, and I also told stories from all four of my adventures traveling down the river. We showed photos from each trip, shared stories, and answered questions from the audience. It was a wonderful evening that brought back many memories of my time on the mighty Mississippi, the beautiful part of America that means so much to me.

—————

I have also traveled to Alaska regularly for the past thirty years or so in order to enjoy the fishing and escape the Arkansas heat in the summer. These trips have been a wonderful chance to travel and make memories with my children, their spouses, my grandchildren, and friends. We try to use those opportunities to engage with local congregations, which are often fairly isolated from one another due to extremely long distances, yet we still often find ourselves running into brethren in the most surprising ways.

Fishing in Alaska with Kevin, Ashley, Louisa, and a guide

On one trip, John Richard Duke, David Duke, and I flew to Anchorage, rented a car, drove down to the Kenai Peninsula, and stayed with Bob Townsley and his wife to go fishing for silver salmon in the Kenai River. We also drove from his house down to visit KNLS, the short-wave radio station that broadcasted church messages to Russia and China. While we were there, we paid a visit to the art studio of

Russell Lowell, a member of the Church of Christ and an excellent artist. He had a beautiful studio in the wilderness, and we enjoyed seeing all the paintings of the landscape and life in that area of Alaska.

On another trip, when we brought our boat back in after a Saturday of fishing we noticed a three-hundred-pound halibut hanging up at the dock. We discovered at church in Soldotna the next day that it had been caught by one of the members there, a petite woman who weighed no more than 125 pounds. She invited us to have lunch with her after church, since she obviously had quite a bit of halibut to share.

On the trip back from Anchorage one year, we happened to meet a young lady who had just graduated from Harding and was working on her doctorate at UCA in Conway. We visited with her, and a few minutes later we heard a man call my name. He was one of Harding's track stars almost forty years ago who now works in Arkansas government and lives in the Little Rock area.

But even more than people, fishing in Alaska means getting to see seals, sea otters, and sometimes whales. On one occasion, a whale circled our boat and played up and down on the top of the water for some time. On another occasion, I saw an orca swim at our boat. Then, it dove under the boat and came up on the other side. We also got to see ducks and puffins, which are very small seabirds. We've also seen families of bears on the shore – the mamas are six hundred or seven hundred pounds, and the babies are about 250 pounds. Once, we just took our poles out of the water and for two hours watched the cubs wrestling with each other and catching fish.

The yield of these fishing trips is always unpredictable. We always go with an aim of catching our daily limit of salmon and halibut, and some years that happens within an hour; other years, we never hit it at all. Whatever we catch with the intent of keeping, we weigh and load into a Styrofoam case covered with ice, then we drive it to wherever the nearest commercial company is that offers packing and sealing for fishermen. I don't think we have ever returned home with less than 150 pounds of vacuum-sealed frozen fish in seventy-five individual two-pound filets. There have been plenty of years when we've brought home closer to three hundred pounds because the fishing just happened to be especially good. I like to think of it as an elaborate grocery shopping trip for the coming year – or, since I often preached for Alaskan churches that we visited, as "sermons for salmon."

―――――――

Some of the most personally meaningful trips, however, have been when I was able to reconnect with my past in a new way. During the Christmas holidays in 2005, Louise and I took our grandson John Richard to New Orleans to see the results of Hurricane Katrina that had devastated the city in August. We only saw wind damage as we drove in, but when we arrived in New Orleans proper, I could really see the effects of the storm. On West End Boulevard there were great piles of tree trunks, branches, and wood chips from fallen trees. Many homes had been damaged by the flooding. A few could be rebuilt, but many others had to be razed completely.

Naturally, I was especially interested in seeing how Lakeview fared, since that was where I had spent most of my time when I lived there. I was amazed at the destruction in that part of the city. My nephew's house on Marshall Foch Street was under ten feet of water and had to be demolished. My brother's house, a few blocks away, had been deluged with six feet of water and also needed to be demolished. My mother's old home had about a foot and a half of water, but it had been salvaged. My sister-in-law, Doris, had a home built on reclaimed soil, which was elevated; the water stopped one inch short of entering her home. She was able to sell her home for a very good price, despite the wind and rain damage, because there was such a shortage of housing in the city at that time.

What impacted me most was seeing the home where my parents lived when Louise and I were married in 1943. My mother had always worried about the canal, which was actually higher than the house. She was terrified it would break loose and flood the house, and that's close to what happened during Katrina. The levee nearest the house held, but water from the 17th Street Canal completely flooded the house, so it had to be demolished, too. The last time I was in New Orleans, the lot was still vacant, but I am sure that a house will be built there someday.

The church building at Carrollton Avenue was under six feet of water on the outside and four feet on the inside. The main auditorium was not badly damaged, since it had a concrete floor and brick walls; the only repairs were to rebuild the rostrum and replace the carpet. The back part of the building with all of the classrooms, however, was completely destroyed and had to be replaced. It was interesting to hear stories of church members who came to the building for safety. They had to go up to the balcony during the flooding. Fortunately, they had a little boat with them and could paddle to places where they could get food. On one occasion, while two young men had taken the boat out, a rescue boat came by to remove everyone from the church building to safety. The people there explained the situation and asked if they could wait until the boys came back, but there were told that wasn't an option. They either had to go right then or wait until the flooding was over. They had to evacuate, and it was two whole days before the parents were able to reconnect with their teenage sons.

I also had a chance to talk with some people at Tulane University, who all expressed concern about the millions of dollars required to restore the campus. Other residents of the city talked about seeing homes swept off their foundations or having to camp on rooftops for two days until rescue came. We passed a service station that had been under seventeen feet of water. The devastation was hard to grasp, even after seeing the results of it with our own eyes. It broke my heart to see my hometown so thoroughly gutted and destroyed, but I am encouraged that, since Katrina, the government has spent a great deal of money and done an awful lot of work not only to repair but also to strengthen the levee system so that such a tragedy will not happen again.

Seeing this damage to my hometown got me to thinking about my parents' hometown. I knew that my mother was born in Menlow, Texas, just a few miles from Hillsboro, where I was born, and I had always wanted to see the town but never had taken the opportunity to go there. So during the Thanksgiving holiday of 2016 I decided that Louise and I would go to Menlow and accomplish some other objectives. One was to take some fish that I had caught in Alaska to Richard Gibson, one of our board members; the other was to do a little family research. Louise and I left Sunday afternoon, driving without stopping to Longview, Texas, about a five-hour drive. While we were there, Richard invited us to go to Bodacious Bar-B-Que for dinner, which I readily accepted. After dinner, we drove on to Corsicana, where we spent the night at a motel.

The next morning we awakened and drove about seventy miles to Waco, where my grandparents on the Ganus side lived when I was a teenager. After visiting the area where the home was once located and realizing that only business establishments were located there now, we drove on north to West, Texas, a small town a few miles from Hillsboro. My mother had mentioned that one of our relatives had once served as mayor of West. Just north of West is the little town of Abbot, which has approximately three hundred people; all the business establishments have been shuttered and only the post office was still in operation, though it was closed when we were there. I did manage to speak to one of the residents who told me where I could find Menlow. We drove four and a half miles west where it was supposed to be, but when we got there we saw nothing but a clump of trees. I drove past it and soon decided that I had gone too far, so I turned around and stopped at a farmhouse and asked a man where I would find Menlow. He said, "I'll tell you something better. Two doors down lives an elderly man named Etter. He has lived here most of his life and knows all the history of this area. Why don't you see him?"

I thanked the man and went over to the house, and the gentleman came to the door. We started a conversation, and I gave him a little of my background and told him why I was there. He was interested in talking about the history of the area and explained it to me. Where the clump of trees exists, there was once a large store, which was the center of the community. Mail was delivered there, newspapers arrived there, and people came to get the news of the community. Many years ago it burned, and there is nothing there now. I also learned more about the community, including the school at Scott's Field where my mother probably attended elementary school before she moved to Hillsboro in order to get a better education. He said, "It is not often that we get to talk with educated people, and if ever you're back in this vicinity, please stop by to visit with me."

When we left Menlow, we went to Hillsboro, where I was born. I went to the T.B. Bond Pharmacy, the oldest pharmacy in the state of

Texas, dating back to the 1800s and owned by Joe Cunningham, whom I had visited a couple of years ago and who had given me a pictorial book on Hillsboro. He is a member of the Church of Christ and knows about Harding. I enjoyed visiting with him once again. This was the drugstore where my mother used to buy candy on Saturdays when her father would hitch the team to the wagon and drive into town to shop.

From Hillsboro, we went to Dallas to the Christian Care Center and visited with Carl and Frankie Mitchell and Will Ed Warren, all of whom we had known for years at Harding, but who were living in the center now. We had a good visit with them and then drove back to Searcy, arriving at 11:15 p.m. In one and a half days, I drove 944 miles and visited in five different communities. We were glad to be home but really enjoyed the experience, and I was grateful for the chance to reconnect with my roots.

CHAPTER 29

A LEGACY OF LOVE

A ll my life I have enjoyed participating in sports, and some of my most enjoyable moments were competing against the students at Harding. I did this until I was seventy-six years old, when I played my last softball game; shortly afterward I gave up playing handball. Since then I have only been able to watch our students participate, but it truly is a joy. I've tried to see every game that I possibly could, especially football, basketball, baseball, and softball games, and watch the other sports occasionally. I have become slower in my walking and more unsteady on my feet, but I still climb to the top of the football stadium to sit in the press box and enjoy watching our teams play.[33]

---

[33] The most enjoyable season was 2016-2017 when our football team lost only to the eventual national champs; our girls' basketball team fell in the playoffs to the eventual national champions; and our softball team lost in the super-regionals to the eventual national champs. It was a remarkable year!

Watching Harding football with Louise, Lucy, Avey, and Laura

I try to stay as active as I can, and I still travel to see friends and longtime Harding supporters when I am able. For close to forty years, I enjoyed visiting Dale and Joan Coleman in Dumas, Texas. I've also been visiting the Kendall family for about fifty years, beginning with George R. Kendall, and now I fly up to Chicago to see his grandson, George Kendall, and his wife Maryann, who live just north of Chicago. They have just about made me one of the family, and they're still very strong supporters of Harding University.

In 2015, my beloved Louise was diagnosed with a slowly progressing dementia, but the doctor in Little Rock assured us that she could live anywhere from five to twenty-five years more. That's not a bad promise when you're already in your nineties.

Dessert reception at the Governor's mansion for the longest married couples in Arkansas, with Debbie and Governor and Mrs. Asa Hutchinson, February 2019, married almost 76 years

Louise's health condition has made it necessary for me to be at home much more than I have in the past. I have learned to do much of the housework and don't mind doing it, although we have a lady who comes part time to assist us. When I am out of town, we get someone to stay with Louise and to see that things go well. It's also wonderful to have all three of our children in the same town with us. I spend more time at home than I have in years gone by, but I have continued to be heavily involved in church activities and in Harding campus affairs, such as daily chapel, athletic events, drama productions and musicals, board meetings, and other activities on the campus. I have enjoyed staying active and maintained my same office in the Administration Building for some fifty years. I thought it was quite special when Dr. David Burks, Dr. Bruce McLarty, and I were all together at Dr. McLarty's inauguration ceremony in 2013. Most of the time, the president leaves the university before the next president arrives, or they are not very friendly with one another. This has not been true with Harding. We all care for each other and work together very well. We feel privileged to have had the opportunity to serve in that capacity at a wonderful institution.

My greatest joy, however, will always be our family. Today, counting myself and Louise, our three children, ten grandchildren, eighteen great-grandchildren, and those whom they married, our family is forty-four strong, with more on the way. Louise and I have been amazed and pleased with the diverse abilities and interests in our family. All of our children and grandchildren graduated from Harding University, and our children and all but two of the grandchildren attended Harding Academy. They all seemed to enjoy school, and they have all done exceptionally well in varied studies.

Most of the family at Ashley's wedding, December 2018

Cliff III started Harding Academy in the first grade and early on began to show signs of musical ability. He began playing the cornet when he was eleven years old, and as soon as he was a freshman in high school he began to play with the Harding College band. He also played football and basketball, was editor of the *Wildcat*, the school newspaper, and was named valedictorian at his graduation. In the beginning of his college career, he decided on a music major and sang in the chorus and the Belles & Beaux while playing in the band and participating in athletics as well as student government. He received his BA in Music in 1966. In 1967-1968 he taught at Ohio Valley College. In 1968, he received his Master of Music Education degree at North Texas

State University and returned to Harding to continue his teaching career, which included many overseas experiences with the Belles & Beaux, chorus trips, and various other activities.

He fell in love with Debbie Lynn from Memphis. They married in March 1972 and soon moved to Boulder for Cliff to get a Doctor of Musical Arts degree at the University of Colorado. They returned to Harding in 1974. Debbie completed her degree in Bible and a master's degree in education at Harding and did graduate work at the Harding Graduate School of Religion in Memphis before getting a D.Min. from Bakke Graduate University in Seattle. She is a licensed professional counselor. Cliff and Debbie have taught with Harding's programs in Florence, Athens, Chile, and London. Cliff has received the Distinguished Teaching Award twice.[34]

Their first child, Sherrill, born in July 1978, was active in basketball, tennis, chorus, drama, and the yearbook at Harding Academy. She graduated from the university in 1999, having studied social work and been involved with the theater, married Chris Daugherty, and worked at the University of North Carolina. They have two girls, Annalise and Juliette.

Cliff and Debbie's first son, Bill, was born January 4, 1981. He played football and basketball and sang in the chorus. He was a good student and excelled in soccer, playing on the Searcy state championship team. He was a National Merit semifinalist and yearbook assistant editor. He graduated from Harding University in 2004 with a major in Chemistry. Later, he almost completed his doctorate before beginning his work with Buckman Labs in Memphis. After working with them for a few years, he decided to be an entrepreneur and developed several different businesses in the Memphis area. He married Jessica Osgatharp from Georgia. Bill and Jessica spent two years teaching in Ningbo, China, before having children. They now have three children: Layla, Ralston, and James.

Cliff and Debbie's next son, J. Cliff, was a good student at Harding Academy where he performed very well in drama and chorus, including a lead role in *You're a Good Man, Charlie Brown*. He was football and basketball manager and worked on the yearbook. He was very involved

---

[34] Cliff received a third Teaching Achievement Award in the spring of 2020.

in drama and theater at Harding University, graduated with a degree in Public Relations, worked for a year in Philadelphia in the publishing business, and then decided to become a medical doctor. He took the medical school prerequisite courses; taught for one year in South Korea; entered med school at St. George's, on the island of Grenada; completed his rotations in Brooklyn, New York; and finished his residency in Springfield, Missouri.

Cliff and Debbie's fourth child, Landon, sang in the Academy chorus, played basketball, played football on their state championship team, placed second in the high jump in the state meet, and loved outdoor activities. He graduated from Harding University in 2009 with a degree in Kinesiology and married Cassie Beagle from Batesville, Arkansas, who graduated from Harding with straight As and then completed Harding's Physician Assistant program. Landon earned the Doctor of Physical Therapy degree at Harding, and he and Cassie now work in Searcy as physical therapist and physician assistant. They have two children, Abigail and Samuel.[35]

Our daughter, Deborah Lynn, also attended Harding Academy. Since young ladies could not participate in athletics at that time, except in intramurals, she represented the Academy in academic matters, such as typing, shorthand, and parliamentary procedure, in which her team placed in the top five in the National FBLA contest in Washington, D.C. In the tenth grade, when she was studying with Katherine Ritchie, she fell in love with algebra and decided to pursue a career in mathematics. She was a very good student and graduated as valedictorian. She enjoyed playing in the Harding College band while she was still in high school and sang in the chorus as well. When she was in college, she sang in the A Cappella Chorus and went on tours to Europe with the group. She served on the *Bison* and *Petit Jean* staff and graduated in 1972, Summa Cum Laude, with a BS in Mathematics. After graduation, she spent a summer in Vienna in mission work with Otis Gatewood and had a plan to return to get her doctorate in mathematics, but, instead, she got married. She met Richard Duke from Florida on one of the Harding chorus trips. They began dating and married in

---

[35] Their third child, Anna Grace, was born in December of 2019.

1973. Later, she completed an MSE at Harding with an emphasis in mathematics and an Ed.D. from Memphis State University. Debbie began teaching at Harding and received the Distinguished Teacher Award twice and other honors for her work. She teaches mathematics, but she also directs the Preprofessional Health Science Program. She assists students by counseling them in their academic work and then helps them with their admissions to medical school.

Richard Duke was a Bible major who also certified to teach biology. After he graduated, Richard and Debbie moved to Paragould, and he taught at Crowley's Ridge Academy. Later, he went to Florida State University to earn his Ph.D. in Education. They returned to Paragould where he taught for another year and then was invited to join the Education Department at Harding University. He taught for twelve years at Harding and received a Distinguished Teacher award. He enjoyed his teaching at Harding, but when he was thirty-eight years of age, he changed course and was admitted to University of Arkansas Medical School in Little Rock. It took him seven years of driving back and forth from Searcy to Little Rock to complete his classwork and the required residencies to become a doctor. He established his own clinic in Searcy and has done very well in this profession.

Richard and Debbie have four children: Johnna, John Richard, David, and Louisa. Johnna attended Harding Academy where she graduated as valedictorian. She was an athlete and participated in track. At the same time, she sang in the Academy chorus and with a small women's singing group. She majored in Chemistry and Ministry at Harding University. After graduation, she married Bret Raymond, who also attended Harding and graduated as an Accounting major. He later received an MBA from Pepperdine University. They spent three years in Uganda as missionaries and two years in Rwanda with MANA. Now, they live in northwest Arkansas, and he serves as co-founder and CEO of the Pack Shack, a company that prepares packages of food to distribute to indigent people across the United States. They have three children: Isaac, Anna, and Luke.

Richard and Debbie's second child is John Richard Duke, Jr. At Harding Academy he played football and basketball and then attended Harding University, where he majored in history and graduated with a four-point average. While at Harding, he was a good basketball player and received the M.E. Berryhill Award, given to the senior athlete who exhibits the true spirit of Harding. He led the NCAA in 3-point shooting percentage with a 53.8% average for the season. After graduation, he played on the national champion basketball team in El Salvador and then served as an assistant coach at David Lipscomb Campus School. He received his master's and Ph.D. in History from the University of Mississippi where he was the head manager for the men's basketball team. He taught for several years at the University of Mainz in Germany and was active in the Wiesbaden Church of Christ. He is now teaching History at Harding University and helping to lead student groups to visit and study in Germany.

Their third child is David Loyd Duke. At Harding Academy, he played both football and basketball and added track to his activities. He won the state meet in his division in the 300-meter hurdles and was sixth in the overall decathlon. In addition, he sang in the Harding Academy Chorus and was a National Merit Scholar. At Harding University, he majored in physics and mathematics and completed his work with a four-point grade point average. He played basketball in college but was saddled with several injuries. After graduation, he taught for a year in a small Kenyan village high school and spent some time in Uganda. He married Lanny Hardman, who was a Marketing major. She also received an MBA from Harding and spent a year as missionary in Jinja, Uganda, before they married. David received his Ph.D. from Carnegie Mellon University in Robotics; however, he was diagnosed with Type 1 diabetes and then switched his research interest to diabetes. He also spent almost five years as a teaching assistant at Carnegie Mellon in Doha, Qatar, where he continued his research. David and Lanny's first two sons, Eli and Caleb, were born in Qatar. They have since settled in the Indianapolis area where he works in diabetes research with Roche Pharmaceutical Company as a project director. Their third son, Asher, was born after their arrival there. Lanny teaches online for Rochester College and is very active with their three sons as well as church activities.

Louisa Ann Duke is the fourth child of Richard and Debbie. At Harding Academy, she played basketball, softball, and ran track. She was in the chorus and was valedictorian when she graduated then graduated from Harding University with a major in Exercise Science with a four-point grade point average. She spent six weeks in an internship in Uganda while she was at Harding. She also studied at HUF in Florence, Italy, as did all of her siblings. She completed a degree as a Physician Assistant at Trevecca University in Nashville, Tennessee, and then moved to Zambia for two and a half years to work at Namwianga as a medical missionary in orphanages and outreach clinics in that area. Later, she returned to work in Ft. Worth, Texas, at a clinic that served school-age children. After a while, she came back to Searcy and worked with her dad at the Duke Medical Clinic and at Prime Care in North Little Rock. She has been back to Zambia twice to help with the Harding program there and taught in Harding's PA program. Louisa married Dan Wicks from Australia. He came to America and studied at Harding University for a BA in General Studies with an emphasis in the College of Sciences. They have one daughter, Avey Louise, born in Searcy, and a son, Samuel James.

Our third child is Charles Austin Ganus. Like the other children, Charles went to Harding Academy and excelled in sports and other activities as well as making good grades. He was all-district in football, played basketball, ran track, and was the state singles and doubles champ in his classification in tennis. He sang in the chorus and served in student government. He was also a part of the parliamentary procedure team that finished in the top five in the nation. Upon finishing at the academy, he attended Harding College and graduated in 1976, majoring in Bible and minoring in History. He sang in the chorus, was active with the TNT social club, and was inducted into Alpha Chi and Who's Who in American Colleges and Universities. He also played on the Harding tennis team. For three years, he won his division in singles at the conference championship, and the team won the conference his senior year.

He fell in love with a young lady named Patty Sapio from Atlanta, Georgia. Charles earned a Master's of Education at Harding with an emphasis in History, and then taught history and American government at Cabot High School for the next two years. When Patty graduated in the spring of 1979, they married in May in Atlanta. I had the pleasure of performing the ceremony. Patty had attended Greater Atlanta Christian School, where she was All-State in chorus, was captain of the cheerleading squad, and was selected as Miss Greater Atlanta

Christian in her senior year. At Harding, she studied in the nursing program and did well in her college work. She became a registered nurse and worked while Charles went to graduate school. He graduated from the University of Alabama with JD and MBA degrees. He graduated from the Harvard Business School's Advanced Management Program in July 1995. After graduate school he went to work in the law department for Murphy Oil Corporation in 1984 and worked in different areas of the corporation, retiring as Vice President of International Downstream on June 30, 2010.

We were happy that Charles and Patty decided to settle in this area. He was already a board member of Harding University, and he quickly became involved in other activities, serving as an elder at the College Church and on the board of World Bible School and the United Way of White County. Patty is very active in church matters as well as Harding organizations. She also serves on the board of CASA.[36]

Their first child is Ashley Lynn Ganus, born September 10, 1985, in El Dorado, Arkansas. She attended school in El Dorado and was an excellent student as well as a good athlete. She played tennis on the high school team and graduated fourth in her class of over three hundred students. She received a state award for combined excellence in athletics and academics. Ashley graduated from Harding University in 2007, where she was active in the Ju Go Ju social club and was president her senior year. She majored in Interior Merchandising and was an excellent student. She went to Zambia to work for five months at Namwianga Mission. Having become interested in working with children, she decided to earn her doctorate in Occupational Therapy, which she completed at Belmont University in Nashville, Tennessee. She then went to work for LeBonheur Children's Hospital in Memphis. Ashley married Loren James in December 2018. I had the pleasure of performing their ceremony. They live in Memphis, where she is an OT, and he works with the Tennessee Bureau of Investigation.

Charles and Patty were then blessed with a son, Kevin Austin Ganus, born August 12, 1988. Not only was he a good student but a very fine athlete as well. He played quarterback on the El Dorado High football team and played first base on the baseball team. I got to

---

[36] Charles and Patty took over the work at Harding Christian Academy in Uganda.

watch him play a couple of times and saw him hit home runs. I have two of those home run baseballs that he gave to me. He was All State in baseball.

When he finished high school, he came to Harding University and played on our baseball team. He was an excellent athlete and a very fine student. He graduated from Harding in 2011 and later earned a MAT from Harding in 2015. Kevin is a teacher and coach at Harding Academy in Searcy. He is married to the former Betsy Carr who graduated from Harding in 2009. She has a Master's of Science in Speech Language Pathology from Abilene Christian University. They have three vivacious and energetic daughters, Lucy Carol, Laura Nancy, and Mary Austin.[37]

Since Louise and I have been involved with Harding University for more than seventy-seven years, it is understandable that our family should be so very interested in some form of education. What is unusual is the variety of educational areas that have been chosen for both undergraduate and graduate degrees. It has been wonderful to watch our biological family grow and achieve. I know that we have had many bumps and bruises, and there are many things we could have done better, but overall, this has been a great journey. We have loved the Lord and His creation and have tried to do His will.

The family at the visitation, September 20, 2019

---

[37] Kevin and Betsy moved to Bentonville, Arkansas, in 2020.

Many of our family members have been involved in mission work overseas and have done extensive travel, sometimes on business, sometimes for pleasure. It seems that we are always praying for some of our family who are overseas. We also pray for the safety of our last journey to Heaven at the appropriate time. So far, we have been fortunate in not being ravaged by death but have lost only one of our members. Cliff and Debbie had their first born live for only minutes. I can still see Cliff carrying her in a small, wooden coffin on a rainy day to bury her in a cemetery just southwest of Searcy. I still mourn that baby, but I praise God for how richly He has blessed our family.

In addition to our biological family, Louise and I have another family we love: It is the family of God, the church of the Lord Jesus Christ. There are millions of brothers and sisters in this family all over the earth. Of course, we do not know them all, but I am amazed at how many we do know and how we have worked with so many of them in different parts of the globe.

When Louise and I came to Harding, we became members of the College Church of Christ, which met first on the campus in Godden Hall and later on Race Street, where it now occupies a much larger building and facility. For several years, I preached away almost every Sunday, but my family was usually in Searcy, and we served under the oversight of the elders of the College Church.

Since June of 1965 I have served as an elder of this congregation, and we have been blessed by the wonderful lessons that we have heard and by the examples of Christian living that have been set before us. We have sat at the feet of good and godly teachers who loved the Lord, loved us, and loved God's word. This has been a great benefit to our family.

And finally, we dearly love the many thousands of staff and students from Harding University whom we have known for decades. There is no way to measure the good that the Harding family has done for us.

They taught us when we were ignorant, supported us when we were weak, and encouraged us when we were sad. They led us when we didn't know the way and corrected us when we went astray. They walked with us in the darkest hours and held up our hands when we were feeble. They nurtured us when we were weak and helped us fight our battles with sin. They visited us when we were sick. They cheered us when we were unhappy. They helped us rear our children, grandchildren, and great-grandchildren. We can find the Harding family all over the world. Being part of the Harding family for all of these years has been a little bit like heaven on earth. Of course, it has never been perfect, because human beings are involved, but I think you would have to go a long way to find a better group of people working together with the spirit of Christ.

We cherish our families.

And he cherished his wonderful life journey, determined to make the most of every encounter with life's opportunities, joys, challenges, and adventures, always caring for others and looking to God for direction and counsel.

ACKNOWLEDGEMENTS

M any hands contributed to the creation of this book, but the Ganus family offers special thanks to Dr. Ganus's longtime secretary, **Edwina Pace**, for her meticulous transcription of his recorded memoirs, as well as the **staff of Brackett Library** and **Nancy Tackett** and **Carina Gibb** in the Provost's Office for compiling, organizing, and scanning Dr. Ganus's papers.

Thanks are due, as well, to **Tiffany Yecke Brooks**, for converting those hundreds of pages and many additional interviews into book form. **Kelly Wiggains**, who helped order and craft the material; **Larry Hunt**, who edited the final manuscript; and **Ken Bissell**, who provided important proofreading assistance along with advice, were also invaluable to the finished product.

TIMELINE OF EVENTS MENTIONED IN TEXT

1922: Born in Hillsboro, Texas, on April 7

1929: Ganus family moves to New Orleans, Louisiana

1932: Cliff Ganus, Sr., starts A&G Number 1

1939: Graduates from Warren Easton High School, attends Harding College

1942: Louise Nicholas graduates from Harding College

1943: Graduates from Harding College and marries Louise Nicholas on May 27

1943: Begins preaching at Charleston, Mississippi

1945: Moves to New Orleans to begin graduate school at Tulane

1945: Cliff Ganus III is born

1946: Receives master's degree in History

1946: Moves to Searcy to begin teaching at Harding

1948: Begins work on doctorate at Tulane University

1950: Debbie Ganus is born

1952: Becomes Dean of American Studies Institute at Harding College

1953: Completes dissertation and receives Ph.D. in History

1954: Charles Ganus is born

1955: Clifton L. Ganus, Sr., passes away

1955: Attends Columbia University for professional diploma in College Administration

1956: Appointed as first Vice-President of Harding College

1957: Travels to Europe with Louise and Bud Green to study socialism in seven countries

1961: Travels with brother James Ganus to South America to study socialism

1965: Becomes President of Harding College, founds President's Development Council and Associated Women for Harding

1965: Travels with son Cliff III to the Middle East

1967: Travels to Japan to visit Ibaraki Christian College

1969: Harding constructs the Stevens Art Center and Keller Hall and renovates the Claude Rogers Lee Music Building

1969: Mrs. Ganus (mother) passes away on April 10

1970: Travels to Eastern European capitals with Louise, Debbie, and Charles

1972: Travels with Louise to Brazil and southern African countries

1972: Navigates his first boat trip down the White and Mississippi Rivers with brother James, son Charles, and nephew Robert

1973: Visits southeastern Russian cities

1973: Travels with Louise in November to Mexico City for Pan-American Lectureship

1974: Harding College celebrates 50 years

1975: Travels with Louise to Spain, Portugal, and Morocco

1976: Travels with son Charles to Norway, Sweden, and Denmark

1976: Harding completes the Athletic Center

1977: Travels with Louise to Cuba

1978: Travels to China, Pakistan, and France with "People to People"

1979: Travels with Louise, Ken Davis, and the Harding Chorus to Poland, Russia, and Germany

1979: Harding College becomes Harding University

1980: Harding completes the Benson Auditorium and new Harding Academy building

1980: Harding starts HUF: Harding University in Florence, Italy

1981: Travels to Russia, Siberia, and Mongolia

1982: Visits Poland as the Church of Christ is recognized as an official religion by the government

1982: Travels with Louise to China

1982: Harding completes J.C. Mabee Business Building

1983: Travels with Louise to the Caribbean Lectureship for the first of 34 years to speak at the Lectureship

1984: Harding purchases the villa for HUF

1985: Works with Sam Walton to develop the Walton Scholars Program

1987: Retires as president of Harding in May; becomes chancellor of Harding University

1988: Travels in August with Louise to fish in Alaska; would return with various friends and family members annually through 2018

1990: Travels with Louise to Romania

1993: Celebrates 50th wedding anniversary with a trip around the world with Louise

1994: Travels to Uganda to help the Jinja missionary team

1994: Travels with Louise to Guatemala on one of a number of recruiting trips for the Walton Scholars Program

1994: Preaches in Bucharest, Romania, May 22-June 20

1994: Travels to Uganda for ten days, the first of twenty-seven trips to Uganda, the last in 2013, variously taking Louise, children, grand-children, and others

1995: Travels with Louise to Turkey, Albania, and Italy

1995: Travels with Louise to Uganda, Ethiopia, Ghana, and Togo

1996: Travels to Ukraine to work with churches in Gorlovka and Torez

1997: Travels to Uganda

1998: Travels with Cliff III and the Harding Chorus to Eastern Europe and Russia

1999: Travels with Louise to Greece with the students from HUF

1999: Travels with Louise to San Salvador, El Salvador, to speak at the Pan American Lectureship

2001: Travels with Louise to Greece to teach at HUG for the semester

2001: Travels with grandsons John Richard and David Duke, and John and Scott Picken, down the Mississippi River

2002: Travels to speak at Pan-American Lectureship in Estonia

2002: Travels with Louise to Uganda for a national meeting of the Churches of Christ

2003: Travels with Louise to Greece, Italy, Croatia, and Slovenia

2003: Travels with Louise to the Bahamas for the Caribbean Lectureship

2003: Travels to China for the 100th anniversary of Central China Normal University

2004: Travels with Louise to Greece to spend time with Cliff III at HUG

2004: Travels to Jinja, Uganda, to meet with advisory council regarding churches in Uganda

2005: Speaks at the Caribbean Lectureship held in Cuba for the first time

2010: Travels with Cliff III and Jim and Tim Woodroof down the Mississippi River

2010: Travels to China to recruit students for Harding

2012: Travels with Cliff III and Lathan and Phil Garnett down the Mississippi River

2012: Tours Eastern European countries with the Harding Chorus

2013: Tours Haiti with Healing Hands

2014: Harding History House hosts event to commemorate the Mississippi River Trips

2017: Travels with Louise and Charles and Patty Ganus on a cruise through Central America

2019: Passes away on September 9, 2019